About Island Press

Island Press is the only nonprofit organization in the United States whose principal purpose is the publication of books on environmental issues and natural resource management. We provide solutions-oriented information to professionals, public officials, business and community leaders, and concerned citizens who are shaping responses to environmental problems.

Since 1984, Island Press has been the leading provider of timely and practical books that take a multidisciplinary approach to critical environmental concerns. Our growing list of titles reflects our commitment to bringing the best of an expanding body of literature to the environmental community throughout North America and the world.

Support for Island Press is provided by the Agua Fund, The Geraldine R. Dodge Foundation, Doris Duke Charitable Foundation, The Ford Foundation, The William and Flora Hewlett Foundation, The Joyce Foundation, Kendeda Sustainability Fund of the Tides Foundation, The Forrest & Frances Lattner Foundation, The Henry Luce Foundation, The John D. and Catherine T. MacArthur Foundation, The Marisla Foundation, The Andrew W. Mellon Foundation, Gordon and Betty Moore Foundation, The Curtis and Edith Munson Foundation, Oak Foundation, The Overbrook Foundation, The David and Lucile Packard Foundation, Wallace Global Fund, The Winslow Foundation, and other generous donors.

The **DESIGN**ER'S

Atlas of Sustainability

The DESIGNER'S
Atlas of Sustainability

Ann Thorpe

◐ ISLANDPRESS | Washington | Covelo | London

ISLAND PRESS is a trademark of the Center for Resource Economics.

Library of Congress Cataloging-in-Publication Data

Thorpe, Ann.
  The designer's atlas of sustainability / Ann Thorpe.
      p. cm.
  Includes bibliographical references and index.
  ISBN-13: 978-1-59726-099-2 (cloth : alk. paper)
  ISBN-10: 1-59726-099-1 (cloth : alk. paper)
  ISBN-13: 978-1-59726-100-5 (pbk. : alk. paper)
  ISBN-10: 1-59726-100-9 (pbk. : alk. paper)
  1. Sustainable development. 2. Design, Industrial—Environmental aspects. I. Title.
  HC79.E5T486 2006
  745.2098'4—dc22

                                    2006035007

Printed on recycled, acid-free paper ♻

Manufactured in the United States of America
10 9 8 7 6 5 4 3 2 1

for Torbjørn and Storm

CONTENTS

ACKNOWLEDGMENTS

This book is, in some measure, an atlas that reflects my own global travels through the ideas of sustainability. My ideas started forming in my native U.S. homes of the Pacific Northwest and the San Francisco Bay area, as well as my adopted home of Europe, especially England, the Netherlands, Denmark, and France. Australia and India also have been significant outposts for me. These places supply many of the book's examples and are the homes to several of the many people who helped me along the way, either specifically with this book or generally.

The book also charts my travels through the economy where I've been lucky to experience the challenges of design and sustainability through work at a large, publicly held corporation and several small businesses, at a regional public agency and various public universities, and at several non-profit organizations. I appreciate all the insights my colleagues have shared with me.

The book's genesis was in the BA (Hons) Product Design Sustainable Futures program at the University College for the Creative Arts (formerly known as the Surrey Institute of Art and Design, University College) my support team there included Julian Lindley, Miles Park, Roni Brown, Anthea Bailey, Tom Portlock, Seymour Roworth-Stokes, Ian Dumelow, Katie Hamilton-Boxall, Tipu Miah, and Tom Griffin.

Early drafts of the manuscript received vigorous and very helpful reviews from Julian Lindley, Miles Park, Joanna Lambert, Philip White, John Wells, Helen Lewis, Michael Herrmann, Alex Young, Tim Kasser and Lynne Elvins, who all pushed me to be clear, thorough, and fair. Later drafts benefited enormously from the help of reviews by Annie Breckenfeld, John Manoocherhi, and Lucia Athens, who helped refine the atlas concept and further clarify the ideas.

Another important group of reviewers consisted of my students, and for working through this material in various versions I would like to thank them all. They provided useful feedback and key insights. In particular, discussions with Ryu Tabu yielded many of the seeds that grew into the section on culture.

Kate Fletcher, Julian Lindley, Roni Brown, Miles Park, Jim Hanford, and Michael Herrmann all contributed some great ideas to illustrate the concepts in the book. John Gertsakis, Emma Dewberry, and Lucia Athens heroically provided not only much general encouragement but also crucial support for funding applications.

This book was generously supported by grants from several organizations, as follows:

United States
Graham Foundation for Advanced Studies
   in the Fine Arts

United Kingdom
 Arts and Humanities Research Council (AHRC)

University College for the Creative Arts at Canterbury, Epsom, Farnham, Maidstone, and Rochester

Many people helped on the development and production of the book. I'm grateful to all the authors, researchers, and designers who provided, with their research, practice, and writing, the terrific foundation for this book. Research assistant (and former student) Estelle Crow provided enthusiasm and commitment that are unrivaled. The visual aspect of the book came together with a great deal of help from photographers Andy Crawford and Finn Brandt and book designer Brian Barth. Tom Portlock helpfully assisted with the illustrations. Many of the photographs are graced by volunteer models, including Nasir Ali, Pete Buckland, Estelle Crow, Gurpreet Flora, Charlotte Gibson, Lena Gratton, Gunvor Karup, Diana Kiesel, Tamara Kocan, Carl Larsen, James Lobley, Edward MaKgill, Jotis Moore, Kevin Morris, Laura Newman, Caitriona Ni Riain, Thomas Portlock, Mary Ryan, Souro Sircar, Blodwen Strachan, Torbjørn Thorpe-Brandt, Hannah Waheed, Kim Wilson, and Kei Yamamoto.

I'm thankful to Jon Koomey, Anne Bikle, Ed van Hinte, Thomas Keenes, and others who shared their knowledge and insights on getting this book published. My thanks also go to Megan Arrivey Hall for the book's index. The whole Island Press team, including Shannon O'Neill, Todd Baldwin, Jeff Hardwick, Maureen Gately, Jessica Heise, Heather Boyer, Brian Weese, and Alexander Schoenfeld, also gets my sincere thanks for seeing the potential in this book and helping bring it to fruition.

I've been lucky to receive tremendous support from my friends and my family, not only throughout this project, but throughout my life. Thanks everyone! This project has given me even more appreciation for all the writers in my family, especially my late father, Peter Thorpe. All aspects of my life, extending right into this book project, are made much richer by contributions from my mother, Lynn McAllister, who has provided every conceivable type of assistance and encouragement, from practical to intellectual. During the process of writing and illustrating this book I've also gotten married and had two children, so thanks to my husband and kids for sharing me with this book, which frequently has felt like a third child.

PART 1

INTRODUCTION

**DEFINITION:
Atlas**

a collection of
maps, charts or
visual plates that
systematically
illustrate a sub-
ject. The visual
nature of atlases
in general is part
of what inspired
this atlas.

WHAT IS AN ATLAS, ANYWAY? Why is this book called *The Designer's Atlas of Sustainability*? By definition, an *atlas* is a collection of maps, charts, or visual plates that systematically illustrate a subject. The visual nature of atlases in general is a large part of what inspired this atlas. Pictureless, black-and-white texts on the substantive questions of sustainable development, no matter how well written, have not reached the design audience that is not engaged by them. My purpose with this book is to integrate information about sustainability and design with a sophisticated visual approach that designers expect, to attract new readers to the topic as well as reenergize readers who already know something about it.

An atlas is a reference book, albeit a visual one. As with any other reference book, the atlas cannot be used in isolation; it cannot be all and do all. Below are a few of the characteristics of this atlas, explained in terms of how they work.

Like other reference books (dictionaries, encyclopedias), an atlas presents a range of concepts, ideas, and facts. But it is the reader who must interpret the information. For example, an atlas may give you information about mountain height, ocean depth, population size, coastline shape,

square mileage, and perhaps the dominant religion or industries. But your assessment of the importance of the information will depend on whether you are a mountain climber, a real estate developer, a shipbuilder, or a devout religious person. This atlas is intended to provide a concise, yet thorough, guide to key concepts underpinning sustainability so that designers can decide where they want or need to go next, depending on the constraints, criteria, and priorities for any given project.

The atlas, like other reference books, does not build toward a single conclusion—there isn't one. The reader provides these conclusions. There are a number of other books (see the further reading section) that provide visionary statements or universal principles about sustainability and sustainable design.

Likewise, reference books don't provide instructions on how to combine the elements they contain. In the same way that a dictionary does not provide a recipe for how to write a paragraph using its words, this atlas does not provide recipes for design solutions using its concepts. Designers are trained in synthesizing a wide range of ideas and materials in imaginative new ways according to a particular design context. In an atlas, for example, we can look at Iceland and then Morocco; although there is no obvious connection between their cities of Reykjavíík and Casablanca, there are endless interesting ways to compare them and combine elements of the two. My aim is to avoid limiting innovation by describing design solutions.

In addition, by providing ingredients rather than recipes, the atlas can be relevant to a range of design disciplines. To be sure, the atlas includes general examples and ideas meant to suggest avenues of approach for using the atlas's material, the way a dictionary might give an example phrase showing a word's usage. A number of existing books already catalog "green" and sustainable design solutions as well as specific design techniques. These books tend to be oriented toward one discipline or another (e.g., architecture, product design, interiors). By showing existing sustainable-design solutions and providing "how-to" approaches, they serve as "recipe" books for those who seek recipes.

What is missing among the books on sustainable design is one that systematically and visually presents the concepts of sustainability in a way that designers can access. Until now a visual approach has not been used to tackle economic and cultural elements of sustainable design, nor have these two elements been comprehensively combined with ecological elements. Yet it's very important that these three elements of sustainability be considered together, as this atlas does.

Although design in all its forms has a tremendous effect on the natural world, ecodesign alone will not lead us to long-term sustainability. With the arrival of the twenty-first century, we entered the second phase in the debate about how design contributes to sustainability. The first phase, characterized by terms such as "eco-design," "green-design," or "environmental design," focused largely—and appropriately—on energy and materials. The second phase requires an additional exploration of the role of design in economic and social aspects of sustainability.

And here lies another, more poetic reason for calling this book an atlas—because sustainability can be thought of as a new *landscape* within which design must perform. This landscape does not replace other design criteria, such as function or appearance, but adds to them—and some design criteria may look different when seen within the landscape of sustainability.

The territory of ecology, or ecodesign has been much better traveled than the economic and cultural landscapes of sustainable design. Ecodesign has emerged as a design practice, whereas the other two aspects of sustainable design still lack definition. For this reason, you may find that the parts of the atlas covering economy and culture represent not only more new material but also more challenging and daring ideas.

This atlas, then, is a collection of visual materials that systematically catalog and illustrate for designers the most important concepts and ideas about sustainability in terms of its ecology, economy and culture. The atlas suggests that design has a role in sustainability that must be incorporated into the other roles that design already has. The atlas shows you what the dimensions of this role might be and presents some initial thinking on how to approach it.

Before charting out the landscape of sustainability, we first examine the current status of both "development" and "design." The landscape of sustainability suggests some possible synergies between the two. After reviewing some terms of reference for the book, I offer some thoughts on how you can use this atlas.

 TRAVELER'S NOTE: Your Journey

The reward for your travels in the landscape of sustainability is, in addition to knowledge and understanding, inspiration. In the end, sustainability is an amazing tool for creativity. My experience has been that the journey is both a personal and professional one. Designers on this journey may find it useful to remember that we are each allowed, indeed required, to be a "whole person"—to consider that our freedom to design is based on other, more profound freedoms and that our best design emerges from these.[1]

DEVELOPMENT

THE TERM "DEVELOPMENT" HAS VARIOUS MEAN-
INGS. In the most general terms, it suggests
improvement or advancement. In global terms,
international development is aimed at bringing
the least developed countries out of poverty, pro-
gressing toward human well-being at its most
complete. In industrialized societies, particularly
over the last one hundred years, development has
come to mean economic development, usually
linked to further industrial development. These
are seen as closely tied to well-being.

For the purposes of this atlas, we will consider development primarily in terms of industrialized countries such as Australia, Japan, and those
of North America and Europe. If development is
progress toward human well-being, what constitutes sustainable development in the context of
industrialized countries?

The term "sustainable" implies longevity and
is derived from the function of ecosystems that
support themselves over very long periods of
time, such as the ten-million-year-old rain
forests.[2] The term "sustainable development"
first emerged internationally in 1986 amid concerns about global environmental degradation
and its relationship to our notions of "development." In particular, the World Commission on
Environment and Development emphasized the
sustainable use of resources in facilitating the
elimination of poverty. The commission's original definition for sustainable development, that it

"meets the needs of the present without compromising the ability of future generations to meet
their own needs," is still often quoted today.[3]

But this definition, based primarily on ecological concerns related to development, has
proved difficult to apply. How can we forecast the
needs of future generations or their capabilities?
Since the commission's report, the term "sustainable development" has come to encompass social
issues as well as environmental ones. There also
have been many different definitions formulated
for the term. Businesses, for example, have tended to use it simply as a new label for existing activities such as eco-efficiency practices and responsible labor practices. Activists and some governments have defined sustainable development in
relation to current quality-of-life indicators—such
as crime levels, accessible urban green spaces, and
the like—which don't appear to encompass truly
long-term goals.[4]

Although the terms "sustainable" and "sustainable development" have perhaps suffered
from having so many diverse definitions, in the
absence of any other good terms that capture the
spirit suggested by "sustainability," I still feel it is
worth using. The definition of sustainable development that we'll adopt for the purposes of this

atlas is *development that cultivates environmental and social conditions that will support human well-being indefinitely.*[5]

The primary set of environmental conditions that support human well-being indefinitely are the life-sustaining "products and services" that ecosystems provide. Examples of these are breathable air, rendered by plant life, or absorption of wastes, for example through topsoil filtration. Ecosystem functions can be harmed by consuming resources faster than they are regenerated and by putting more waste into nature than it can process and absorb. Part 2 of this atlas examines conceptual aspects of ecosystem functions and investigates how design might support them.

We'll address the social conditions that support human well-being by breaking these conditions into two categories: culture and economics. We might characterize culture as all of our socially transmitted behaviors, including systems of belief and art forms. We can describe economics as a subset of culture, as a system for managing and developing our resources, whatever their form. Many people think of economics in terms of the marketplace and things we buy and sell, but in fact we have many resources, such as human relationships and planetary oceans, that we must manage even without being able to price them. What economic conditions will support human well-being indefinitely? Part 3 of this atlas examines the marketplace as well as the broader economy, which includes our government policies and our charitable organizations. We will investigate the design options for supporting economic aspects of sustainable development.

DEFINITION: Sustainable Development

Development that cultivates environmental and social conditions that will support human well-being indefinitely.

Broader cultural conditions that support human well-being over the long term are perhaps the most controversial because they involve values and beliefs. These seem least related to the ecological origins of sustainability. In the context of culture we are indeed examining aspects of human well-being—such as self-esteem, a sense of identity, participation, and belonging—that are not tied directly to ecological functions. Part 4 of this atlas investigates the notion of human well-being in cultural terms and highlights design's role in supporting cultural sustainability.

And how long is "indefinitely"? Fifty years? A thousand years? Ten thousand years? Given our current fast-paced culture, one hundred years is much longer than most people ever consider, but is it long enough for "long-term" sustainable development? Probably not. The question of time threads through several chapters of this atlas (part 4) in an effort to help designers approach this dimension of sustainability in their work.

Design, in one form or another, has always played a key role in the environmental and social conditions that affect our human well-being. The next chapter looks briefly at the history of design and its relationship to development.

> This book focuses primarily on design in the context of industrialized societies, but it is important for sustainable design to be informed by international development issues.

The gap between developing and developed countries: Measures of inequality

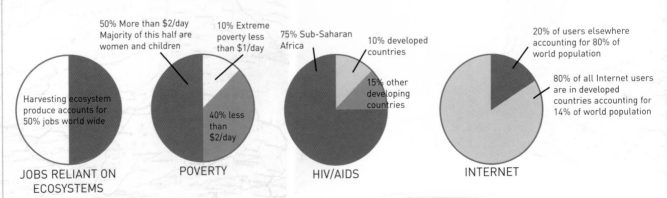

JOBS RELIANT ON ECOSYSTEMS
Harvesting ecosystem produce accounts for 50% jobs world wide

POVERTY
50% More than $2/day Majority of this half are women and children
10% Extreme poverty less than $1/day
40% less than $2/day

HIV/AIDS
75% Sub-Saharan Africa
10% developed countries
15% other developing countries

INTERNET
20% of users elsewhere accounting for 80% of world population
80% of all Internet users are in developed countries accounting for 14% of world population

LANDSCAPE FEATURE: The World's Countries

The world has nearly two hundred countries, but only around thirty of them are considered developed. They are sometimes called industrialized with a common emphasis on mechanization and intensive energy use. Since, except for Australia and New Zealand they are generally located in the Northern Hemisphere (Europe, North America, and Japan), they are sometimes also referred to as the North in the north-south divide or as the first world. They account for about 15% of the world's population.

Most of the rest of the world's population experience poverty. About 60% of this population is in low-income countries that are sometimes referred to as the third world, developing countries, or less developed countries (LDCs). Since these countries are predominately located in the Southern Hemisphere (Africa, Latin America, and Asia), they are sometimes referred to as the South.

About 25% of the world's population is in middle-income countries such as Turkey, Greece, South Korea, and the countries of Eastern Europe. These countries have fewer common names as a group, but they are sometimes called the second world or, depending on their economies, transitional economies or newly industrializing countries (NICs).

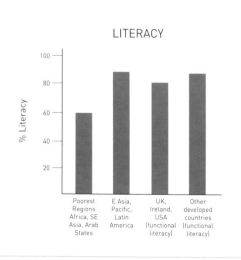

LITERACY

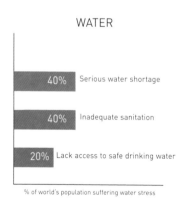

WATER

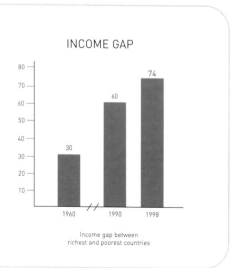

INCOME GAP

DESIGN

A CHAIR MADE OF WOOD, a building made of cement—designers get materials for their work from natural resources, so design directly affects environmental conditions in this and other ways. If we consider social conditions in terms of both economy and culture, we find design has a role there, too. For example, a sleek, shiny design conveys a different meaning than a rough-hewn one, and this is one of design's powerful influences on social conditions, the way design can express social meaning. Design is also used to influence sales in the marketplace, affecting the economic conditions for development. Such wide-ranging influences on the conditions directly linked to development suggest that design has great potential to support sustainability—to cultivate processes that support human well-being indefinitely. Yet to succeed, design will have to find a way to balance current design criteria with some new ones.

Victorians:
Thrilling
Simulations

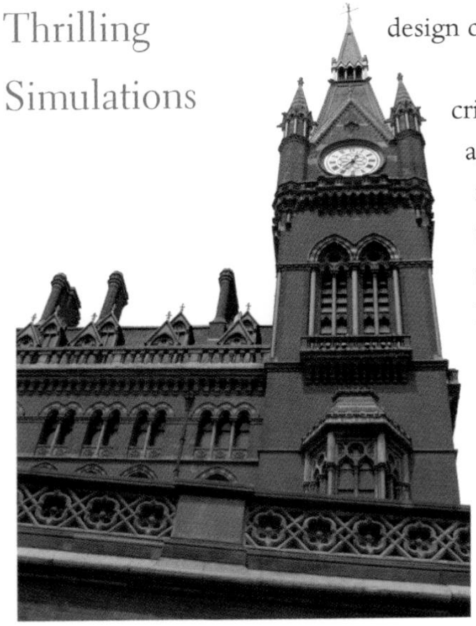

Designers have always faced the challenge of balancing competing design criteria such as appearance and cost. Cost constraints have to be balanced against manufacturing requirements; ease of use has to be balanced against miniaturization pressures. Technical capabilities to achieve suitable forms, textures, and functions limit the expression of social meaning in design. In the context of sustainable development, the struggle to balance the needs of humans, machines, and commerce gets more complex when we add ecological concerns.

Some social and environmental concerns have long persevered at the edges of mainstream design, but the field has typically been dominated by other themes. For the modern profession of design, which grew alongside industrialization, an overriding goal has been to humanize the products of industrialization. After centuries of craft and designer-maker traditions, modern design emerged in a mass production context, using machines and now computers. Initially, the machine capabilities were thrilling, and during the Industrial Revolution there was an early "Gee whiz!" period. The possibilities for machine-made objects were endless; they could have design appearances that in the previous crafts-making mode would have been very expensive and time consuming.[6] A huge range of surfaces and façades could be simulated using mass production techniques. After initial infatuation wore off, designers began coming to terms not only with the question of machine aesthetics but also with mass production, the identical products it created, and the need for a new philosophy for modern design.

These questioning modernists, as if to say, "Get control of yourselves!" proposed design solutions that were stripped-down expressions of function. Ideally, there was very little façade, and the form itself expressed function. This theme of function was best captured in the famous phrase "form follows function."[7] Englishman William Morris (1834–1896) founded the arts-and-crafts movement, which urged that designers should be reunited with the true nature of their materials and that quality should be restored to production. This approach hinted at environmental conditions. At the same time, others such as the German designer Peter Behrens

Post Modernists:
Form Follows Fun

Design expresses social meaning: A sleek, shiny design conveys something different than a rough-hewn one.

(1868–1940) searched for a rational approach, a way to use industry to spread positive social change through design, taking hints from the philosophical movements of the era. The German art-and-design school known as Bauhaus (1919–1933) also pursued rational approaches to design.

The Bauhaus and other design schools produced some severe designs that they characterized as "machines for living," among other things.[8] The idea was that the machines themselves would provide the meaning for the designed forms.[9] The approach encompassed products, buildings, and interiors. The modernist rejection of surface decorations gradually grew fashionable in the 1950s and 1960s in keeping with new interests in science and logic. Consumers also came to be seen more as a bundle of rational needs. The minimalist results lasted up into the 1970s.[10]

Postmodernists rebelled against the severity of the modern period. Their message was "Lighten up!" Design then focused on the theme of emotional expression, putting fun, whimsy, and desire back into the equation. Some have even characterized this as "form follows fun" or "form follows meaning." The main idea is that objects are invested with meaning by the people who use them, and some of those meanings are not rational and machinelike but rather expressive, emotional, and humanlike. And the designer's ability to create fanciful, whimsical forms has been greatly aided by new digital design technology.[11] In terms of development, both modernists and postmodernists were concerned with cultural and economic conditions connected to design.

Postmodernism has coincided with, perhaps grown out of, consumerism. Consumerism, arguably the dominant theme for design in the early twenty-first century, is an economic approach concerned with identifying goods and services and providing them to consumers at a profit to the manufacturer. The element of postmodern design that can identify consumer desires and appeal to them is commercially successful, and in many quarters, good design is now considered any design that sells.[12] Earlier concerns about positive social change and broader social goals largely have been abandoned. The emphasis is on the "form-giving" aspects of design—the appearance of objects themselves, the fantasy of a brand (promises of a better life through association with a brand), and the move toward relatively generic solutions that can appeal in global markets. In addition, short product life cycles are common, with frequent styling updates to draw consumers back before the old product is worn out.

The drive to meet consumer desires cuts across design disciplines. Interiors, particularly "home improvement," have gotten a consumerist boost from do-it-yourself movements as well as the availability of low-cost home furnishings through retailers such as IKEA.[13] Graphic design finds much of its application in advertising, marketing, branding, and the digital retail environment. Although architecture, through the nature of its products, can't allow for such frequent styling updates, in areas of architecture that do respond most directly to consumers, such as residential housing, planning, and sale of the product are very consumer driven. In addition, the attitude toward large public buildings has increasingly moved toward "disposability," as perfectly good buildings are destroyed before their time to make way for newer models.

Despite consumer sales as dominant criteria and as a measure of the success of design, other

 DEFINITION: Sustainable Design

Theories and practices for design that cultivate ecological, economic, and cultural conditions that will support human well-being indefinitely.

issues relevant to sustainability refuse to die out entirely. Among these we find "empathic design" or "inclusive design," beginning not with the form or object to be designed but rather with understanding the users and their context. Successful design here enables users. Rather than being focused on sales, it is focused on needs (including emotional and expressive needs). User groups might cover a broad range, from the elderly to children or from parents to students. In addition, green design or ecodesign has emerged out of concern over environmental deterioration.

Issues that relate to environmental integrity and human well-being have long had a place within design debate and practice, but a defined view of these concepts in relation to sustainable development is relatively new. Considering sustainability as a way to integrate a broader range of environmental and human needs into a design process that currently focuses on balancing economic, technical, and human needs will open new vistas. According to the definition for sustainable development that I laid out in the previous chapter, we can extrapolate a broad definition of sustainable design. Sustainable design encompasses design theory and practice that cultivate environmental and social conditions to support human well-being indefinitely.

Beyond these definitions for sustainable design and development, we need to explore some additional terms. The next chapter clarifies terms such as "design practice" and "design theory" as they apply to this atlas.

What Role do creative
and management processes
have in sustainable design?

TERMS OF REFERENCE

FROM ARCHITECTURE TO INTERIORS TO GRAPHICS, there are a few relative constants in design. Designers usually respond to a "brief," or a description of what type of design is needed. Design activity includes a spectrum from knowing to doing. The "knowing" takes the form of theory (or philosophy) and management. For example, from a philosophical standpoint, should form follow function, or should form follow fun? From a management perspective, design has to be organized within some sort of structure—typically a business such as a design consultancy, corporation, or freelance practice.

The "doing" of design, sometimes called "design practice" or "process," covers the creative research, development, and making processes. Designers develop ideas through research and capture them through techniques such as drawing, mapping, and modeling. Design responses typically operate on many levels, including sensual, intellectual, emotional, functional, and commercial. The design process typically involves visual and, if appropriate, three-dimensional experimentation and testing of ideas, leading to the presentation of a final design concept that can then be implemented through physical production. Designers often work in teams with other designers and other disciplines. When I refer to "design" generally, I mean this spectrum from knowing to doing.

The emphasis of this book is on understanding the concepts behind sustainability and how they relate to design in both knowing and doing. Some argue that sustainable design is primarily enacted through the management function, by making sure that the right policies are in place and that the supply chain is properly managed. Others make the case that the

Machine- or craft-made products

For the purposes of including in the discussion a wide range of designed objects, I'll use the term "artifact" to denote all designed objects, including architecture in buildings or landscape, mass-manufactured products (e.g., clothing, furniture, appliances, computers, garden tools), and craft-made products (e.g., jewelery, ceramics, textiles). We'll consider interior spaces or exhibits as collections of artifacts controlled by the designer.

creative process—ideas, images, and forms—ultimately have a more central role in identifying the breakthroughs and inspiring the change necessary to make sustainability a reality.

In my view not only do knowing and doing each have crucial roles, but they also appear to have new scope when we look at design within the context of a new landscape of sustainability. To the extent that this atlas covers new ground, the thoughts I put forward about the emerging opportunities for theory and practice are like prototypes to be tested and interpreted by designers.

It is worth noting here that each design discipline also has its own scope for working on sustainability. For example, the scope for graphic

design is fundamentally different from that for architecture, yet there also is some overlap. Each designer and each design problem are unique. Some designers work in more than one discipline or "crossover," for example, the architect who designs furniture or the product designer who ends up doing the graphic design for a Web site. In addition, many design briefs are complex and involve a range of disciplines in a team where ideas also may cross disciplinary boundaries. So again, designers draw their own conclusions about which concepts are most relevant to them—and the relevancy of concepts may change with projects. More important, with creative insight you, the reader, may see connections that I would have missed if I had tried to match concepts to disciplines. Some disciplines associated with design, such as marketing, engineering, or planning, also may find some of the concepts in this atlas useful.

In terms of sustainable design, there is another term we need to consider here and revisit

Clothing

throughout the atlas. I'll introduce this term as "purity," but it could also be characterized as thoroughness, completeness, or a matter of degrees. We might define the purist approach as one that accepts no compromises—only 100% sustainable in every way, or nothing. Less pure approaches tend to be more practical and quick, accepting current circumstances to gain, let's say, 20% sustainable results in a short period of time. For example, consider the question of materials. An impure approach would be to concentrate on increasing recycling of our existing materials. A purist would argue for reinvention of our system of material use altogether, striving for that elusive 100% sustainability. Sometimes purist approaches are characterized as radi-cal or "outside the system," since by definition the "system" we have now is not sustainable. The impure approaches are often called practi-cal or incremental because they work from "inside the establishment" and typically allow for much of our daily business to continue as usual. Throughout the atlas I've tried to present a range of concepts across the spectrum from pure to impure.

The debate over purity and over the relative contributions of theo-ry versus practice (or knowing versus doing) is bound to continue. In the end a useful result will be the unified movement of design, in know-ing and doing, in pure and impure initiatives, toward the end point of sustainability. No single type of approach, on its own, is likely to be effective. The individual choices we make about how to pursue sustain-able design will be based on personal situation, skill, and temperament. Individuals may even vary their own approaches throughout one career.

 TRAVELER'S NOTE: Purity of Sustainable Design

The motto for purists might be "I have a dream" or "Reach for the stars," whereas the motto for "impurists", or incrementalists, might be "Don't let the perfect be the enemy of the good." Each approach has merits, and in the end, purists and incrementalists need each other to keep sustainable design moving forward.

Architecture and Interiors

Packaging

USING THE ATLAS

NAVIGATIONAL FEATURES

DEFINITION:
Key terms

LANDSCAPE FEATURE:
Main concepts

TRAVELER'S NOTE:
Design thoughts

THE DIVISION OF THE ATLAS into three main parts presenting ecology, economy, and culture as separate is somewhat artificial but useful in coming to terms with a broad range of ideas. After outlining these parts, I suggest ways you might approach the atlas.

Within part 2, "Ecology" the key issue is that human systems are overwhelming nature's systems, destroying environmental conditions that support human well-being. This part examines ways that design can help harmonize human and natural systems. Two overriding concepts in this part are, first, learning to recognize seemingly invisible connections between nature and design and, second, applying nature's elegance, economy, and sensitivity with materials and energy to human designs.

Within part 3, "Economy," the key issue is that our market system fails to capture important values, many of which are at the core of sustainability. The economy itself is bigger than just "the market," although the market dominates, focusing the attention of society primarily on economic expansion and the generation of material wealth, especially at the global level. This part of the atlas examines not only the market-based private sector where design has traditionally been positioned but also the public and non-profit sectors of the economy. Two overriding concepts in this part are, first, that designers need to develop some economic literacy in order to address sustainability and that this literacy has both a personal (or citizenship) dimension and a professional one. Second, there are options for positioning design in all three sectors of the economy, and each sector provides certain opportunities and barriers to pursuing sustainable design. Understanding these parameters can help designers decide how to organize the "business" of design to support sustainability.

Within part 4, "Culture," the key issue is to understand cultural sustainability in terms of human well-being and how design can support it. Over the last one hundred years we have fundamentally changed the way we try to meet our human needs, from primarily internal mechanisms (such as reflection or creativity) to external ones (such as watching the media or owning materials goods). Design shapes media images and material goods, but research indicates that these external methods meet human needs badly. This part uses four main themes—communication, artifacts, time, and nature—to explore how design might better support human well-being.

Within part 5, "Frontiers," concluding thoughts reflect on how the three previous parts interconnect, as well as the notion of change and how we can accomplish it. Both personal and professional dimensions of change are important, and some of these involve real challenges to our notions of design, compared with what we are used to outside the landscape of sustainability.

If you are new to the topic of sustainable design, you will benefit most from reading the book sequentially. But the three main parts, although connected, also can stand alone to be read separately. If you have one particular area of interest, you can go directly to the part that covers it. On the other hand, if you are familiar with the topic of one part, you might simply skip or skim that part and read the others.

Each main part contains a summary map of its landscape, to be used as a reminder (or preview) of key ideas from that part. The atlas also contains some navigational features to help readers use it effectively. Main concepts within each part are defined as "landscape features." Although each landscape feature is presented broadly in relation to design, in places where more specific design ideas emerge, they are captured in a series of "traveler's notes." Recommendations for further reading and endnotes for each part offer ways to pursue specific concepts more in depth and make it easier to trace the ideas presented. Definitions of key terms help introduce new ideas.

FURTHER READING

The books and articles that served as sources for the introduction to the atlas are cited in the endnotes. The following books, which are generally not featured in the endnotes, provide more information on some of the topics discussed in this part.

How-To's and Catalogs of Existing Sustainable Design Examples

Biologic: Designing with Nature to Protect the Environment by David Wann (Boulder, CO: Johnson Books, 1994)

Design + Environment: A Global Guide to Designing Greener Goods by Helen Lewis and John Gertsakis with Tim Grant, Nicola Morelli, and Andrew Sweatman (Sheffield, UK: Greenleaf, 2001)

The Eco-design Handbook: A Complete Sourcebook for the Home and Office by Alastair Fuad-Luke (London: Thames and Hudson, 2005)

How to Do Ecodesign? by Ursula Tischner, Eva Schmincke, Frieder Rubik, and Martin Prosler (Frankfurt: Verlag form, 2000)

Okala Ecological Design: Course Guide by Philip White, Louise St. Pierre, and Steve Belletire (Portland, OR: U.S. Environmental Protection Agency, 2004)

The Total Beauty of Sustainable Products by Edwin Datschefski (Hove, UK: Rotovision, 2001)

Vision and Principles for Sustainable Design

Cradle to Cradle: Remaking the Way We Make Things by William McDonough and Michael Braungart (New York: North Point Press, 2002)

Design for the Real World by Victor Papanek (London: Thames and Hudson, 1984)

Design for Society by Nigel Whiteley (London: Reaktion Books, 1993)

Ecological Design by Sim Van Der Ryn and Stuart Cowan (Washington, DC: Island Press, 1996)

International Dimension of Sustainable Development

A large body of literature is available on sustainable development and its international dimensions. The United Nations Development Programme, for example, publishes regular updates on the status of worldwide development. A few starting points include the following:

Development as Freedom by Amartya Sen (Oxford: Oxford University Press, 1999)

Human Development Report 2004: Cultural Liberty in Today's Diverse World by the United Nations Development Programme (New York: United Nations Development Programme, 2004)

Small Is Beautiful: A Study of Economics as If People Mattered by E. F. Schumacher (London: Vintage Books, 1973)

RECOMMENDATIONS
OR FURTHER READING END EACH PART

PART 2

ECOLOGY

A TOASTER IN A MEADOW?

The picture looks odd in some ways, but what's right with this image? It remind us where all artifacts begin and end in the natural environment. "But it's made of metal and plastic," you argue. "What does that have to do with trees and birds?" Most mining requires clearing the land of trees and animals to make way for digging and processing activities. In addition, mining chemicals and the metals themselves can make their way into ecosystems and cause harm. For every 1,000 kilograms of iron mined, 600 kilograms of material becomes waste. The energy used to process the iron comes mainly from fossil fuel power plants that emit carbon dioxide, a climate warming gas, and gases that contribute to acid rain. That rain can react with the soil, reducing the calcium available to birds and causing their eggshells to be too thin. There's more connection than you might think. But since we design and interact with artifacts in the human world, we don't register these connections.[1]

Nature has an intrinsic design. We can imagine nature as a product that lasts for millions, if not billions, of years. It's a product that, using only solar energy in the form in which it hits Earth's surface, creates valuable resources. Rather than breaking down over time, nature evolves into newer, more sophisticated forms. It adjusts to changes by cleverly absorbing "shocks" in its smallest, fastest parts but maintains its overall continuity (and durability) through its biggest slowest-moving parts. Its parts are self-organizing, which means that without any central "brain" or control mechanism, each part participates cooperatively, adjusting as needed, to help with the function of the whole product.

Now imagine inflicting rapid changes on this product, changes that are so big and that happen so quickly that the stability of the product as a whole is overwhelmed. Entirely new parts that don't have any function are suddenly added, disrupting the connections between the existing parts that do function. At

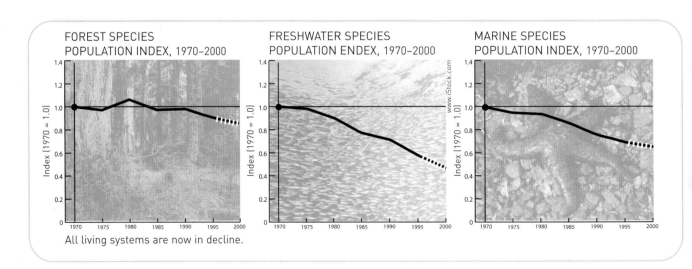

FOREST SPECIES POPULATION INDEX, 1970–2000

FRESHWATER SPECIES POPULATION ENDEX, 1970–2000

MARINE SPECIES POPULATION INDEX, 1970–2000

All living systems are now in decline.

the same time, some of the product's essential parts are broken beyond repair. Other parts, though still functioning, become severely deformed. The product barely resembles its former self. It can no longer maintain its durability and begins to break down.

This is a description of how human designs are overwhelming nature's design. Recent evidence from around the globe suggests that all living systems are now in decline.[2] Losing their ability to re-create themselves, plant and animal populations are decreasing. The World Wildlife Fund, in partnership with the United Nations Environment Programme, publishes a "living planet index" that tracks the abundance of species in forest, freshwater, and marine environments. Between 1970 and 2000 the three indices together show a 37% decline.[3] Research suggests that tropical and southern temperate regions are suffering the most.

We can trace this decline directly to the activities of one particular species: human beings. Until relatively recently, all plants and animals, including people, were evolving in self-organized systems. As humans gained more control over their environment, using fire and tools, in effect when they began *designing*, they rapidly became vastly more dangerous to other living things. People are now capable of transforming most places on Earth, and more and more often, the only other species that survive are the ones compatible with human activities.[4] Yet we don't generally see the connection of our daily quality of life to ecology. Nor do most of us see ecological decline firsthand.

As designers we can frame our challenge as making our artifacts compatible with ecology, with nature's design. The aim of this part of the atlas is to explore the key ways that human design influences nature's design and what designers might do to harmonize the two.

All artifacts begin and end in the natural environment.

DESIGN AND THE ECOSPHERE

EVERY ARTIFACT, FROM LIBRARY BUILDING to telephone, is connected to Earth's four ecological layers, or "spheres"—air, organism, water, and rock. These spheres, sometimes known by the names atmosphere, biosphere, hydrosphere, and lithosphere, are the source of all materials and resources that we need to make artifacts. They are also the depository for all things we discard. In essence these four spheres are all we have. You can identify materials, such as wood, metal, or insulating air, from each sphere that end up in any design. The making of any object also has effects on all four spheres. For example, a T-shirt is not just cotton. Estimates are that it takes one-third of a pound of lithosphere chemicals to produce a cotton shirt.[5] In addition to agricultural chemicals required to grow cotton, the textile itself is treated with softeners and antimicrobial chemicals.[6] Water is used in growing the cotton, but also in washing and dying the textile. Once I purchase a T-shirt, I continue washing it with water and soap at home until, after possible reuse at a second hand shop, it becomes a rag and then gets thrown into a landfill.

As with human designs, nature's design requires the use and distribution of materials. Cycles are a key feature of nature's movement of materials, and ecosystems are the main form of organizing materials. An ecosystem is a network of organisms and their environment, a network that is complex and synergistic. In an ecosystem, the whole is greater than the sum of its parts.[7]

Ecosystems are remarkable because they have sustained a wide variety of species over many thousands or even many millions of years. The Amazon rain forest, for example, is thought to be as much as ten million years old.[8]

If you consider a specific place, such as a mangrove swamp in Australia, then you can see how the four spheres come together to create a unique environment in an ecosystem. The environment includes a weather pattern (atmosphere), plants and animals (biosphere), surface water, groundwater, and precipitation (hydrosphere), and soil and rock (lithosphere).

DEFINITION: Metabolism

A set of complex physical and chemical processes that help sustain life. Carbon is a building block of life and its cycle, or metabolism, involves processes within organisms, regions, and the entire globe.

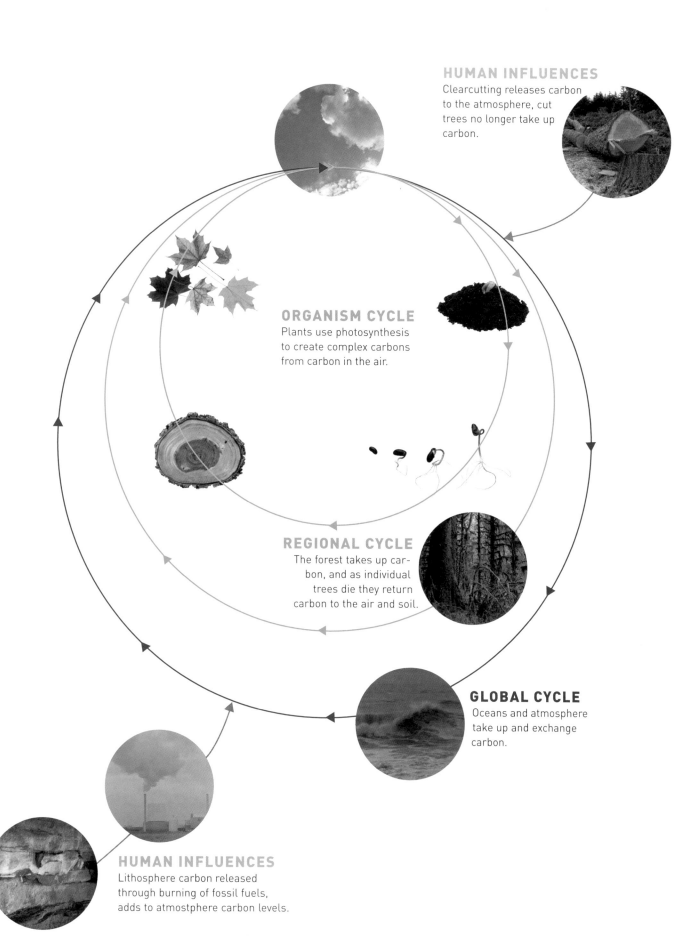

HUMAN INFLUENCES
Clearcutting releases carbon to the atmosphere, cut trees no longer take up carbon.

ORGANISM CYCLE
Plants use photosynthesis to create complex carbons from carbon in the air.

REGIONAL CYCLE
The forest takes up carbon, and as individual trees die they return carbon to the air and soil.

GLOBAL CYCLE
Oceans and atmosphere take up and exchange carbon.

HUMAN INFLUENCES
Lithosphere carbon released through burning of fossil fuels, adds to atmostphere carbon levels.

LANDSCAPE FEATURE: The Ecosphere

Earth is an ecosphere: the source of all materials, the repository for all discards.

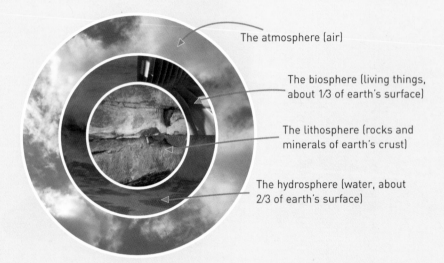

The atmosphere (air)

The biosphere (living things, about 1/3 of earth's surface)

The lithosphere (rocks and minerals of earth's crust)

The hydrosphere (water, about 2/3 of earth's surface)

Every material that we use comes from the ecosphere and eventually goes back to it. Ecosphere is just a fancy name for planet Earth. A sphere, of course, is a circle in three dimensions. And "eco" relates to living systems. At this point Earth appears to be unique; we are aware of no other ecospheres in the galaxy. Our ecosphere is made up of four systems or "layers," which are sometimes called spheres by ecologists. These layers are the atmosphere, biosphere, hydrosphere, and lithosphere. [9]

The atmosphere is the layer of gases that surround Earth and make the surface habitable with breathable air and liveable temperatures. The hydrosphere is the layer of water surrounding Earth, including obvious things like oceans, seas, lakes, and rivers as well as less obvious sources of water such as underground water reservoirs, water in ice caps or snow, and water stored in clouds. The lithosphere is the layer of rock and mineral, sometimes referred to as the earth's crust, that contains many natural resources such as iron, gold, petroleum (used for gasoline as well as a huge range of plastics), and natural gas. The biosphere is a relatively thin layer of living material on Earth's surface containing millions of species of plants and animals existing in a wide range of different habitats.

An ecosystem maintains its delicately balanced cycles using a metabolism—a life-maintaining process. Various nutrients, such as carbon, nitrogen, and water, along with energy from the sun, form the basis of the cycles. Plants use sunlight and nutrients to create starches that other species can then eat. Plants and animals use the energy and nutrients to grow and then die, giving back nutrients to the system through decomposition. Natural cycles also occur on a global scale. The four spheres serve as reference points for some of the most critical global cycles that deliver nutrients around the planet. These cycles are the carbon cycle, the nitrogen cycle, and the water (hydrological) cycle. [10]

The next chapters explore how human activities are putting nature's cycle out of balance.

ATMOSPHERE	BIOSPHERE	LITHOSPHERE	HYDROSPHERE

what we take out

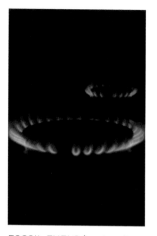

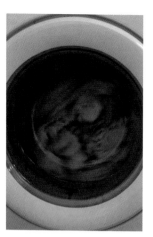

AIR captured between fibers (insulation), in structures (inflatables), and in aerosols and spray paints

NATURAL FIBERS from plants (wood, cotton, linen, hemp) and animals (leather, feather, bone)

FOSSIL FUELS (coal and natural gas), petrochemicals (plastics, coatings), metals (iron, bauxite), and minerals (stone, clay, silica)

WATER in washing, processing, growing, mixing, thinning, drinking

what we put in

GASES (carbon dioxide, sulfur dioxide, nitrous oxide); heat, light, noise, particles from incineration

SOLID WASTE including toxic chemicals; genetically modified and non-native species

CHEMICALS, solid waste, radioactive materials

CHEMICALS, excess nutrients (fertilizer), soil, sewage

SPEED, SIZE AND LOCATION

THERE ARE THREE MAIN WAYS that human designs disrupt nature's material cycles. First, the speed at which we use materials is too fast: Nature can't keep up in regenerating materials. Second, the scale on which we both use and discard material is unprecedented and is beginning to affect nature's cycles. Finally, we are increasingly taking material from the lithosphere and redistributing it to the other spheres, causing damage to living systems. Let's explore these a bit further.

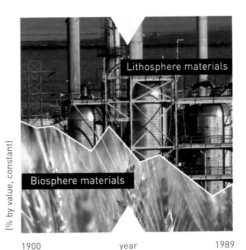

(% by value, constant)

1900   year   1989

Current estimates suggest that we obtain more than 70% of all materials from the lithosphere.

LANDSCAPE FEATURE: Speed and Size

The speed and scale of our resource use is best described with a few examples. Between 1940 and 1982 the production of synthetic materials, namely chemicals, grew roughly 350 times. It's also estimated that we've used more energy since 1900 than in all of human history before 1900.[11] To the extent that materials from the lithosphere are not quickly renewed, we are using up resources too fast. And the overall amount of resource use is growing—we would need three or four planet Earths to sustain the world's population at the current lifestyles of Western countries.

We would need at least three earths to sustain the world's population if everyone consumed as much as Western countries.

Speed and Size

To gain some perspective on the problem of speed and size, consider our resource use in terms of the land area necessary to provide all the raw materials we use as well as to absorb the total amount of our outputs (e.g., solid waste, heat, synthetic materials). This land area is known as our "ecological footprint."

A startling realization occurs when we see that only about one-third (actually less that 30%) of the globe is covered by land. The rest is oceans and seas. Moreover, not all land is productive: Some of it is under ice caps, and some consists of desert or rugged mountains. In fact, less that 25% is bioproductive. If we divide the amount of bioproductive land by the number of people on Earth (about six billion in 2001), we find that only about 1.9 hectares (5 acres) of bioproductive space (land and ocean) is available per person. Not very much considering that lifestyles in the Western world are currently estimated to require 10 hectares per person. We would need three or four planet Earths to sustain the world's population at the current lifestyles of Western countries.[13]

Location

A dramatic shift in the "sphere source" for our material occurred during the Industrial Revolution. Before industrialization, we got a majority of our materials from the biosphere. Furniture was made largely from wood; buildings were made from wood, brick, and straw; and clothing was made from wool, leather, silk, and other natural fibers. Now, it is estimated that we get more than 70% of all materials from the lithosphere.[14] Furniture is still made of wood but also of metal, plastic, and synthetic upholstery. Buildings, though still constructed using biosphere materials, also contain metal, cement, glue, paint, plastic piping and fittings, and many other lithosphere-sourced materials. Many materials that we used to get from renewable

TRAVELER'S NOTE: Ecological Footprint

An ecological footprint is an analytical tool that, for a given population (any size from a household to a city or a country), allows us to estimate that population's resource consumption and waste absorption needs in terms of an amount of corresponding land area. Another way of thinking about it is to imagine a human population, such as the city of Chicago, as an organism, like a cow in its pasture. The cow needs to eat resources and eliminate waste without entirely fouling its own pasture. So, how big a pasture is necessary to support the "cow" that is Chicago? From a design perspective it is possible, although very complex, to calculate an ecological footprint for a given artifact such as a product or a building. For example, preliminary research suggests that a personal computer accounts for about 9% of the overall ecological footprint of a "world-average" citizen. The PC's footprint was estimated at 1,790 m^2 or 0.18 hectares over its three-year life span. This area is bigger than the PC itself by more than a thousandfold. Much of the footprint area is determined by energy use during the PC's useful life.[12]

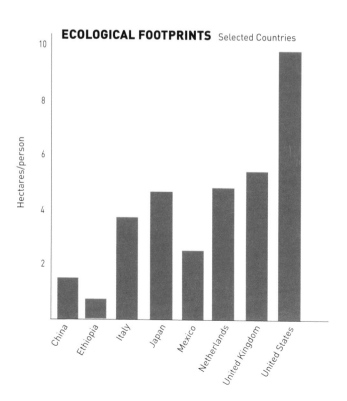

ECOLOGICAL FOOTPRINTS Selected Countries

LANDSCAPE FEATURE: Redistribution of Materials

The design and development of artifacts, from clothing to buildings, is one of the main ways that society redistributes materials from one sphere to another. Most often we take material from the lithosphere and put it into the other spheres where it causes problems (such as destruction of habitat or toxicity) and has little value. It's been suggested that most of the environmental impact of artifacts, and thus much of the redistribution of material, is "locked in" at the design phase when materials and function are decided.[15] The speed and scale of this redistribution through design increases with frequent styling updates, population growth, and an increasingly materialistic global lifestyle.

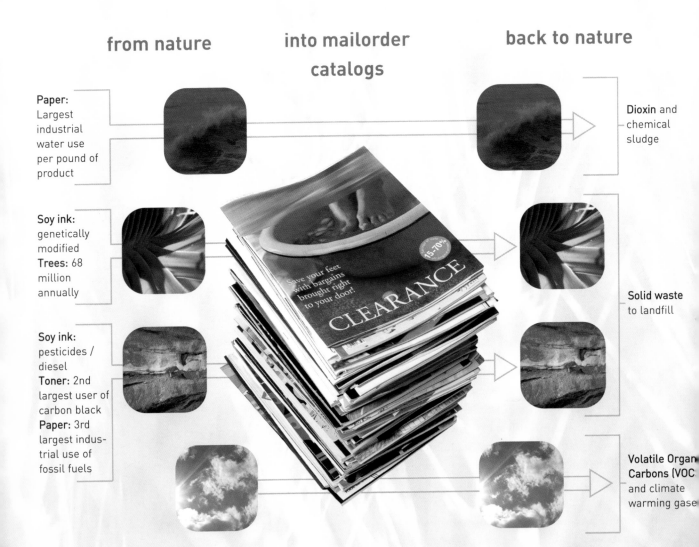

from nature

into mailorder catalogs

back to nature

Paper: Largest industrial water use per pound of product

Dioxin and chemical sludge

Soy ink: genetically modified **Trees:** 68 million annually

Solid waste to landfill

Soy ink: pesticides / diesel **Toner:** 2nd largest user of carbon black **Paper:** 3rd largest industrial use of fossil fuels

Volatile Organic Carbons (VOC) and climate warming gases

resources—everything from indigo to rubber— are now generated synthetically using chemicals, especially petrochemicals, from the lithosphere.

Intensive energy use, itself almost entirely from lithosphere material such as coal, oil, and gas, has brought increases in our use of metals, particularly iron, copper, zinc, aluminium, and lead. Use of nonmetallic minerals such as stone, sand, and clay, often used in construction, also is on the rise. Although we take this material from the lithosphere, we can't put it back into the lithosphere. It gets spread out across the atmosphere, biosphere, or hydrosphere. Carbon, for example, is transformed from fossil fuels in the lithosphere into carbon dioxide gas in the atmosphere, which is a key culprit in global warming.[16]

The accumulation of lithosphere materials in the biosphere is of concern for several reasons. First, many of these materials are toxic when introduced into the biosphere. This is the case with many toxic metals such as lead, nickel, and mercury. The health effects of synthetic chemicals, most of which come from lithosphere sources, also are potentially hazardous. One thousand new chemicals are introduced each year. Most of these chemicals have not been tested on human health, but like other processed lithosphere materials, they will end up somewhere in our biosphere.[17]

Our second concern about the relocation of lithosphere material is speed and magnitude of use because these materials are not renewable except within geologic time scales (e.g., millions of years). Finally, lithosphere materials cannot be easily removed from the other spheres because they are so widely distributed. We will explore this distribution more in upcoming chapters.

In general, we can trace most of our environmental problems to rapid resource depletion (faster than resource renewal rates) or to the redistribution of sphere materials.

 ## TRAVELER'S NOTE: The Natural Step

Another way of thinking about speed, size, and location comes from a group known as The Natural Step (TNS). Swedish doctor Karl-Henrik Robèrt developed TNS in a consensus-based process with many other scientists, struggling to answer the question, "Under what conditions would we have a sustainable system?" The answer emerged as four conditions that we must meet:[18]

1. Materials from the lithosphere must not be allowed to systematically increase in nature.
2. Persistent substances produced by society must not systematically increase in nature.
3. The physical basis for Earth's productive natural cycles and biological diversity must not be systematically deteriorated.
4. There must be fair and efficient use of resources with respect to meeting human needs.

In terms of TNS, "systematically" means that something happens automatically because of the way the system is designed. For example, your body systematically takes in oxygen through breathing—you don't have a choice because that's the way you're designed.

As we will see, none of the four system conditions are currently being met. The TNS organization has typically approached companies and governments to adopt TNS as a guiding framework for their operations. For example, Interface, IKEA, and the Swedish McDonald's have used TNS principles to set corporate goals.

WHAT'S ALLOWED, WHAT'S PREFERRED

BECAUSE OF THE PROBLEMS having to do with the speed, size, and location of material use and disposal, designers are already experiencing some restrictions of choice. These restrictions arise either from rules that dictate what's allowed or from policies that dictate what's preferred.

Rules and regulations typically control what types of materials are acceptable, how they can be used, or what levels of waste can be tolerated. For example, in Europe polyvinyl chloride (PVC) is banned from use in mouth toys for babies because it contains a class of chemical plasticizers—phthalates—that is implicated in increases in cancer.[19]

People are sometimes surprised to find that regulations don't cover many of the materials that are of environmental concern. For example, CO_2 is not regulated, even though human emissions of CO_2 are the main source of new climate-warming gases in the atmosphere.

A chemical plasticizer, banned in Europe for use in baby toys, has been implicated in increases in cancer occurrence.

LANDSCAPE FEATURE: Rules and Recommendations

Design choices are already restricted because of their environmental impact. In the past this was accomplished mainly through regulations, but increasingly organizations are adopting recommendations or guidelines that, to protect the environment, curb the range of options designers have. For example, toxic materials, even if allowed, are not recommended. Virgin materials (as opposed to recycled materials) and those materials that come from sensitive ecosystems are also discouraged.

Where regulations haven't yet been created, some companies (Volvo is a good example) develop their own "blacklist" of materials that should not be used because of their extremely harmful effects.[20] There may also be a "graylist" of materials that are bad but for which no alternatives currently exist. Designers are beginning to encounter policies that promote or favor a certain type of material performance. For example, some organizations have policies to "buy recycled" and will choose products, including building materials, containing recycled content over other products, if all else (e.g., price, quality) is equal. These policies are part of a larger scheme known as "green procurement of supplies."[21] There are also policies, both from governments and nonprofit groups, that offer ways of rating the environmental performance of products and buildings. For example, the U.S. Green Building Council offers the LEED (Leadership in Energy and Environmental Design) rating system for commercial buildings.

Since cutting down on the overall quantity of materials usually saves money, this is also an incentive to be more efficient. Reducing use of hazardous material saves money because it eliminates costly management requirements for handling, storing, and disposing of the material.

In general, the list of allowed and preferred materials is changing all the time. It's not the purpose of this book to provide details but rather to make it clear that these are the mechanisms currently affecting design.

Unfortunately, most of these mechanisms are reactive. That means they don't appear until after there's a problem and oftentimes not until the problem has grown large. For example, overflowing landfills and difficulty in siting new landfills brought home the importance of reducing waste and recycling, and then governments adopted "buy-recycled" policies.

These reactive mechanisms typically aim to get only the worst materials out of the biosphere, leaving many black- and graylist materials legal at some level. As a whole, these techniques are sometimes referred to as ecoefficiency. They aim to be efficient with ecological resources and ask for minor adjustments rather than for a fundamental rethinking of our industrial methods.

The appeal of ecoefficiency lies in its measurable, rational approach. A fair amount of work has gone into developing tools and techniques that designers can use to improve the ecoefficiency of artifacts. Several good books on this topic are available, and I've referenced them in the "further reading" section.

But is ecoefficiency enough? Estimates are that to achieve "sustainable" material flows (not depleting our stocks more rapidly than they are restored), we would need to cut material and energy intensity by 50%. Since developing countries need to use more resources just to meet basic needs, we find that most of the reduction in material and energy intensity will need to occur in developed countries, which equates to a 90% reduction in intensity—or factor 10 improvement in efficiency.[22]

In addition to ecoefficiency, are there other ways to organize our productive systems so that they are compatible with natural systems? How would the role of design change, or indeed, how could designers begin contributing to a more harmonious productive system? The next chapters explore these questions. The first step will be to understand more about materials and their human and ecological cycles. The second step is to assess how ecological cycles could inform human design.

Some governments have policies to "buy recycled" and will choose products with recycled content over others, all else being equal.

SEE ME!

MATERIALS ARE INVISIBLE. This sounds nonsensical, and almost any designer will point out that materials are the most visible aspect of an artifact, whether it's a plastic bowl or a brick building. Yet in four very important ways, materials are invisible. First, most materials used to produce an artifact are not in the artifact itself. Second, because artifacts are distributed throughout society as private possessions, we are unaware of the large stockpile of materials many in mothballed artifacts. Third, in many cases the actual contents and source of a given material are unknown, and indeed, the designer and producer are not required to know them. Finally, materials contained in artifacts escape through mostly invisible processes such as off-gassing, abrasion, leaching, and incineration.

Let's explore these four aspects of invisibility in more detail before considering how designers might teach themselves to see the "material trails" in their work.

Volume of Material

The first aspect of invisibility is the volume of material use. Estimates suggest that 90% or more of all materials used in the production process don't end up in the product but go straight to being waste.[23] That means for every one kilogram of artifact, nine kilograms of material waste are generated. That's the invisible nine kilograms that the designer, the consumer, and most other people don't see.

Metals are a good example of this phenomenon, because a great deal of raw ore and soil (known as the "overburden") must be dug and processed to generate a finished kilogram of "pure" metal. Gold is one of the worst culprits. Two gold wedding rings require an amount of ore 10 feet long, 6 feet wide, and 6 feet high, and to make matters worse, the toxic chemical cyanide is used to separate the gold ore from the overburden. As we mine more aggressively, we have to process larger volumes of ore with much lower concentrations of metal, meaning that at current rates of use, volumes of waste will only increase.[24]

Stockpile

The scale of materials also is invisible because we tend to see or consider distributed artifacts one at a time or in small groups on the store shelf. In fact, the amount of materials "stored up" in products and buildings is huge. When these products contain hazardous materials, we can forecast a

Waste in Production

Materials are invisible in four important ways.

Stockpile

looming environmental problem. For example, each computer contains a certain small amount of hazardous material. When we consider these small amounts, it doesn't seem so bad. But estimates are that in the United States alone, 315 million computers were retired between 1997 and 2004. These old computers sitting in garages and attics each contain about 4 pounds of toxic materials. That amounts to about 1 billion pounds of lead, 400,000 pounds of mercury, and 1.9 million pounds of cadmium.[25] Each of these toxic metals is very dangerous when released into the environment and possibly before.

Contents and Origin

What about the ingredients in materials or their geographic origin? In many cases, we simply do not know what a material contains or where it came from. Sometimes suppliers of the material don't even know its origin or won't reveal the information (perhaps they will claim it is proprietary). Designers and producers are not required to know what is contained in the materials of their artifacts. With global sourcing of lowest-cost materials and labor, substances banned in "developed" countries can be used in "developing" countries and then enter developed countries as finished products.[26]

 LANDSCAPE FEATURE: Invisible Materials

Although we might think that the material aspects of an artifact are the most obvious ones—it's made of wood or it's made of metal—in fact, the true material implications of our designs are largely invisible. This invisibility occurs through four mechanisms:

1. Materials are used to produce an artifact that are not present in the artifact, because a large percentage of the production material ends up as waste.
2. Distribution of materials throughout society conceals the scale of materials and particularly those tied up in dormant artifacts such as old computers and mobile phones.
3. Designers frequently don't know the contents or origin of materials.
4. Materials contained in artifacts frequently escape through invisible processes.

Contents

Escape

Escape

Once these undesirable substances (whether legal or not) are encased in an artifact, the next aspect of invisibility emerges—routes that materials follow to get back into the environment.

Off-gassing happens when products and furnishings give off gasses in the indoor environment. The combination of harmful gasses found indoors is typically called "indoor air pollution" and has led to a concern for indoor air quality as people tend to spend more and more time indoors. Carpet glue, paint, medium-density fiberboard (MDF), and other building materials contribute to indoor air pollution, but electronic products do, too. Recent studies showed that during use a wide range of ordinary household products off-gassed hazardous chemicals. In the worst cases, instances of "sick building syndrome" have affected entire office buildings.[27]

Abrasion occurs when particles of a material are rubbed off, for example, to form dust in a house. Recent research shows that common house dust typically contains traces of dozens of chemicals, many known to be toxic and some that have been banned for many years. Invisible escape also happens through waste incineration and plain old litter. Research in the United Kingdom found that tiny particles of plastic are now distributed throughout the environment.[28]

How to See

A critical challenge for designers is to actually see the "material trails" in their work. One method for doing this is to think about an artifact's whole life, from raw material through to waste material. Typically, designers have focused most on the construction and use of an artifact. Understanding that each artifact has a life cycle is a useful start.

Although ecodesign tools ("further reading" section) can help you decide how to act once you have the whole picture of an artifact's material trail, there are no ready-made answers for where to find that material picture or develop it. Indeed, in a complex global system, there probably should not be ready-made answers because these will often mean universal solutions. And a one-size-fits-all solution doesn't allow for the diversity found in real life. Indeed, universal solutions are the antithesis of genuine efforts to harmonize with nature's design.

Seeing the true amount, type, and source of materials behind artifacts, as well as in them, is a good step toward understanding the challenges of harmonizing with nature's design. Another important step is thinking about how material in human designs could better relate to nature's cycles.

 DEFINITION: Life Cycle Approaches

From a building to a small electronic device to a brochure, the general outline of a product life cycle is the same. From a designer's perspective, it is important to recognize that the life cycle starts with the idea or concept for the design. Next comes the collection and shaping of materials. Some people will choose to look as far back as the harvesting and transfer of raw materials; others will choose to consider only the processing and assembly of refined materials. Typically, after assembly there is some level of packaging and distribution. Once the end consumer begins to use the artifact, the "use phase" of the life cycle begins. The term "end-of-life" often is used to describe the last phase of the cycle, when the product falls out of use or is discarded. Beyond the life cycle, it's also helpful to understand each artifact as part of a system—both a natural system and a human system. We will explore this concept further in the upcoming chapters.

TRAVELER'S NOTE: Material Trails

Investigation is the main tool that designers can use to get the whole picture of the material trail attached to an artifact. Common investigation techniques include:

Asking questions

Designers at Nokia are asking their suppliers to provide complete material content lists for all components in the phone. You can also ask experts in the field what they know about materials, chemicals, and their risks.

Doing estimates

If Nokia phones contain a milligram each of a substance, let's call it substance A, and if there are 100 million phones sold next year, that's 100,000 kilograms of substance A. If consumers update their phones every two years, then that's 100,000 kilograms more of substance A in two years' time.

Doing some tests

If you're not sure about materials or want to understand more about existing artifacts, consider having them tested and get help interpreting the results. Make friends with a chemist or a chemical engineer. There might be one resident at larger nonprofit environmental groups. William McDonough (a designer) and Michael Brangart (a chemist) have done this type of testing on a variety of products. Greenpeace also has tested mobile phones and children's sleepwear, among other things.

Lifecycle of an $18 waffle iron

Design Concept

Materials and Manufacture: Mining, Drilling, Molding

Packaging and Transport

End of Life

Consumer Use: Energy, Batter, Water

Consumer Purchase

DOWN-CYCLE, UP-CYCLE

THE MOST COMMON IDEA for cycles with materials used in human designs is recycling, and unfortunately, one of the most shallow claims for an "environmentally friendly" artifact is that it can be recycled. In theory, almost anything can be recycled if there is someone to collect it, sort it, and reprocess it. The problem is that aside from the most commonly recycled materials (such as steel, aluminium, glass, and paper), no other recycling systems exist.

Still, the ideal behind recycling is laudable and borrows principles from nature's cycles. When a material can be safely reabsorbed, it becomes "food," or nutrients, for the metabolism. Otherwise, it is processed by global cycles.

Ultimately, all matter and energy are "conserved," meaning that they never disappear, they just change form. For example, when we consume energy and other types of materials such as wood, metal, or any kind of food, we don't really destroy them. They are just converted into something else—usually something less useful than before. We are changing their structure or concentration, causing them to dissipate—be spread around into less concentrated, less useful forms.

But nature doesn't just churn materials around in cycles. Nature "adds value" to material by using the sun's energy to concentrate simple ingredients and structure them to make them useful. Green plant cells use photosynthesis to turn sunlight into plant matter by converting carbon dioxide into carbohydrates, making plants the basis of support for life on Earth.

Over time these carbohydrates concentrate further and become fossil fuels. Over even longer periods they become diamonds. The sun's input of energy to Earth counters the law of entropy, which is the tendency for all resources to lose their structure and concentration.[29]

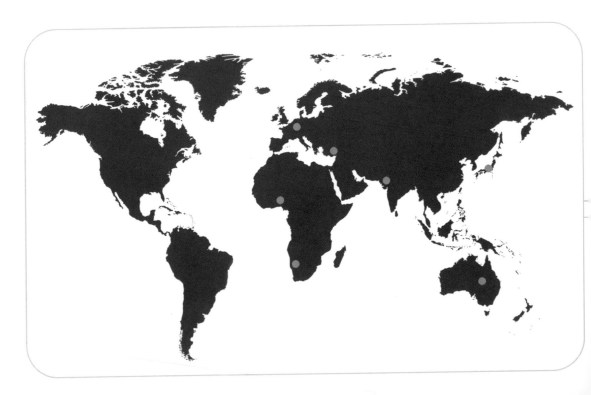

 TRAVELER'S NOTE: Design is Unstructuring

Design is usually an activity of unstructuring and deconcentrating energy and materials. Although we may argue that we use "pure" or "natural" materials, which are no doubt helpful in recycling efforts, the result of mass production is to spread these materials globally, often into places where they would not otherwise occur, where there is no mechanism to collect or reuse them.

For example, a pair of jeans draws together materials from all over the world. Synthetic indigo comes from Germany, pumice for stonewashing comes from Turkey. Cotton for denim comes from Benin and cotton pocketing comes from Pakistan. Polyester fiber for thread comes from Japan and copper for fasteners comes from Namibia and Australia. Bound together in a pair of jeans, these diverse materials are deposited in European stores.[30] The jeans represent the long process in which raw materials (cotton, copper, polyester) lose their original structure and concentration, their potential, and get spread in less useful forms around the globe. Our current human systems offer no practical way to structure and concentrate the materials from billions of pairs of jeans.

LANDSCAPE FEATURE: Structure and Concentration

Nature's own recycling system "adds value" to material by using the sun's energy to concentrate simple ingredients, structuring them to make them useful. This cycle is facilitated by the fact that in nature, one organism's waste is another organism's food. Structure and concentration are what give a material its potential to be useful. Consider an industrial-sized chunk of pure PET plastic compared with a bunch of used soda bottles discarded across a large urban region. Which has more value as a material? Not only are the soda bottles dissipated, that is to say, spread around in a disorderly manner, but also the PET plastic, which is their main material component, is contaminated by paper labels stuck on with adhesives, dyes, and possibly other plastics used to protect the bottle's contents. By becoming thousands or millions of soda bottles, the PET has lost its structure and concentration. Human recycling systems to date have had great difficulty structuring and concentrating materials as well as nature does. In fact, most recycling is actually down-cycling in terms of material quality.

Human recycling systems to date have had great difficulty structuring and concentrating materials as well as nature does. Unfortunately, most recycling actually degrades material quality resulting in "down-cycling," With each recycle, the materials lose structure and concentration.

Material becomes less concentrated primarily because of contamination. Contamination has many sources including inaccurate separation of materials and poor storage. In most cases an artifact is made of different materials that are hard to separate. For example, clothing might be 100% cotton—except for the buttons, zipper, and thread.[31]

The relatively low quality of down-cycled materials means that additives are often required to make the material perform. Additives might include chemical stabilizers or other introduced material. Contaminants can be hazardous when recycled material begins its new life. For example, when recycled paper is used as building insulation, inks and waterproofing chemicals from the original paper can off-gas into the indoor environment. Down-cycled steel from automobiles contains paints and plastic residues from other car components. These contaminants can become a source of toxic emissions when the down-cycled steel is refabricated.

Contaminants present one version of "danger-cycling." Danger-cycling also can occur when a material designed for one use is recycled into another use for which it was never intended. Polyethylene terephthalate (PET) soda bottles are being recycled into fleece sweaters. Yet the material composition of a soda bottle in not necessarily suitable for prolonged contact with human skin. The bottles contain the toxic chemical antimony, potentially harmful plasticizers, ultra violet (UV) stabilizers, and other chemicals.

A conceptual alternative to the current down-cycling is up-cycling. Up-cycling means the material is remade into a high-quality (structured and concentrated) material. One example is a waterproof book that William McDonough and Michael Braungart have published. Rather than being made from a mix of different materials, the book is made of one pure plastic, enabling it to be easily up-cycled. Eventually, a sort of up-cycling imprint could be embedded in every kind of artifact, identifying all the substances contained in the product and how to reuse them, separate them, or return them to their "spheres."

Danger-cycling: Some materials are being recycled into products that could pose hazards to the user. Plastic water bottles are transformed into fleece, but what are the effects of plastic chemical composites on skin?

Spun into yarn

Wool from sheep

Made into carpet

RETHINKING MATERIALS

ORGANIC MATERIAL CYCLE

To stop the high-speed, large-scale distribution of lithosphere materials into the other spheres, some designers have proposed adopting the idea of metabolisms for human material flows. The scheme involves classifying all materials as either organic nutrients or technical nutrients. Organic nutrients are generally biological (or natural) materials that will safely biodegrade. Technical nutrients must remain in a closed-loop industrial metabolism because they are unsuitable for release into natural systems.[32]

Biodegrades back to soil

This metabolism concept suggests an elegant system that protects nature while also meeting the material needs of modern civilization.

But its material designation would be difficult. The chair you're sitting in probably has both organic and technical nutrients in it, but it is hard to distinguish which is which. More important, one of the materials alone may contain both organic and technical nutrients. Even if you knew which materials your chair contained, what's the best and easiest way to get them out—when the chair breaks or you buy a new model? What else could these materials conceivably be used for?

There are other questions as well. In the current industrial system, many materials that might seem to be "organic nutrients" actually are not because they become contaminated during industrial processing. So while cotton could be made to safely biodegrade, current practices in growing, processing, and finishing cotton products mean that they can't biodegrade safely now.

In addition, there is the issue of renewability. Many organic nutrients are biological materials that are renewable within the time frame of a human life. Some materials that are grown as agricultural products (cotton, hemp, or bamboo) are rapidly renewable on a seasonal basis. Tree and forest products tend to be slower—on the order of decades. If the pace of use remains so fast that nature cannot cope with the loss of biological materials, then an organic nutrient loop won't work. Moreover, with limited agriculturally productive land area on Earth, much land will need to be dedicated to growing food as the population grows to nine or ten billion.

Finally, where and how will our organic materials biodegrade? We know that landfills are airtight and that little biodegradation takes place within them. What about community compost heaps? Where would the compost, when ready, be distributed? For technical nutrients, how can they be collected, disassembled, and reprocessed on a mass scale? If artifacts are made overseas, do the collected nutrients get shipped back overseas to be used again, or do technical nutrients find a new home closer to where they end up? We know that natural cycles work within regional ecosystems but that some materials are handled by global cycles—how would technical nutrients split themselves between local reuse and global processing?

High-tech composite materials pose another challenge for technical nutrient cycles. Composites like hemp–fiber polymers or ceramic–metal composites are the wave of the future in terms of materials development.[33] Since composites involve a tight integration of two material types, they suggest yet more new material streams needing management and renewal. In addition, as "old" technical nutrients such as PVC are phased out, where would they go in the technical nutrient cycle in order not to accumulate in the biosphere.

The challenges associated with this concept make good design problems in themselves, but they reaffirm that an artifact is never alone. It is always part of a system, and the designer needs to think about it that way to realign human and natural systems. Using technical and organic nutrient classifications is an intriguing idea. Indeed, creating "industrial" metabolisms is the work of a new field, industrial ecology. The next chapter explores this and other nature-inspired design.

A PAGE FROM NATURE'S BOOK

WHY NOT GROW A BUILDING instead of constructing it? How far could we go in adopting nature's patterns and techniques? To date, designers' adaptations from nature have been largely aesthetic—a leaf motif on printed fabric or a building in the shape of an animal. But nature's structures and functions, as we've seen, may suggest useful design approaches.

Biomimicry involves taking inspiration from nature in order to solve design problems. Nature has ways to manufacture super strong material and high-performance composites all without artificially high temperature or pressure and without any life-threatening synthetic chemicals. By operating within the defined boundaries of ecosystems that are highly adapted, nature, at a global scale, produces no waste.[34]

Natural ecosystem boundaries require plants and animals to become extremely well adapted to their environments. This is nature's way of "thinking locally." Camels and penguins are two extreme examples. Camels are particularly well adapted to hot, dry environments such as the Sahara desert. Meanwhile, nature has designed a special type of feather that keeps penguins super insulated even in the icy conditions of the Arctic.[35]

 DEFINITION: Biomimicry

Biomimicry in design involves taking inspiration from nature to solve design problems. To date, biomimicry largely has been the domain of engineers and biologists, but designers of all types should consider it (see the "traveler's note"). Shark skin has inspired new textures for airplanes and swimsuits to make them more aerodynamic. Lotus leaves have inspired a new paint that has a self-cleaning surface. Perhaps the most famous example is that of Velcro, which is patterned after a burr—a seed pod that sticks to your clothing. In another example, natural weather patterns have served as inspiration for building ventilation.

Shark skin

Swimsuit

Burr

Velcro

Biomimicry looks for inspiration from nature's many specialized adaptations.

Biomimicry looks for inspiration from nature's many specialized adaptations. The ecosphere holds somewhere between 10 and 30 distinct biomes (depending on how broadly you characterize them), from desert to polar ice cap. Within each biome is a range of unique regions (sometimes called "bioregions" or "ecoregions") that illustrate adaptations that can inspire design ideas. It is the physical boundaries of ecosystems that promote the diverse and specialized adaptations throughout nature. By specializing in local conditions, individuals within an ecosystem use energy and materials most productively.

In "industrial ecology," the aim is to make industrial facilities perform more like ecological systems. This has been demonstrated most prominently in Kalundborg, Denmark, where a series of industrial facilities are linked together using each other's waste products as "nutrients" for their own processes. [36] Included are a power plant, a wallboard factory, and an oil refinery exchanging things such as fly ash (for asphalt), steam heat, and sludge (for fertilizer). The development of eco-industrial parks so far focuses on industrial processes rather than designed artifacts. Yet by being aware of materials and the local region, designers may be able to identify industrial ecology opportunities.

The idea of mimicking nature's cycles and structures is a useful starting point for design. Further possibilities for design arise from investigating the sophistication of nature's structure, as we do in the next chapter.

LANDSCAPE FEATURE: Bioregion and Biome

Bioregion describes a geographic area that is characterized by a distinct range of native plants and animals, watershed, soils, and climate. A related term is "ecoregion," which also describes a more regional-scale unit of biodiversity. A third term is "biome," which describes a major ecological region, such as tundra, tropical forest, or grassland, that, when considered on a global scale, may contain a large range of different ecoregions or bioregions around the world. There are several ways to characterize Earth's major biomes, resulting in estimates ranging from about 10 to 30 for their total number. Detailed studies of Earth's ecoregions have yielded estimates of 867 terrestrial (land-based) ecoregions.[38]

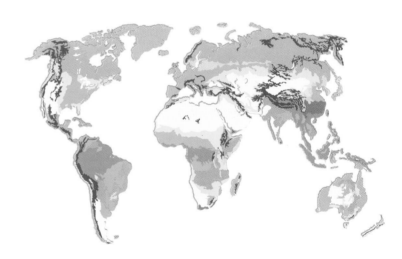

There are between 10 and 30 major biomes on earth.

TRAVELER'S NOTE: Biomimicry

Consider applying biomimicry to answer a specific design question. For example, if you were working on insulation, you would look to places in nature where plants or animals have to insulate themselves—how do they do it? This was the starting point for the idea of using penguin feathers to create clothing insulation.

Designers also could consider the biome or bioregion in which their artifacts will be made and used. By working with the conditions of those systems and adapting to them, rather than overwhelming them, designers can better harmonize with nature.[37]

ECO-STRUCTURES AND FUNCTIONS

WHEN WE THINK ABOUT ARTIFACTS as part of systems, it becomes clear that each artifact is more than the sum of its parts. Being connected in a web of people, places, and technology, each item gains important attributes that give it function and meaning. A phone doesn't amount to much on its own; only when it's connected to a system does it serve a purpose. Similarly, an ecosystem amounts to more than the sum of its parts. To what extent then, could we develop product ecologies?

In healthy living systems the community and the individual strengthen and support each other in self-organizing systems, without any central control mechanism or "boss." Organisms are made up of individual living cells, and ecosystems are made up of individual living organisms. In each case the individual participates cooperatively in a whole system. For example, although the cells in our body individually control their own boundaries, deciding what to let in and out, they also freely share their resources to support the whole body on which they all depend.[39]

The main activity of an ecosystem is to reproduce itself and carry on its existence. Earth has a living history of billions of years. Living systems, whether individual organisms or whole ecosystems, continually re-create themselves by transforming or replacing their components. Through continuous re-creation of themselves, living systems can change their structures but maintain general patterns of organization. For example, a rain forest contains trees and frogs, but as these individual organisms die, they are replaced by a new generation so that the overall pattern of the rain forest remains the same. But living systems also have the capacity to adapt in response to catastrophes and opportunities.

One particularly interesting perspective suggests thinking of an ecosystem as a structured cycle. The cycle has four phases.

At first, the system exploits new conditions, but gradually a conservation phase establishes itself, emphasizing accumulation and storage of material and energy. Then a release occurs, when material and energy are freed and then reorganized, followed by a new exploitation phase. Ecosystems naturally fluctuate between states of relative stability and bursts of "creative destruction" (such as forest fires, drought, insect pests, or overgrazing).[40]

The resilience of an ecosystem lies partly in its ability to function along a continuum of points. It doesn't have to return to one given state, nor does it have a set sequence of interactions that play themselves out repeatedly like a videotape playing over and over again. Rather, an ecosystem is more like a deck of cards, continually reshuffled and inventively reorganized. A single ecosystem can have a wide range of functional states. It is diverse and adaptive, yet it also maintains productivity and life-sustaining cycles.

LANDSCAPE FEATURE: Recreation and Resilience

Ecosystems carry on indefinitely—in many cases for billions of years—by being resilient. They survive potentially destructive events because the small, faster parts react quickly while the big, slower parts maintain the overall continuity of the system. In continually re-creating themselves, ecosystems change their structures but maintain their overall pattern of organization. For example, the rainforest will be home to countless generations of tree frogs over a thousand years, but the roles of tree frog and forest are stable over that time period. Roles may change and evolve but the ecosystem recreates the right conditions for life; conditions can vary and still be viable. This room for variation and invention allows ecosystems to adapt in response to catastrophe and opportunity.

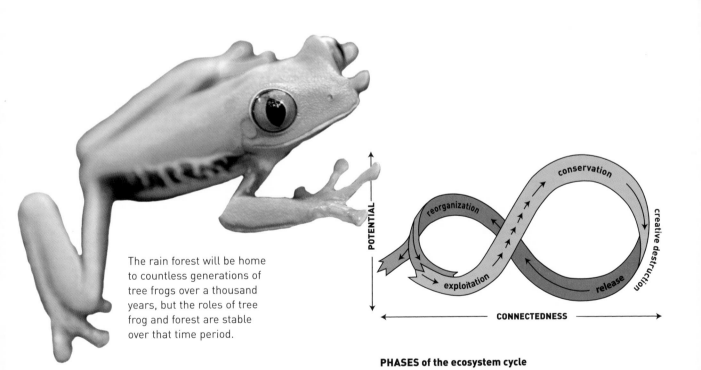

The rain forest will be home to countless generations of tree frogs over a thousand years, but the roles of tree frog and forest are stable over that time period.

PHASES of the ecosystem cycle

Life sustaining conditions within an ecosystem can respond to changing conditions

RESILIENCE

EACH ECOSYSTEM STRUCTURE HAS ITS OWN CYCLE time and its own boundaries. For example, a rain puddle is a short-lived microecosystem, but a large mountain range has a very long life. When we step back and look at the range of things people design, we see the same patterns emerging in terms of how long artifacts last and how big they are. At the short and small end of the spectrum are things like disposable food packaging. At the long and large end of the spectrum are things like grand museums. Urban designers might say they design on an even longer and larger scale, deciding where to draw urban boundaries and orchestrating the long-term development of cities and the countryside.

Ecosystems use size and time strategically to adjust to change. At a large scale, things generally happen slowly (e.g., the formation of a mountain range). At small scales, things usually happen

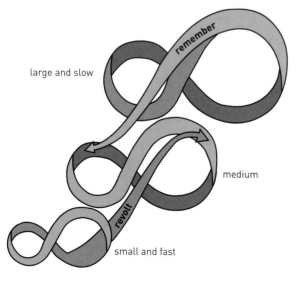

Adjusting to change using size and time

faster (e.g., the life span of a fruit fly). In any shock to the ecosystem, the fast parts respond quickly, allowing the slow parts to "ignore" the shock and maintain the continuity of the system.[41] Nature combines small-and-fast with large-and-slow to create resiliency.

The fast levels serve to invent, experiment, and test; the slower levels stabilize and conserve the memory (e.g., genetic combinations) of past successes. This method of combining learning with continuity is a way of describing sustainable development.[42]

At first glance, the nesting of ecosystems from small to large looks like a "top-down" structure, where the top levels dictate what happens in all the rest. This is actually not the case, since there are many instances in which the fast, inventive levels of the ecosystem drive the direction of the layers "above" it. For example, after a forest fire, it is the smallest ecosystems that start the recolonization

Nature uses small, fast elements (such as leaves) and large, slow elements (such as whole forests) to adjust to change.

> We cannot understand the individual, whether living thing or artifact, without understanding the networked system of which the individual is a part.

process. The contents of these microecosystems set the stage for forest regrowth. Each structure has its own boundary at the scale of its cycle. For example, the tree has its own boundary, but it is part of a forest, which has its own boundary. These structures also operate across the scale of time, as well as space (from local to global).[43]

The nesting structure doesn't indicate a hierarchy, but it does illustrate the dynamics of systems, where change in any one part affects all others.

Ecosystems have adapted to changes over time, but their capacity to adjust is not infinite.

For example, each ecosystem structure has the capacity to support a limited number of species and a limited population size of each species. This limit is known as the ecosystem's carrying capacity, and it is governed, in part by the ecosystem's reliance upon global cycles to transform materials back into usable forms.[44]

The nested and dynamic structures of nature leave us with a better understanding of sustainability. Nature sustains itself by conserving its ability to adapt to change. Until recently, it had flexible responses to uncertainty and surprises. It is through adaptation that nature also creates

 TRAVELER'S NOTE: Holism

Holism, or understanding by seeing parts in relationship to the whole, is an approach already familiar to design. Designers frequently use iterative techniques that require them to go back and forth between the big picture and the small details of individual parts. The big picture, though it may include only the artifact and the immediate user, often includes some broader aspects of the context for an artifact. For example, in designing a suitcase do we consider only travelers and their belongings, or do we consider the wider transportation and storage system, including airports, baggage handlers, and cargo holds? The designer also considers many small parts such as a handle on the suitcase.

Design is already the process of experimenting with how all the parts can be balanced elegantly in a big picture. What we learn from natureís holism is that, first, we must see artifacts as parts of systems. Second, design must face the challenge of further enlarging its "big picture" to consider more thoroughly the entire system or network in which the artifact interacts. In the landscape of sustainability the system includes ecological aspects we've reviewed in this part, as well as economic and cultural aspects that weíll examine in upcoming parts. As far as ecological systems are concerned, our challenge is to develop an ability to see materials and their use in such a way that we can help our designs harmonize with nature's design rather than overwhelm it.

novelty. Ecosystems grow, collapse, reassemble, and renew.[45] The results of human activity, including design, are now jeopardizing nature's ability to adapt.

It's clear that human designs need to be thought of in terms of systems that create and absorb them rather than in terms of just the artifacts themselves. To see the system and work with it requires approaching it holistically. We cannot understand the individual, whether living thing or artifact, without understanding the networked system of which the individual is a part. Much of the individual's definition comes from the interaction, or relationship with its broader context. In addition, nature demonstrates that adaptation through local variety is the best way to capture the potential value in a system, but that these local systems benefit by being linked to a background global system.[46]

As for whether systems of human artifacts can borrow from the structures and functions of ecosystems, we return to that question in part 5, after we've considered the dynamics in the other two landscapes for sustainability.

DEFINITION: Holism

Holism takes its meaning from the word "whole." It is an approach that tries to understand something by seeing how the parts relate to the whole. Holism is an important aspect of working with systems, because they are dynamic. A system is a group of interacting or interrelated elements that form a collective entity. That means that any change to one part of a system affects the other parts of the system. To see the system and work with it requires approaching it holistically. To the extent that artifacts are part of systems, such as ecological systems, designers need to use holistic approaches.

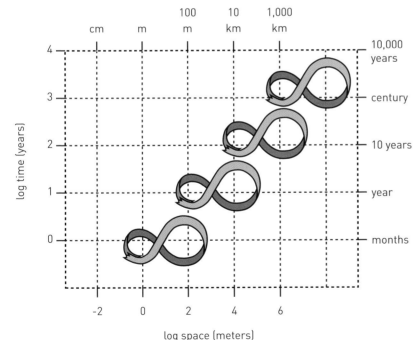

Individual ecosystems are part of the whole ecosphere. Their cycles interact at different times and sizes.

CONCLUSION

AFTER VISITING THE LANDSCAPE OF ECOLOGY, we can think of ecodesign in terms of the four layers of the ecosphere. The process of human design takes materials, frequently from the lithosphere, and distributes them, in a relatively useless form, in all the other spheres. Although this results in some major problems for the ecosphere and human health, the challenge is that, in many ways, materials are invisible. The task of really seeing materials, what they are made of, where and how they travel, continues to be a key issue for sustainable design.

We've considered a range of responses for design. Incremental steps include recycling and making full use of existing recommendations (such as black- or graylists of materials) and policies or regulations (such as ecoefficiency). In terms of larger steps that design might take, among the possibilities is using inspiration from nature's structures and functions for individual design solutions and striving to create an actual materials metabolism. This metabolism could take the form of an industrial ecology or a nutri-

ent system in which all materials are either technical or biological nutrients.

A more sophisticated understanding of ecosystems shows us that they use size and time strategically to manage change. The nesting of ecosystems from a local to a global level also better illustrates how sustainability works. Local systems spawn nature's elegant, specialized design solutions, whereas at the global level, input of solar energy and global cycles of materials allow the ecosphere to thrive. The adaptive capability of the ecosystem allows it to respond creatively to changes, and the continuity in the system maintains development opportunity over the long term.

An important conclusion is that our designs are part of systems that include, and indeed rely on, the healthy function of the ecosphere. Once we understand the connections among nature's systems and our work, we can begin to consider how design can contribute to the environmental conditions that truly support human well-being indefinitely.

FURTHER READING

Human Influence on the Environment/State of the Environment

A large body of literature is available on the environment and environmental management. Several groups publish regular updates. For example, the United Nations Environment Programme publishes a global environmental outlook (GEO), while the Worldwatch Institute publishes an annual state-of-the-world report. A few starting points include the following:

GEO Yearbook 2006: An Overview of Our Changing Environment by the United Nations Environment Programme (Nairobi: United Nations Environment Programme, 2006)

The Human Impact on the Natural Environment by Andrew Goudie (Oxford: Blackwell, 2000)

State of the World 2006 by the Worldwatch Institute (New York: W. W. Norton, 2006)

Environmental Aspects of Materials

Lightness: The Inevitable Renaissance of Minimum Energy Structures by Adriaan Beukers and Ed van Hinte (Rotterdam: 010 Publishers, 1998)

Materials and Design: The Art and Science of Material Selection in Product Design by Mike Ashby and Kara Johnson (Oxford: Butterworth-Heinemann, 2002)

Stuff: The Secret Lives of Everyday Things, New Report, No. 4, by John C. Ryan and Alan Thein Durning (Seattle: Northwest Environment Watch, 1997)

Biomimicry and Complexity in Nature

Biomimicry: Innovation Inspired by Nature by Janine Benyus (New York: Quill William Morrow, 1997)

By Nature's Design by Pat Murphy and William Neill (San Francisco: Chronicle Books, 1993)

The Hidden Connections: A Science for Sustainable Living by Fritjof Capra (London: HarperCollins, 2002)

Industrial Ecology by T. E. Gradel and B. R. Allenby (Englewood Cliffs, NJ: Prentice Hall, 1995)

Journal of Industrial Ecology by the International Society for Industrial Ecology (New Haven, CT: Yale School of Forestry and Environmental Studies)

Nature in Design: The Shapes, Colours, and Forms That Have Inspired Visual Invention by Alan Powers (London: Conran Octopus, 1999)

Zoomorphic: New Animal Architecture by Hugh Aldersey-Williams (London: Laurence King, 2003)

SUMMARY MAP of the LANDSCAPE FEATURES for
ECOLOGY

When we look at design within the landscape of ecology, these features are critical to understanding sustainability.

1 ECOSPHERE

The atmosphere = air
The biosphere = living things, about
 one-third of Earth's surface
The hydrosphere = water, about
 two-thirds of Earth's surface
The lithosphere = rocks and minerals
 of Earth's crust

Although we don't normally "see" it this way, every material that we use comes from somewhere in the ecosphere and eventually goes back to it someplace else.

2 SPEED AND SIZE

Material use increases: Overall material use is growing, causing both ecological loss and resource depletion. We would need more than three planet Earths if everyone on the planet had the lifestyle of those in the United States.

[% by value, constant]

1900　　year　　1989

3 REDISTRIBUTION
OF MATERIALS

The balance of our materials comes increasingly from nonrenewable materials in the lithosphere. Environmental problems result when lithosphere materials pile up in the other spheres. For example, carbon from fuel goes into the atmosphere and contributes to climate warming.

4 RULES

Regulate and recommend: Some materials are not allowed, others are controlled. Relatively harmless materials and better efficiency are preferred. For example, many types of materials were preferred for construction at the Sydney 2000 Olympics.

5 THE FOUR WAYS MATERIALS ARE INVISIBLE

1. Ninety percent of production materials end up as waste rather than in the products.
2. Our existing product and buildings contain large stockpiles of problem materials, but because artifacts are so broadly distributed, we don't see the scale of the problem.
3. We frequently don't know the contents or origins of materials we use.
4. Materials escape invisibly into the environment as tiny particles, dust, and gases.

6 STRUCTURE AND CONCENTRATION

Nature's recycling system structures and concentrates materials, adding value to them. Human recycling systems so far are mostly down-cycling and danger-cycling. We have not found a way to structure and concentrate materials the way nature does. Creating an industrial metabolism of organic and technical nutrients is one proposal for improving our material cycles.

7 WORLD BIOREGIONS

Earth's major biomes illustrate how nature's adaptation to local conditions creates elegant design solutions. Biomimicry is the practice of taking inspiration from these adaptations to solve design problems more elegantly and in harmony with the ecosphere.

8 NATURE'S SYSTEMS

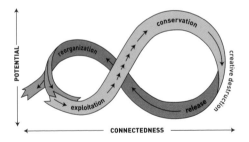

PHASES of the ecosystem cycle
life sustaining conditions within an ecosystem can respond to changing conditions

Ecosystems have a four-phase, self-organizing cycle that continually re-creates the ecosystem with the right conditions for life. The nesting of ecosystems, from micro to global, results in dynamic interaction among them because they have their own cycle times and boundaries. For this reason, the conditions for life can vary and still be right. This is how nature conserves (always the right conditions) and innovates (conditions may vary).

9 RESILIENCY

Nature combines small-and-fast with large-and-slow to create resiliency. The fast levels invent, experiment, and test, while the slower levels stabilize and conserve the memory of past successes. We also can categorize artifacts in terms of how long they last and how big they are, but human artifact systems appear to lack the kind of resilience nature has.

THINK FOR A MOMENT of your vision of success. How will you know when you've "made it"? What is the first thing that comes to mind? For many people, it will be money: not having to worry about money, being able to win generous budgets for design projects, creating artifacts that people buy, or perhaps working for exciting clients who can afford to do really interesting design work. Although it's possible to imagine a vision of success that includes nonmonetary elements, it is nearly impossible to imagine a vision of success that does not include some measure of money.

When you think of success, money is one of the first things that comes to mind.

58 / 59

Why is money such an important measure in society—so important that it drives most decision making from the personal to the global level? What kind of decisions does money drive us to make? For example, cost is one of the largest obstacles to harmonizing human designs with nature's design. There are plenty of instances when it costs more to use safe, biodegradable materials than it does to use dangerous, toxic ones. This is a strange result for a system that is supposed to capture value.

Money is part of a market system. The mechanism of a marketplace allows us to efficiently distribute valuable things, such as food, housing, clothing, office space, or electronic appliances. Money, our medium of exchange, allows any participant to exchange goods and services with others even when only one of them has a material

Money is seen as all-important in society. But what kind of design decisions does money drive us to make?

item that the other wants. Money also makes it possible to sell services, such as design, and store wealth. These features combined have become known as the "free" market and are certainly useful in society. We might see the marketplace as a means of accomplishing the things that are important to us, such as raising a family.

Yet our current free market, in the form of modern capitalism, has focused the attention of society more and more exclusively on economic expansion and the generation of material wealth. Rather than being a means to an end, capitalism has itself become society's aim. But there are a number of important values (happy families, breathable air) that are not captured by the market, so a big challenge for a sustainable economy is to find a system that allows us to capture these

values as well as trade the goods and services that are easily valued by the market. To do this, we need to consider the economy as a whole, not only the private sector (or free market) where design has traditionally been positioned, but also the public and nonprofit sectors of the economy.[1]

The challenge for designers is twofold. First, we need some economic literacy in order to address economic sustainability, and this literacy has both a personal (or citizenship) dimension and a professional one. Second, there are options for positioning design in all three sectors of the economy, and each sector provides certain opportunities and barriers to pursuing sustainable design. Understanding these parameters can help designers decide how to organize the "business" of design to support sustainability.

THREE-SECTOR ECONOMY

When the market decides,
what priorities are emphasized?

MOST DESIGNERS WORK IN THE PRIVATE SECTOR, which we recognize as the free market, where their tasks involve expanding markets or pioneering new ones by improving the consumer appeal of products, improving profitability, and so forth. The private sector is made up of individuals and for-profit enterprises, usually companies. The main objective of private sector entities is to create as much profit as possible. To accomplish this, companies are motivated to continually cut all costs (such as employee salaries, materials, and transportation) that eat into their profits and to channel as much money as possible toward directors and shareholders.[2] The private sector describes the marketplace in which individuals and businesses exchange goods and services using money as a medium of exchange. Exchange of goods and services in the private sector is sometimes also called "commerce" or "commercial activity."

But the market does not operate in isolation. Consider the example of a designer who, although pressed by his client (a large corporation) to use the cheapest possible method of cooling a building, is required by the building code to meet certain energy efficiency standards. The public sector, namely government, provides a consistent set of operating conditions, standards, and rules that govern competition in the market. Through courts of law, governments make possible business agreements and legal contracts. The government also provides public services such as security (e.g., police, firefighters) and transportation (e.g., road networks, public transit). The public sector raises money through taxation of the private sector. This is the price that individual people and organizations agree to pay in exchange for the consistent operating conditions that the public sector provides. But the reliance on tax money puts tremendous pressure on public agencies to justify all expenditures and follow strict rules to keep the public trust. The public sector also has concerns about basic public services such as health and safety, waste and recycling, fairness (democracy), and a range of other issues for the greater good of the general public.[3]

Consider that the same designer, although engaged in commercial design practice, also uses some of his spare time to participate in a charity that designs sports equipment for children with special needs. These organizations, sometimes collectively called the "third sector of the economy" or the "social economy," are typically motivated by a passionate concern for important issues that are not well addressed elsewhere in the economy. Unlike the private sector, the third sector's objective is generally social rather than financial. Religious organizations have historically been the largest part of the non-profit sector, ministering to people's souls and helping those in need. From this tradition has grown a large non-profit sector with a largely moral or compassionate mission, such as protecting endangered species or defending human rights. Participants in the nonprofit sector are moti-

DEFINITION: Public Companies

One point of confusion is that companies that sell shares in their business to anyone who wants to buy some, for example, through the stock exchange, are known as publicly held companies. This does not mean that the companies are in the public sector, only that the shares are traded among members of the public as opposed to being held exclusively by the company's founders or controllers.

Private
- Individuals
- For-profit companies
- Designers

Public
- Nations
- Cities
- States

Not for Profit
CHARITIES
- Religion
- Education
- Environment
- Health
- Social well-being

THE ECONOMY

vated to ensure that other values, besides increasing profits, are addressed by the economy. Funding for nonprofit organizations comes from a wide range of sources in the public and private sectors.

It has become common to think of the free market as the ultimate decision maker in society, expressed by phrases such as "Let the market decide." In this sense, the free market has come to be the dominant sector of the economy, with its priorities generally put ahead of those in the public or nonprofit sector. From the standpoint of sustainability there are several problems with this. First, unlike the other two sectors of the economy, the free market has only monetary values, and specifically it values generating more money. In other words, the market has no intrinsic ethics or morals. The market is governed by

the "bottom line" of profits and, on the whole, the private sector resists the idea that human values should be allowed to interfere with the economic bottom line.[4] Second, some entities within the private sector, namely corporations, have gained an enormous amount of power because our capitalist system results in the extreme concentration of wealth. These large corporations, powerful entities within the private sector, can and do pressure the other two sectors of the economy for unquestioning and favorable treatment of private sector interests.[5]

For sustainability to succeed, we need a balanced economy that allows us not only to capture a wide range of human values—such as clean air or healthy families, which cannot be easily expressed in monetary terms—but also to trade the goods and services that can be more easily measured by the money. In the following chapters we will look in more detail at both the dominance of the free market in society and its weaknesses in terms of supporting sustainability; then we will examine the designer's option for working from within each of the three sectors of the economy.

LANDSCAPE FEATURE: Three-Sector Economy

There are many ways that people divide up the economy and its activities. These divisions might be by industry type (health care versus electronics) or by business size (sole proprietors versus large corporations). Often these divisions are called sectors, which simply means parts or divisions. To look at sustainability from an economic perspective, it is helpful to divide the economy into three sectors—private, public, and nonprofit—and consider their broad financial aims. The private sector, made up of individuals and for-profit enterprises, has the financial aim of generating profit. Profits arise from the marketplace where labor, material goods, and services are bought and sold. In the public sector, made up of governments (such as cities, counties, states, and countries), the financial aim is to collect a modest percentage of citizens' money (largely in the form of taxes) and use it to provide collective public services such as military defense, education, and legal systems. The nonprofit sector, made up of organizations that are neither businesses nor governments, has the financial aim of marshaling resources to better meet social needs, such as the environment or children's welfare that are passed over or underserved by the market and government. Nonprofit organizations go by a range of names such as charities and nongovernmental organizations and get much of their funding through donations from the other two sectors.

MONEY IS THE MEASURE

Designers have had an important role in the drive for economic expansion. It started with the arrival of industrialization in the 1800s and the birth of the industrial artist, whose job it was to humanize machine-produced goods. But it was mass production that required designers to keep up the consumer appeal of goods so that sales would increase and the market for goods would expand. A classic example of this styling activity occurred with automobiles, which were updated annually to encourage more frequent purchases. Designers and marketers were so successful at generating consumer appeal that by the 1950s and 1960s, most people in industrialized countries were no longer in need of material things but still desired them. By 2000, instead of saving, many Americans were going in to debt to meet their desire for more consumer goods.[6]

In their contribution to suburban development, architects have participated in the process by which housing has become a commodity first rather than part of a community. In the development of cities, architects often have been called upon to glorify the agents of economic expansion, corporations, and their centers of political and financial power.[7]

**DEFINITION:
Economic Expansion**

The terms "economic expansion" and "economic growth" mean growth in the amount of market activity in society, particularly as measured by the amounts of money accumulated and amounts of money exchanged through the market. Our debt-based economy and our measurement tools, such as the GDP, make economic growth a primary goal in society. Designers have played an important role in fueling economic growth.

But why is economic expansion so important? Why has it become the primary goal in society? Two of the main reasons are our debt-based economy and our use of economic measurements as an indicator of national well-being.

Our economy is based on debt that must be paid back with interest, stemming from the fact that the government has delegated the power to issue new money to commercial banks. For the purposes of creating new money, banks are authorized to lend into existence as much as twelve times the amount they have on reserve (e.g., as customer deposits).[8] The interest payments owed on the new money have to be generated over and above the amount of new money issued. If the economy doesn't keep expanding, then the money to pay back interest won't be available and the economy collapses on itself.

We also have institutionalized a measurement method that portrays economic growth as the single indicator of well-being. We have come to a point of tracking almost everything in terms of

Designers push economic growth through frequent product styling updates and "Power" architecture.

money, and unless something has a price, our modern economy perceives it as having no value and ignores it. As one economist notes, "economics equates changes in the happiness of a society with changes in its purchasing power—or roughly so" and, as we will find out, wrongly so.[9]

The national economic measurement tool, known as gross domestic product, or GDP, formalizes our reliance on money to indicate well-being. The problem is that the GDP counts any monetary transaction as a contribution to "economic growth." That means if someone gets sick because of exposure to toxic chemicals, all the medical expenses (economic transactions) show up as a positive contribution to economic growth and make the economy "better." If a forest is cut down and a species lost forever, only the economic activity associated with the logging shows up as a "positive" contribution to GDP. Crime and divorce also are good for GDP, because they generate monetary transactions in terms of legal services, housing, and security, among other things. Meanwhile, time voluntarily spent caring for our children or our elderly has no value according to the

GDP. Like a giant calculator that adds but can't subtract, the GDP makes no distinction between "mere monetary transactions and a genuine addition to a nation's well-being."[10]

The nonprofit sector has attempted to call attention to this failing of the GDP by adjusting it in two ways. First, money transactions resulting from harmful activities are subtracted rather than added and, second, nonmonetary values are added. A few national governments also have begun investigating alternative ways to measure our progress in terms of human development and not just economic growth. The result for the United States, known as the genuine progress indicator (GPI) and shown at right, indicates that over the last fifty years there has been little improvement in well-being and some periods of decline, despite nearly continuous "growth" in GDP.[11]

When we consider natural and social systems, which are declining even though money systems showed growth, the GPI hasn't changed much from 1950. Items subtracted in the GPI include loss of natural resources, cost of chemical pollution, the cost of long-term effects from energy use, costs of family breakdown, crime, loss of leisure time, and the costs of underemployment. Items added to the GPI include value of housework and parenting and

**DEBT BASIS
OF THE
ECONOMY**

If the economy doesn't grow by $100, the system collapses.

Customer deposits: $100

Bank loans new money into existence (10 x deposits): $1000

Borrowers pay back principal plus interest (10%): $1100

**MAKES ECONOMIC
GROWTH A PRIMARY
GOAL IN SOCIETY**

the value of volunteer work. Other factors decreasing the GPI include indebtedness to foreign lenders and the unequal distribution of income.[12]

Sustainability requires that we do not exclude or ignore important human values simply because they don't fit within a monetized market system. The next chapter examines in more detail how the free market fails to capture important values and how the public and nonprofit sectors of the economy have tried to correct this problem.

 DEFINITION: GDP/GPI

The gross domestic product (GDP) measures all monetary transactions within a country. An increasing GDP means economic growth and is generally equated with an improvement in well-being. Yet the GDP does not subtract economic transactions that result from damage or harm to our well-being, nor does it add values that have no monetary price. In the end it is not a good measure of real well-being. Alternatives to the GDP, such as the genuine progress indicator (GPI), attempt to measure economic transactions in terms of human values rather than monetary ones by subtracting transactions associated with damaging our well-being and adding nonmonetary values that improve it.

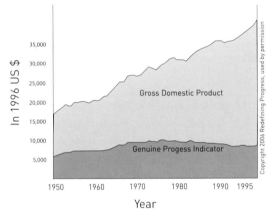

 LANDSCAPE FEATURE: Economic Growth

Ever-present pressures for economic growth are likely to influence us against the maintenance of social and environmental resources that are not properly valued by the market. Indeed, the decline of these resources results in expenditures that appear as "growth," such as money spent on environmental cleanup or prisons. The pace of economic growth also harms social and environmental resources. For example, forests and freshwater are actually being borrowed from future generations, and our voracious use of chemicals (and their dumping) amounts to an experiment on the health effects of future generations. At the same time, the pressures for economic growth generally require us to work longer hours and lose leisure time. These pressures influence us, sometimes subtly and sometimes brutally, to shift many of our traditionally unpaid activities to the monetized economy. For example, we cook fewer of our own meals and instead buy prepared foods or eat out. We provide less care and instead pay for care facilities for our children and our elderly. These outcomes from the pressures of economic growth, particularly as encapsulated in the GDP, lead some observers to comment, "The GPI reveals that much of what we now call growth or GDP is really just one of three things in disguise: fixing blunders and social decay from the past, borrowing resources from the future, or shifting functions from the traditional realm of household and community to the realm of the monetized economy."[13]

ZERO PRICE

DESIGNERS WHO TRY TO REDUCE the ecological impact of their artifacts often turn first to materials. It's then frustrating to find that ecologically "better" materials often are more expensive than conventional, ecologically harmful ones. Why is it cheaper to use wood that has been obtained through destructive forest practices than wood that has been sustainably harvested? Why is it cheaper to use conventional cotton, with all its harmful pesticides, water consumption, and soil loss, than organic cotton, which preserves soil productivity?

As we saw in the discussion of GDP, the damage that human activities cause to ecosystems is not counted by our private sector markets even though all other forms of wealth rely on the foundation that the ecosphere provides. In money terms, this foundation has a price of zero so the market treats its value as zero.[14] It's not surprising then that ecosystems are deteriorating across the board. The same problem applies to social values. Like the ecosphere, the time and energy spent on care of a parent or a child has no price, so the economy treats its value as zero. Perhaps it's not surprising that our social systems also are in decline when we have no way to capture their value.

Just as a parent provides the service of caring for a child, nature also provides services, such as creation of fresh air, clean water, and nutrient cycling (among others). Nature's services are estimated to be worth $36 trillion annually. This figure is probably a conservative estimate considering that we can't live without nature's biological services, and many can't be replaced at any price.[15] Yet the market counts these as "free" because we don't pay money for them. Nature also has value for reasons other than being useful to people—like all life-forms, it has intrinsic value, meaning value just for existing.

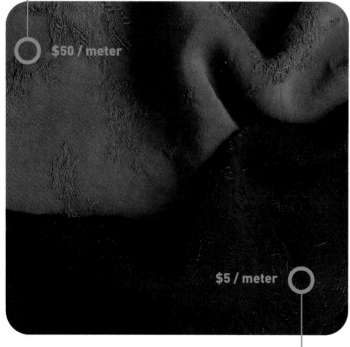

- No harmful toxins used in production
- Renewable, natural fibers
- No harmful sizers or softners
- No flame retardants
- Safely biodegrades

$50 / meter

$5 / meter

These fabrics look similar but have a very different eco impacts.

- Heavy metal finishers
- Toxic carriers for dye
- Brominated flame retardant coating
- Dry clean solvents

LANDSCAPE FEATURE:
The Market Fails

Many important values and resources, such as clean ocean water or diverse languages, are difficult or impossible to price in the marketplace. The market in effect gives these a price of zero, and the result is that we treat them as though they have no value at all. At the same time, the damages caused to these unpriced resources are not measured by the market either.

As long as we let the free market make decisions about the ecosphere, it will appear to be cheaper to destroy ecological resources than to preserve them. Compared with the "free" destruction of nature's resources, the activity of improving and preserving nature costs money. Only a few designers, producers, and consumers will choose to pay extra for ecologically better products. Those who do choose to pay extra are essentially putting their private resources toward the greater public good in contrast to companies that freely extract public resources for private gain.

Both the public and nonprofit sectors of the economy have offered some solutions to the problems inherent in the free market. In the public sector one of the key questions is whether or not we should attempt to create artificial markets for difficult to price goods. For example, the government has experimented with a trading system for air pollution. The government caps the overall amount of air pollution allowed, then polluters who reduce their air emissions gain "credits to pollute" that they can sell to other businesses that feel they need to pollute more, say, through increasing production.[16]

Another approach is to try to establish artificial prices, for example, by asking people how much they would pay to preserve a pristine wilderness. But some argue that these types of artificial markets and prices are inadequate and, worse, they wrongly put even more emphasis on money values where they are not legitimate. Consider an example of being asked to sell your child or otherwise place a value on a human life. You would place an infinitely high price on your child to make it impossible that you would have to sell your son or daughter. Those who try to value nature (or other unpriced but infinitely valuable things) in this way often find that in a market context their valuations are ignored as extreme and unreasonable. And this is one of the difficulties with trying to apply market-based approaches. Alternatives to artificial markets and pricing involve democratic processes and other collective decision-making methods available largely through public and nonprofit organizations. These are perhaps more legitimate, if more difficult ways to determine how we capture non-money values across society.[17]

The current approach of letting the market decide that zero price means zero value is a significant barrier to sustainability. The next chapter explores some of the public and nonprofit approaches to countering the zero-price problem of the private market.

Your Child

Nature

How would you price them?
Who's to say what's resonable?

INFINITE VALUE

DESIGNERS, AS BUSINESSPEOPLE, ARE CAPTIVES within the current market-driven system of measuring growth and progress. There are few ways to reflect nonmoney values in your design work, no matter how infinitely high those values might be. Even if you're personally willing to pay more, you and your artifact are still part of a system that is based on the free exploitation of natural and social capital, which are public resources, for private gain. Public and nonprofit groups have put forward several approaches to solve this problem such as regulation, labeling, and other consumer awareness campaigns, standards, ecorents, and other forms of subsidy and taxation.

Government regulation has been the primary vehicle for correcting the zero-price/zero-value problem associated with nature. Environmental regulations restrict emissions of hazardous material, protect wilderness areas, and ban the hunting of endangered species, which would permanently and irreversibly damage ecosystems. But regulations vary by country, and some countries, for example, allow harmful chemicals that have been banned elsewhere.[18]

Observers contend that regulations are diluted by corporate interests and haven't captured the real values of natural capital. And indeed, in response to the weakness of governmental regulation, several key nonprofit groups, including the Environmental Defense Fund and the Natural Resources Defense Council, made their mark by successfully suing government agencies that were not adequately enforcing environmental regulations.[19]

Both public agencies and nonprofit groups have taken steps to improve the consumer's awareness of natural and social capital, often through product labeling. Since sustainable designs may look the same as any others, labeling systems such as Green Cross in the United States, Green Dot in Germany, or the Nordic Swan label in Scandinavian countries make consumers aware of environmentally preferable products. Many appliances now carry energy performance labels. Some of these are visual in terms of energy costs relative to other appliances in the same range. Wood may be certified as sustainably harvested by the Forest Stewardship Council. Fair trade, organic, and animal-safe labels also are becoming more common.

Labels are one way of improving customer's awareness of natural and social capital. Shown here: Polyethylene low density, Forest Stewardship Council, and Green Dot (German label).

These labels, however, have tended to be quite limited in terms of what they reveal about a product. Typically, they cover only a few elements of environmental performance such as the use of recycled content materials or the source of one material contained in the product.[20]

For buildings, several rating systems have been developed to help consumers identify the level of environmental performance of the building. The U.S. Green Building Council's LEED rating system awards commercial buildings platinum, gold, and silver levels of performance, which cover materials, energy, landscape, and transportation.[21] Various residential building rating systems also exist, many of which focus heavily on energy.

A range of nonprofit groups have worked on consumer awareness campaigns that include activities such as boycotting certain products, engaging in nonviolent protest (such as "tree hugging"), or bearing witness to and reporting on environmental and human rights abuses that occur in overseas production (such as sweatshops).

Another incremental step is the creation of international standards, such as the ISO14000 series, a standard for environmental quality. These standards do not rate environmental performance; rather, by meeting the standard, the company uses agreed-upon measurement and management techniques by which the company itself and others can gauge their performance.[22] For example, the standard might dictate the highest quality method for measuring air quality, but it won't say which air quality standard you should meet.

Some progressive economists have proposed collecting ecorents for the value subtracted from natural resources. Companies, governments, or individuals who want to use natural capital would pay the ecorent to a general fund. The underlying principle is that all citizens, including future generations, should enjoy an equal share in the value of common resources that are provided by nature. Ecorents could allow for the fact that nature has some value in and of itself, recognizing that people are not the only living organisms that value nature.[23] Ecorents are not tied to any artificial prices but instead would be decided by a democratic or collective process, thus illustrating one way that society could make decisions outside the market to capture unpriced values.

The long-term benefit of the ecorent is that it makes all prices across the economy reflect some costs for environmental damage and some benefits if companies reduce environmental damage. The more accurate prices would make ecologically efficient materials less expensive than ecologically harmful ones. That would change behavior throughout society. Since the ecorent charge would be applied at the source—at the beginning of the supply chain—the costs get distributed throughout the economy and resource-intensive activities cost more for producers and consumers alike, universally. In addition, those who use more resources, such as people in industrialized countries, pay more ecorent. In the end, it is a system that directs us toward activities we do want (systems of production that harmonize with nature's systems) and away from activities we don't want.

Governments also are developing policies that withdraw corporate subsidies. For example, governments have historically taken on the job of waste disposal. Under new legislation in Europe, Australia, and some U.S. states, governments will no longer provide this service for electronic products. After consumers are done with the products, companies will have to take back their own electronic product waste and manage it themselves—including all costs.[24] Governments have historically subsidized the extraction and destruction of natural resources, for example, providing free roads into the forest for clear-cutting. But now some governments (sometimes only under pressure from nonprofit organizations) are starting to reexamine these policies that have the effect of making cheaper the activities we don't want and making more expensive those we do want.[25]

What all these mechanisms have in common, from boycotts to ecorents, is their effort to bring unpriced values into the realm of our market decision making. Even with these efforts, there is still another aspect of the market, known as "discounting," that thwarts our efforts to capture nonmoney values. We examine discounting in the next chapter.

 TRAVELER'S NOTE: Reflecting Value

Designers can use many of the solutions proposed by public and nonprofit groups. Clearly, designers can create artifacts that earn the relevant environmental or social labels. Consider a brochure or booklet. The designer could specify paper with recycled content or alternative (nonwood) fiber that meets targets promoted by environmental advocates. From a social perspective, is the brochure printed by a cooperative, worker-owned printing company, or by one who exploits overseas workers? Designers also can consider the idea that regulatory requirements represent a *minimum* level of performance rather than a statement of the most that needs to be done. In the eyes of some, if you only just meet regulatory requirements, it's the equivalent of admitting that "if I could have made it worse, I would have."[26]

NO MORE CLASSICS?

CONSIDER THE EAMES LOUNGE CHAIR AND OTTOMAN FROM 1956. The chair is still carried in the Herman Miller catalog fifty years later and will probably continue for another fifty years. When an artifact stands the test of time, it becomes a classic and it stays in demand. It retains its value over time—it might even gain in value. This kind of classic is the exception, not the rule. The market rule assumes that everything from money to materials will have less value in the future than they do in the present.

Classics are less common these days. After all, to fuel continuous economic expansion, we need continuous consumption of new things rather than long-lasting classics that don't need to be replaced. If I keep my Eames chair for fifty years, it could replace five or ten lesser chairs that I need to "update" each time I redecorate.

A classic.
It retains or even gains value over time.

Future generations may have more money than we do today, but they will probably have fewer old-growth forests, making the forests more valuable in the future. To the extent that discounting leads us to over-use forests at the expense of future generations, we are simply borrowing from the future to gain economic (monetary) growth in the present.

Discounting the value of money makes sense on some levels. As long as we are concerned primarily with money, people do have a time preference for money—they prefer to have money now rather than in the future.[27] With continuous economic expansion, future generations will have more money than current generations, so a given amount of money will have less value in the future than it does today. Indeed, we see this phenomenon within our own lifetimes, when we consider that houses our parents probably bought for $20,000 will cost us $200,000 today.

Nature, however, is a classic. So is cultural knowledge such as diverse languages or tribal use of medicinal native plants. The practice of discounting nature and culture presents a problem. We cannot assume, for example, that given current patterns of deforestation, future generations will have more old-growth forests than we have today; most likely they'll have less. Since they'll have a bigger population with less available old-growth forest, they should value it even more than we do today. If so, it would not be appropriate to discount the future value of old-growth forests or of nature and culture in general. Some

people argue that the discount rate for nature should be negative to demonstrate this probability. For example, for decisions we make today, we should count $100 worth of natural capital as being worth $120 a year from now.[28]

Our economy's consideration only of monetary values may be shortchanging us of real future well-being. If we consider the example of food, once we finish a meal, we don't want more food right now. We prefer to have more food in the future when we are hungry again. Money in the future is valuable only to the extent it helps us meet future needs for well-being, such as growing more food.[29]

But there are uncertainties about nature. In many cases we do not know what the future

Nature is a classic.

effect of our current actions will be. This is the case for the tens of thousands of chemicals that we use but that haven't yet been tested for health effects. In addition, some effects may be irreversible, such as the loss of species. Finally, there is uncertainty about the size of the effect, such as with global warming—how much temperature will increase, how much sea level will rise, and so on.

The uncertainties around nature lead some to argue that we should retain a small discount rate or at most set the discount rate to zero. As it is, private organizations value money in the present more heavily than public or nonprofit groups do because these latter groups typically consider the needs of future generations.[30] Those in favor of discounting argue that expending some natural resources today might turn up a new technology that would benefit future generations in some way we can't imagine now. Since we in the present use the discount rate to make decisions about the future, there will always be trade-offs to consider. Discounting future values puts subtle but distinct pressure on designers to focus on the short term, and we will return to this theme in future chapters.

Discounting and the zero-price problem of the previous chapter are two examples of how the market fails to capture important but unpriced values. But there are other ways in which the economy tends to put money first, making sustainability more difficult. For example, design and sustainability are affected by the ways in which the economy concentrates wealth and grants access to money. The next chapters examine these features.

> Since we in the present use the discount rate to make decisions about the future, there will always be trade-offs to consider.

DEFINITION: Discounting

The economic term for devaluing things in the future is discounting. That is, we discount the value of future money to make investment decisions in the present. The rate at which we discount future income is called the "discount rate."

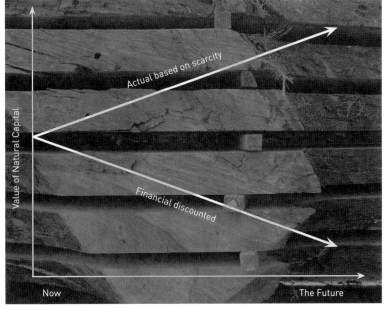

Discounting the future.

"FREE" MARKETS

THE IDEA THAT ANYONE CAN WORK HARD AND ACHIEVE MONETARY SUCCESS is relatively recent. Historically, your economic and social position would have been determined by birth and you would take on the position of your family. If your father was a lowly shoe cobbler, you, too, would be a shoe cobbler. You wouldn't have had the chance to work your way to the top. Throughout the history of civilizations, the masses were mostly poor and survived by subsistence production (making everything they needed for themselves). Wealth was concentrated in the hands of the nobility—the class of people who were "chosen" to be at the top of society and who acquired wealth and social standing as a birthright. This system, based on inherited privilege, is sometimes called an "aristocracy," and those at the top were known as the "nobility."[31]

Although our current free market suggests the possibility of a much wider distribution of wealth based on merit and hard work, what we might call a "meritocracy," in reality the concentration of wealth today is just as severe, perhaps more severe, than it ever was historically.

When the market economy was emerging roughly two hundred years ago, many Western countries were in the process of revolting against the aristocracy and forming governments based more on fairness and less on inherited favor. The French Revolution (1789–1799) and the American Revolution with its Declaration of Independence (1776) exemplify the trend. This period also was the beginning of the Industrial Revolution and of a factory system that began to replace feudal agriculture.[32]

An early economist named Adam Smith (1723–1790) recognized that a market economy, unlike the feudal system, had the potential to result in a fair and socially optimal distribution of resources, as though an invisible hand were directing the individual activities to benefit society as a whole. He based this idea on several assumptions. He assumed that the market is made up of a large number of small traders, none of whom could individually influence market prices. He also assumed that information was freely available, with no "trade secrets," and that all sellers would bear the full cost of their products and pass those costs on to consumers. Along with a few other assumptions, Smith proposed a sort of self-organizing economic democracy that gradually gained the nickname of the "invisible hand."[33] In theory consumers would use their dollars as "votes" to express their preference and keep the market in check.

Karl Marx (1818–1883) also contemplated the nature of wealth. Although industrialization and a market economy would in theory allow anyone to gain wealth (Smith thought the market economy would be socially beneficial in this regard), Marx considered different outcomes. He identified key aspects of producing material wealth, and these means of production he famously called "capital" (land, money, or equipment). But capital by itself does not generate wealth. It requires labor to make it productive. Marx noted that those who owned the means of production—the capitalists—typically accumulated wealth and those who provided the labor did not.

The vast majority of us, including designers, are laborers. When you graduate from college as a designer no one is concerned about your ability to become a capitalist—to own productive assets and accumulate wealth. The main concern is about your ability to find a job. Despite our system being called capitalism, few of us are actually capitalists, or owners. Jobs are still the most common connection that most of us have to the economy. And if we rely only on savings from our wages, almost none of us will ever build real wealth.[34]

The system we have today is called free market capitalism, and it emphasizes the accumulation and concentration of capital in the hands of, well, the capitalists. Although it is based on markets and private property, our economy does not act as an invisible hand the way that Adam Smith suggested it could.

Adam Smith (1723–1790) foresaw a potential economic democracy where $1 = 1 vote.

Like everyone else, the vast majority of designers are laborers, who rarely accumulate capital and thus fail to build wealth.

Karl Marx (1818–1883) foresaw that wealth would concentrate most among those who already have it—the rich get richer.

Although economic expansion has resulted in the creation of more and more wealth, the nature of the economy is to concentrate that wealth in a very small percentage of the population. It happens within individual countries and among countries in the world. The world's richest 1% of people receive as much income as the poorest 57%, and the richest twenty-five million Americans have income that is nearly equal to that of the world's poorest two billion people.[35] Wealth is also concentrated among men—less than 1% of the world's assets are held in the name of women.[36] The concentration of wealth is apparent in the field of design, just as it is in every other aspect of society. Although some designers will always rise to the top on their merits, the forces of capitalism will hide the merits of many others.

As Marx suggested, we have a system in which an increasingly wealthy and powerful pool of billionaires has considerably more influence in the marketplace, in the form of "dollar votes," than everyone else.[37] Since those who have money can and do buy more representation (also known as "influence") in our political system, democracy—our process for collective decision making—is weakened. Studies have also shown that dramatic inequality in wealth makes the poor majority less healthy as the stress of financial insecurity and loss of control drag them down physically as well as mentally.[38]

Instead of an invisible hand that fairly distributes wealth in a meritocracy, we have a market system that invisibly but systematically concentrates wealth in the hands of a few. The next chapter looks more closely at how this works.

THE GENDER OF WEALTH

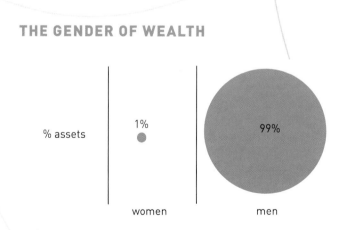

% assets   1%   99%

women   men

LANDSCAPE FEATURE: Concentration of Wealth

The concentration of wealth prevents a real economic democracy. We often are urged to "let the market decide," on everything from the types of housing to be built to the range of products available in the supermarket. We assume an economic democracy, where $1 = 1 vote. In theory consumers use their dollar votes to express their preferences and keep the market "in check." The problem with this theory is that, of course, wealth is not spread evenly. In the United States, for example, the wealth of the top 1% of households exceeds the combined wealth of the bottom 95%. And in global terms, the combined wealth of just three Americans (Bill Gates, Paul Allen, and Warren Buffett) is now larger than the combined wealth (GDP) of forty-one of the poorest nations and their 550 million citizens.[39] An increasingly smaller but extremely wealthy segment of the population has considerably more influence (dollar votes) in the marketplace than everyone else. Similarly, wealth is concentrated in large corporations that influence market decisions far more than an individual can.

CONCENTRATION OF WEALTH

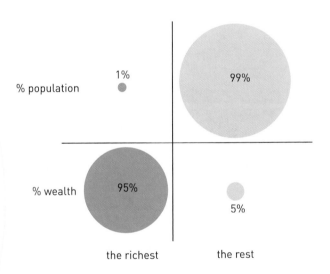

The economy invisibly yet systematically concentrates wealth in the hand of the few.

A few designers rise to the top in salary and celebrity, partly due to the way the economy concentrates wealth.

SHALL WE FINANCE?

THE CONCENTRATION OF WEALTH that is a feature of our economy applies to designers as well. A few designers rise to the top, becoming celebrities and enjoying huge financial success, while many others toil uncelebrated and struggle financially. Somewhere along the line, the lucky few will get a financial break that allows them to jump onto the middle rungs of the economic ladder. The economy itself does the rest.

The economy has several key features that enable the rich to get richer. One of the main features is that only those who have already accumulated wealth have access to finance (the primary means of acquiring more wealth). Other features, such as inheritance, interest payments, and the global movement of money, ensure that those who already have wealth have a better chance of gaining more wealth. Let's look at some examples. The scenarios below, starring Designers A, B, C, D, E, and F, are simplified and fictitious, but they demonstrate how the market concentrates wealth.

Designer A is born into a middle-class family and completes her education to become a designer. She produces her first line with small backing from a wealthy family friend. The line is successful, and again with the help of the family friend, she is able to get a loan to develop her next, grander line.

The wealthy family friend is Designer A's main route to finance. Designer A can't get financing on her own because she doesn't have any property (any form of material wealth—such as land, a business, or equipment—also sometimes called "assets") that she can use as collateral. In this sense only people who already have material wealth, or access to others with material wealth, can get access to finance. Capitalism expands mostly without creating new capitalists. It is largely a closed system.[40]

Designer B is born into a wealthy family. He uses his family resources to design and build his

Modest savings   Wealthy family friend   Corporate wealth   In debt   Inheritance   Wealthy family

The stories of these designers show how wealth is typically drained from the bottom and accumulated at the top.

first building, a high-end house. His parents' wealthy friends are invited to see it, and he gains three commissions—including one for a small office building. In this case inheritance is Designer B's ticket to ride, and inheritance also contributes to capitalism acting as a closed system. Of the wealthiest people in the United States as measured by the Forbes 400 list, nearly 40% of them inherited some or all of their wealth.[41] These are the modern nobility or aristocracy.

Designer C did very well at college and was recruited to the design department of Big Company. Big Company is large and financially successful. But because Big Company wants to grow further, it still needs to raise money to expand into new markets. The latest venture is a new line of wireless consumer handheld devices for the Asian market. Big Company, like all corporations, has both internal and external mechanisms to raise funds. External sources, which typically account for about 25% of funding, include borrowing money and selling shares. Internal sources include use of earnings and depreciation. Of these two internal sources, 90% typically comes from depreciation.[42]

Depreciation is a tax/finance concept that turns out to be very important to understand, and actually, as Designer C learns, it's not that complicated. For the new venture, Big Company wants to outfit its design department with a lot of new computer equipment, consumer testing labs, and studio space. Some of what the company earns can be set aside to replace worn-out assets (such as the old computers and the buildings that will be replaced by the new lab and studios).

DEFINITION: Finance

Finance allows you to buy assets before you have the means to pay for them. Assets are property or other forms of material wealth (land, a business, or equipment). The assets that you acquire with finance then pay for themselves—they become self-financing. But finance is accessible only to those with collateral (some form of material wealth used to secure the loan).

These old assets decrease in value over time (depreciate). Companies are not taxed on the income they use to replace old assets. In that sense, companies shelter their income from taxes and can use "write-offs on today's technology to purchase tomorrow's technology."[43] Their material wealth (the old property) is the basis of gaining a tax advantage. When Big Company's new consumer device hits the stores, Designer C, who led the well-financed design team, is catapulted into the press by Big Company's well-financed marketing and advertising campaigns.

Designer D was born and raised in Africa, where he still lives. As an architect he ekes out a modest living in a poor West African town. He manages to save some money every month, which he puts into an investment fund. The fund takes his money and sends it to the United States, to invest in companies like Big Company and others that earn a lot more money than any companies native to West Africa. The movement of money is another way that the rich get richer while the poor get poorer. When people in poorer communities do manage to save money, their money is typically sent away to richer communities where it will earn a better return on the investment.[44]

Designer E comes from a wealthy family. Although she doesn't make money on her design work, she loves to do it anyway. Fortunately, her family's financial adviser has helped ensure that her trust fund is well invested, and she can live off the interest alone. Designer F, unfortunately, doesn't have a wealthy family. As a furniture designer-maker, he struggles to make ends meet. He uses his credit cards more than he would like to keep his business afloat, and the credit card interest rates are so high that he has little hope of being able to pay off the debt soon. Interest payments contribute to the concentration of wealth because those who do not have material wealth are typically more indebted through consumer debt such as credit cards. These working people, typically with access to much less favorable interest rates than the wealthy, pay much more in interest on debt than they gain in interest on their savings. Whereas the wealthy are not only paying interest at a lower rate on money they borrow, they are also gaining much more interest on their investments than they are paying on their debt. Using financial sophistication, they also are able to move their money to places with the highest interest payments on their investments.[45]

These features of the economy—access to finance, inheritance, interest, depreciation, and the mobility of money, especially combined—make it likely that the new wealth that results from economic expansion will continue to concentrate among the wealthiest. These features also make it likely that those who are struggling to make ends meet will continue in the struggle and perhaps fall further behind. Continuous economic expansion puts most of us on a carousel of borrowing and spending that we can never get off. Since interest will always have to be earned and paid back with whatever we borrow, we'll always be trying to get ahead of it but rarely succeeding. Moreover, as the extreme concentration of wealth continues to grow, the "benchmark" for being wealthy is continually rising.

From a design perspective, if most wealth is concentrated among a few individuals, then the market for design is not very vibrant or robust. As the poor majority get poorer, it ultimately means fewer opportunities for design. By contrast, if wealth were more evenly distributed, demand for and access to all products and services would be broader and deeper, increasing opportunities for design.

Continuous economic growth: a carousel of borrowing and spending that we can never get off.

WE CHOOSE

DESIGNERS, LIKE EVERYONE ELSE, PARTICIPATE IN THE ECONOMY on at least two levels. First, we are individual citizens who can vote, express our opinions, and engage in public debate about values and how society should capture them. Second, we are "economic actors" who, mostly through our jobs and businesses, make decisions about how to spend money and at the same time are affected by the countless, often invisible features of the market.

LANDSCAPE FEATURE:
The Market: Not a Given

This market, and the larger economy of which it is part, is something that most of us tend to take as a given or not see at all. Indeed, it is not a system that any of us have chosen, but rather it has developed over time. If given the choice, how many of us would vote in favor of extreme concentration of wealth that excludes most of us? Or in favor of ignoring values that have no market price? By our active involvement in the economy, we can change it. As one observer noted, "Money is a human invention that has changed over the years, and if it does not perform the way we want it to, we can reinvent it."[46]

> How many of us, given a choice, would vote in favor of a system that concentrates wealth and ignores values that have no price?

The rules and procedures of the market, and the larger economy, have been developed more and more by those experts in finance who appear, to those of us without economic literacy, as masters of a mysterious world. The one rule that dominates this world, which is perhaps now less mysterious, is that the money flow through the market must expand at all costs. No one has been in charge of reviewing the economy to make sure that it "does no harm," to make sure it actually, does some "good," or even to identify what some of the costs of economic expansion have been. No one has been in charge of balancing moral, ethical, or other human values against monetary ones.[47]

Within a certain scope, the scope of goods and services that are easy to exchange for money, the market can play a very valuable and powerful role in society. But as we have seen, if we want to pursue ecological and cultural sustainability, then it is inappropriate to let the market be the primary decision maker in society. The issues of economic expansion, unpriced values, discounting, and concentration of wealth all suggest that the market alone will not lead us to sustainability. In fact, these money pressures make the pursuit of sustainability appear as an issue of individual altruism, a reliance on the selflessness of others rather than a reasoned decision about real values that are important to us all. Genuine pursuit of sustainability in the economic realm requires that we, as civic individuals and as actors in the marketplace within the profession of design, make choices that steer the economy toward sustainability, which will ultimately be of benefit to us all.

The previous chapters in this part have provided background to give you some of the general economic literacy that's required to begin making choices, particularly as a civic individual. The next chapters look in more detail at the options that design has for positioning itself within each of the three sectors of the economy. Each sector provides different avenues for steering the economy toward sustainability, and each contains obstacles. We've already explored a few of the more significant obstacles within the private sector, or the "free" market. The following chapters examine both the opportunities for placing sustainable design within the private sector and a few more of the obstacles. Then they explore the opportunities and obstacles for placing sustainable design in the public and nonprofit sectors.

DESIGN FOR PROFIT

IN THE PRIVATE SECTOR, design is a tool to improve profits and expand market share. Design itself is often seen as a for-profit industry, sometimes referred to as part of the "creative industries."[48] Indeed, the majority of designers work in for-profit businesses. The private sector, however, is quite varied in terms of how design can organize itself. A designer can work alone as a freelancer, a sole proprietor (or "sole trader") for his or her own business. Designers can join together in small groups to form design consultancies and partnerships or find work in the design departments of large multinational corporations.

Yet for all these varied organizational forms, much for-profit design work is still driven, either directly or indirectly, by large corporations. For example, small- and medium-sized design consultancies are frequently called upon to supplement the in-house design teams of large multinational corporations. Freelance designers routinely work for these consultancies and other companies who, in the end, supply large corporations. One way or another, the design process often is marked by the presence of a financially powerful client, typically a corporation.[49]

Consider, for example, an architect working on a new corporate headquarters. The architect soon becomes aware of how her client gained financial power. The company uses persistent cost-cutting measures such as sending production overseas for cheap labor, laying off workers, reducing employee benefits, and negotiating favorable treat-

 TRAVELER'S NOTE: Private Sector Design

Design is often seen as a for-profit industry, with a primary responsibility to add value to business profits without compromising, or by minimizing the compromise to the user's experience. Yet by positioning itself in the private sector, design has a real struggle to reflect a wide range of human values that the free market doesn't acknowledge.

Sole trader / freelance

Consultancy, small business

Medium-sized business

Global corporation

Design fits into a range of different business organizations.

ment from the government, particularly for tax relief. In fact, the company got a financial incentive from the local government for locating its new corporate headquarters in their town. The company also makes huge contributions to politicians who influence the regulations that affect the company. The company focuses on short-term economic gains and constantly pressures the architect to cut corners on the design. The architect also notices that all these measures are in the service of one group of people involved in the company—the shareholders.

This is a common scenario. Corporations are the primary vehicles for accumulating wealth. If we think of corporations as "economies" in themselves, the way we would think of, say, the French economy, we find that of the largest hundred economies in the world, fifty-one are corporations. It's currently estimated that three hundred companies control 25% of the world's productive assets.50 Yet as corporations have grown very large they have increasingly narrowed their focus and responsibilities to just one group—their own shareholders—and just one objective—increasing financial returns. This pressure to continuously increase shareholder value also contributes to the need for continuous economic expansion.

The structure and power of corporations further limit design's ability to pursue sustainability within the private sector. The financial power of corporations buys them many freedoms but requires little responsibility to the rest of society. The next chapter explores this situation in more detail.

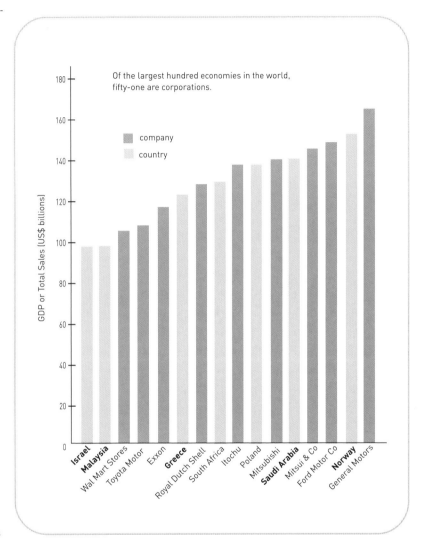

Of the largest hundred economies in the world, fifty-one are corporations.

company
country

GDP or Total Sales (US$ billions)

Israel, Malaysia, Wal Mart Stores, Toyota Motor, Exxon, Greece, Royal Dutch Shell, South Africa, Itochu, Poland, Mitsubishi, Saudi Arabia, Mitsui & Co, Ford Motor Co, Norway, General Motors

CORPORATIONS

A MODERN CORPORATION is actually a bunch of contradictions. Although legally owned by shareholders, a historic U.S. court decision grants corporations the same rights as individual people in terms of free speech and the ability to participate in the political process. Individuals are also mortal, whereas corporations have no defined life span—they can be immortal. A multibillion-dollar corporation, particularly an immortal one, has greater ability to pursue its interests than individuals. In addition, most individuals have a wide range of interests, whereas the corporation has just one— increasing shareholder profits. Many corporations are no more than the sum of their employees, although as a form of property the company can be bought and sold.[51]

So what do corporate shareholders actually do to deserve such attention? Although shareholders are said to own the company, their main role, aside from extracting the corporate profits, is to provide liquidity for other shareholders. Liquidity means the ability to convert value to cash. Otherwise, owning stock would tie up money, as it does when you buy a house, until the company is sold. Turnover in stocks is now so rapid that shareholders may own stocks for as little as several hours or even minutes. Although over the past few years an increasing number of average citizens have become shareholders through pension schemes and the like, figures show that of the gains in stock market wealth from 1983 to 1998, more than half went to the richest 1% of shareholders.[52] Modern shareholders rarely provide investment dollars to a company. In fact, the productivity of shareholder investment through the stock market is now actually negative.

Many corporate managers and executives are also large shareholders, since shares are often a part of their compensation (or pay). In this sense many companies channel as much wealth as possible to their top management. This amounts to pressure to concentrate wealth within companies. In the United States it is common for a company executive's wages to be four hundred times higher than the wages of the average factory worker, and it is not uncommon for executive pay to be much, much higher, especially when CEO's stock options are included—not only do these drive CEOs to keep stock prices up, but they easily amount to additional tens of millions in pay.[53]

In the largest companies the situation is extreme. For example, in 1998 the chief executive

EMPLOYEES

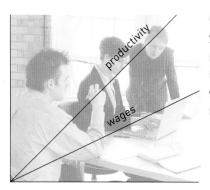

Over the past 20 years, employee productivity has increased, but wages have not kept pace.

SHAREHOLDERS

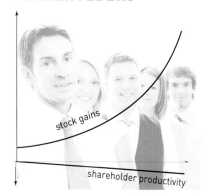

Meanwhile, the productivity of shareholder investement through the stock market is now actually negative.

officer of Disney, Michael Eisner, received pay totaling $575.6 million, which was twenty-five-thousand times the average Disney worker's pay. Various experts who study workplace dynamics suggest that if the highest-paid workers earn more than twenty times what the lowest-paid workers earn, the workplace is badly affected, some even say "poisoned." Even in Europe where executive pay traditionally has been less extreme, recent years have seen rebellions against excessive pay in the United Kingdom for CEOs and boards of directors, whose pay rose 23% at a time when average earnings were up only 3% and share prices actually fell 24%.[54]

Stock ownership is a form of wealth, and owners have the right to vote in company affairs, such as the pay level of the company officers. But the modern corporate structure simulates an aristocracy in which "noblemen" shareholders "own" all the wealth generated now and for the corporation's perpetual life, even though they have done nothing to create it. Those who don't own property (e.g., employees) can't vote, much like peasants in feudal times. This system constitutes discrimination on the basis of wealth.[55]

In a modern democracy, generally, "new wealth flows to those who create it."[56] What about employees, including designers, who create actual wealth with their knowledge and skills? At a time when shareholder productivity is negative, employee productivity is rising. But compensation is not keeping pace. Employees are a cost, and one to be minimized. Companies strive to maximize shareholder earnings and minimize employee pay. Employees do not appear at all on the corporate balance sheet that includes assets and liabilities. This is particularly problematic when we consider that many shareholders now participate in the company for a matter of days or months, whereas employees typically participate in the company for a matter of years, if not decades. The communities that provide and support the employees (e.g., families, schools, clubs, sports) also are at the mercy of shareholders, albeit more indirectly.[57]

Corporations have a large degree of freedom, being a hybrid of owned property and legal "individual," but they actually have little responsibility—to their employees, the communities in which they operate, or the general public. In many ways modern corporations stand out as undemocratic because they buy special treatment and have many freedoms without specific responsibilities.

The brutally financial corporate approach to people and communities amplifies, or even adds to, the limitations on sustainable design in the private sector. The attention to money above all else, combined with the power and freedom of large corporations, makes it even more difficult to capture a wide range of social and ecological values in the design process of the private sector. Yet it is happening. There are many ways that corporations are beginning to pursue sustainability, and it is possible for designers to engage in these, as we explore in the next chapter.

> The brutally financial corporate approach to people and communities—all in order to generate money for shareholders—amplifies and adds to the limitations to sustainable design in the private sector.

Many companies channel wealth to top management while continually cutting the amount paid to all other employees.

Executive Pay > + 23%

Average Earnings + 3%

- 24% < Share

In 2004, Europe catches up to American excesses in high-priced executives.

THE GOOD CORPORATION

IT'S IMPORTANT FOR US TO REMEMBER that all businesses, including corporations, are made up of people who, in their private lives at least, probably already hold a wide range of human values. As individuals we recognize that some things—such as protecting a species from extinction or the health of our children—have an infinitely high value so they are impossible to price. What can we, as businesspeople, or corporate employees and consultants, do to counter private sector views that treat these difficult-to-price items as having no value? Some strategies for this are described below.

Philanthropy (Charitable Giving)

Many companies, especially large multinational ones, form non-profit, philanthropic offshoots. Microsoft has the Bill and Melinda Gates Foundation. Xerox has the Xerox Foundation, and Nokia has the Nokia Educational Foundation. These foundations are usually directed toward helping in areas that are underserved by the market and by the public sector, such as education, the environment, or health. Some provide money, some offer paid sabbaticals for employees to donate large amounts of time. Some companies choose to provide this support in proportion to their own financial success. One way of doing this is through tithing, which has come to mean voluntarily contributing 10% of your time or money to charitable causes. Historically, a tithe was levied as a tax for the support of the clergy or church. The term "tithe" comes from Old English for "one-tenth," the amount typically levied.

Companies like Patagonia make annual charitable donations proportional to their own success: either 1% of sales or 10% of profits, whichever is larger.

A company might choose to donate 10% of its gross or net income. It may choose to support its employees by allowing them to spend, on some regular basis, ten hours of work time volunteering for important causes. The outdoor equipment company Patagonia is probably the best-known example of tithing. Patagonia's founder, Yvon Chouinard, cofounded a charitable organization known as 1% for the Planet, an alliance of businesses that tithe 1% of their annual sales to charitable causes. For the past fifteen years Patagonia itself has tithed 1% of annual sales or 10% of profits, whichever is larger, to grassroots environmental groups. That amounts to over $18 million given to local community groups.[58]

Shareholder Activism and Investment Screening

There are a few ideas for making global companies more responsible, in keeping with the thought that the greater your power, the greater your responsibility. The first is oriented toward shareholders and is sometimes called "shareholder activism." The idea is that people who own shares in a company take an active role in influencing what the company does. Shareholders can do this in a number of ways. In some cases they can request that there be shareholder votes on certain company activities. In other cases they might organize protests, for example, against certain company policies.

Another approach to shareholder activism happens before an investor even buys the shares. This is known as "responsible investing." In this case investors make sure that they put their money into companies that meet social and environmental criteria, such as using sustainably harvested wood or paying fair wages to overseas laborers. Since design can influence these activities, offering sustainably designed products is one way a company can upgrade its investment rating among discerning investors. In addition, to the extent that designers are investors in companies, they can participate in these strategies

 TRAVELER'S NOTE: Corporate Design

Where has your company already taken action or shown interest in sustainability of any form, and how can you shape design activities to support that action or interest? For example, with philanthropy and tithing, designers can find out if their companies have these types of programs and, if not, propose them. If these programs exist, find out which areas the company targets for philanthropic attention—are any of them sustainability oriented? If not, propose them. Is there a way to relate the company's support for sustainability outside to support for sustainable design inside?

Find out how your company rates in the eyes of those who rank ethical or sustainable investments and even those who rate good companies to work for. If you uncover any marks against your company, do any of the issues relate to artifacts (through labor, material sources/types, safety, or other ethical concerns)? Compare your company's ratings to its competition as a way to gain perspective for yourself and your colleagues, and finally, consider your own personal investments.

Designers can study their company's position on corporate social responsibility (CSR), perhaps by reading the company's report, to find out if there is a way to directly link sustainable design to the company's CSR objectives. In all of these efforts, designers should not overlook the potential value of an external partner who can help champion sustainable design activities of the company.

Corporate Social Responsibility

Another approach to broadening corporate concerns beyond shareholder profits is aimed at corporate cultures and takes the form of business principles. Several different sets of principles have been developed, usually by a coalition of business and nonprofit partners. These principles, such as the CERES (Coalition for Environmentally Responsible Economies) principles, Agenda 21 (developed through the United Nations sustainable development conferences), or the Five Capitals (Forum for the Future), typically address environmental and some social practices. Companies then make a public statement adopting the principles as their own and may voluntarily report on how they are adhering to the principles. Even before a company formally adopts principles, designers can use them to guide design work. A growing body of literature covers the area of corporate social responsibility, as indicated in the "further reading" section for this part of the atlas.

Partnerships for Sustainability

In some cases corporations recognize that their own financial interests make it difficult for them to pursue sustainable design independently. They recognize the value of outside partners, often public agencies or nonpofits, in providing expertise, recognition, or other encouragement. For example, both McDonald's and Starbucks have worked with the Environmental Defense Fund to design environmentally sensitive packaging. Many public agencies recognize socially and environmentally responsible businesses with awards that can improve the company's public image. In the Netherlands and in Ireland, the governments provided incentives for companies that demonstrate good sustainable design.[59] Designers can seek out these types of programs to help find "champions" for sustainable design from outside the company, as well as to find opportunities for the company to be recognized.

Designers can also seek out public sector initiatives, such as awards programs or even grant funds, to support sustainable design. As buyers, private sector companies can consider their role in the supply chain, helping to develop markets for environmentally or socially preferable products and materials. For example, Nike is supporting the market for organic cotton, and a coalition of California businesses made an agreement to support the market for recycled paper.[60]

Competitive Advantage

Sustainable design can be portrayed as a competitive advantage in the marketplace. This often is referred to as the "business case" for sustainability, because money saved from efficiency can put businesses ahead financially. In some cases businesses do not explicitly see the cost of resources

Sustainable design can be portrayed as a competitive advantage in the marketplace, refered to as "the business case for sustainability."

because they are embedded in other costs. For example, "waste disposal" or "energy" costs might be embedded in a maintenance budget. In these cases it is beneficial to audit the company's actual resource expenditures, identify them explicitly, and then demonstrate how better resource management leads to money savings.

Employee morale will likely improve if employees feel that the company they work for is "doing good," and this can increase employee productivity. Also, more and more of the population is becoming informed and demanding "greener," more socially responsible goods. Finally, anticipating legislation and going beyond it rather than simply fighting any new legislation is a strategic advantage that puts a business ahead of the competition and gives it more control over operations.

See the "further reading" section for more on these types of arguments, which are well developed in other books that concentrate entirely on making the business case for sustainability.

Working within the private sector may provide a way to open hearts and minds, but viewing sustainability as a market advantage still leads to many of the problems in the market that we covered earlier. Some benefits will continue to be unpriced. The business case for sustainability suggests we rely on artificial markets or the altruism of individual companies, both of which are problematic. In addition, if sustainable design provides a competitive advantage—if it really can lead to profit—then only a few, those who can afford it, will have its benefits. Competitors will strive to keep information secret (or "proprietary") so that they can use it to gain profits. So, while there may be benefits from "competitive sustainability," the fact that particularly ecological and social benefits won't

Partnerships: A coalition of California business made an agreement to support the market for recycled paper.

be broadly shared by all has to make us suspicious of the level of real contribution to sustainable development.

On a positive note, any movement toward sustainability within the private sector is positive movement. And no matter the financial pressures, there are many business people genuinely striving to bring a wider range of human values into corporate operations and the private sector.

THE IRRESPONSIBLE CORPORATION

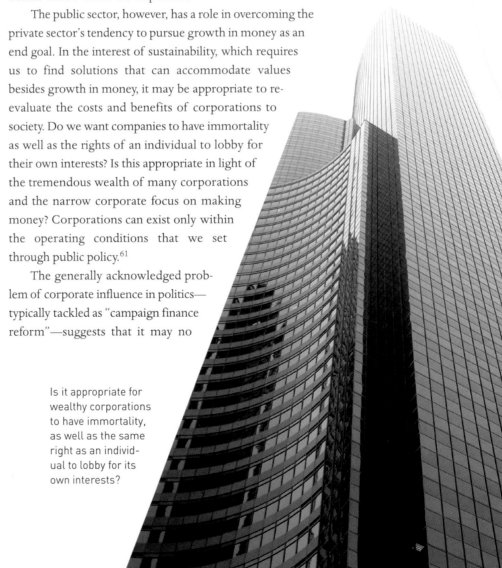

GIVEN TREMENDOUS FINANCIAL PRESSURES, most companies and the designers who work for them will continue to focus exclusively on financial growth and ignore the negative effects of unpriced values, the concentration of wealth, and continuous economic expansion. They will be content to let the market decide which values are important.

The public sector, however, has a role in overcoming the private sector's tendency to pursue growth in money as an end goal. In the interest of sustainability, which requires us to find solutions that can accommodate values besides growth in money, it may be appropriate to re-evaluate the costs and benefits of corporations to society. Do we want companies to have immortality as well as the rights of an individual to lobby for their own interests? Is this appropriate in light of the tremendous wealth of many corporations and the narrow corporate focus on making money? Corporations can exist only within the operating conditions that we set through public policy.[61]

The generally acknowledged problem of corporate influence in politics—typically tackled as "campaign finance reform"—suggests that it may no

Is it appropriate for wealthy corporations to have immortality, as well as the same right as an individual to lobby for its own interests?

longer be appropriate for corporations to be treated as individuals under the law, with rights to "free speech" and other rights intended for individuals within a democracy.[62] Many feel that it is proper to limit the rights of corporations, not only in campaign finance but also in terms of advertising to children and otherwise "expressing views" to the public.

The nature of shareholders, or owners, of the corporation also has come under scrutiny. For shareholders who are company directors or executives, corporate reformers suggest a maximum as well as a minimum wage that should provide guidelines to corporations. Those companies that choose to pay their top employees more than twenty-five times their typical employee's wage would receive less favorable tax treatment reflecting the social costs that result from extreme concentrations of wealth.[63]

Some have suggested that initial investors have ownership of a company for a limited period, after which the company ownership is turned over to a range of stakeholders made up of customers, managers, workers (including designers), and the surrounding community. This approach, sometimes called "ownerizing" or "stakeholder ownership," ensures that those who have a stake in an economic enterprise also have the rights and duties of ownership.[64]

 DEFINITION: Public Policy

The term "public policy" describes the set of approaches that governments take to set up a civic framework for society. Governments establish policies in a number of ways, including laws, but in democratic countries participation of citizens in the decisions that affect them is at the heart of policy formation. Not only can citizens elect representatives whose policy approaches they support, but citizens also usually have a number of opportunities to provide input to policy debates. Citizens can serve in public office. Public policies will cover topics such as health, education, banking, transportation, and the like. Policies will establish requirements, legal limits, basic rights, levels of service, and myriad other issues that affect the structure of daily life and the economy. We can consider the example of car travel. Public policy dictates that we take reasonable steps to maintain and improve travel safety. From that policy stems rules such as the requirement to wear seat belts and the prohibition of both talking on mobile phones while driving and driving under the influence of alcohol.

PENSIONS

Tax-subsidized pensions investments managed to de-concentrate wealth.

Although it might seem impossible at first, there are actually many ways to convert to stakeholder ownership using existing mechanisms such as bank loans, retirement funds, corporate mergers, government contracts, and even media advertising. As briefly reviewed below, each of these economic transactions could be set up so that stakeholder ownership is favored.

Government contracts: Governments buy many products and services. Because of the government's concern for values other than money (such as the environment or flexible work schedules for parents), public agencies will frequently seek out suppliers that can

Price signals in favor of stakeholder ownership.

PROCUREMENT

Government purchasers prefer stakeholder ownership, all else being equal

demonstrate their positive activities in these nonmonetary areas. Similarly, government buyers could favor companies that are ownerized over those that are not, all other things (e.g., price, quality) being equal.

Retirement (pension) funds: Many forms of retirement savings grow tax free; that is, we the public support your retirement plan by not taxing the earnings you make with your retirement savings. This amounts to a large public investment. However, most pension funds are very large funds managed by professional

ADVERTISEMENTS

Advertising is a tax write-off only for companies that utilize locally owned media.

money managers whose only goal is to grow money. In essence, these fund managers have used large-scale public investment to generate steady increases in the concentration of wealth, creating a very few extremely wealthy people. As the rich get richer, the economic landscape for future retirees worsens. As an alternative, pension fund managers could seek to make investments that earn economic returns without ignoring other variables, similar to responsible investing described above. Pension investments could also favor broad ownership patterns by investing in companies that are stakeholder owned or that are converting to stakeholder ownership.

Media advertising: Media companies have increasingly concentrated their ownership among a few megacorporations, arguably against the interests of the general public. Companies that advertise in the media can write off (get tax shelter from) money they spend on advertising. But why not give more favorable tax treatment to those companies that advertise with media companies that have broad-based local ownership?

As we have seen, there are both opportunities and obstacles to sustainable design in the private sector. Although it is essential that we maintain our effort to pursue sustainable design within the private sector, the limitations suggest that it also is important to consider how we might approach sustainability as designers within the public or nonprofit sectors of the economy. These are explored in the following chapters.

PUBLIC DESIGN

Although it's not possible for designers to organize themselves as public agencies, it is possible for designers to find work within the public sector. Fewer designers probably work in the public sector than in the private one, but those who do are able to make a much stronger case for pursuing sustainable design objectives. This is because, in large measure, the public sector is responsible for protecting those things that fall outside the boundaries of the market, such as environmental quality or democratic equality.

Design, especially architecture, has had a role in the public sector in terms of design review, historic preservation, or design guidelines. But graphic designers also work to create communication pieces about public services, and product designers work to create public products, such as the seating at a bus stop. Designers work to create public uniforms and new public buildings. Beyond these traditional roles, design may find or carve out new roles from the insight that sustainability provides. For example, to manage natural resources, public agencies have traditionally been organized into divisions that address different resource types. One division manages air quality, another manages water, a third manages fish and game, and so on. In a sense these divisions were suitable when the task was purely to facilitate the consuming of resources, such as through public utilities for water, drainage, electricity, and so on, but to manage, improve, and sustain the resource is entirely different. Since all these resources are connected, managing fish without managing water quality can be a difficult task. Many environmental challenges involve not only air, water, and soil but also the organisms that live in them.

From this general problem of fragmentation among public agencies arise some of the interesting opportunities for design. The design process is a natural way to create connections among these agencies, as well as to capture links to associated economic and cultural issues. For example, if we use product design as our lens, an integrated resource picture arises that brings in to focus resource harvest, manufacturing, consumerism, transport, energy use, and solid waste. Each of these

This bridge is part of a Seattle project to impr drainage, restore habitat, and provide a place for p ple to connect with their environment.

categories would typically be dealt with by a different public agency. The integrated picture would be hidden from conventionally organized public agencies. The design process highlights the integration uniting people, artifacts, processes, and providing a unique opportunity to address sustainability. In the case of products, the design process also brings into focus the variety of spatial scales, from local to global, that are influenced by a given product sector.[65]

In this sense design offers a lens through which a broad range of interconnected issues are seen and, more important, acted upon. Can a wastewater treatment facility be a source of beauty and inspiration? A place of reflection? Many traditional resource managers would be trying to "minimize the objections" to a treatment facility, but by bringing to bear the skills of artists and designers, such a facility becomes an inspiring park. Other pieces of public infrastructure (overpasses, transit stations, sidewalks) with similar art and design treatment have accomplished equally impressive environmental and social gains.[66] In the public sector, the nonmoney values of design can have an important role in uniting the main concerns of sustainability—ecology, commerce, and culture—and funding exists that enables the creation of physical expressions that succeed at all three.

Still, some designers who have tried public life may find its emphasis on policies above actions not to their taste. In that case, a third option to consider, one that allows a broader scope for the practice of design as well as research, analysis, critique, and education, is the nonprofit sector.

 TRAVELER'S NOTE: Public Sector Design

Although few public agencies may yet be thinking of design as a tool for sustainability, that doesn't mean these agencies can't be convinced of its value. For designers who would like to try their hand in the public sector, the task is to demonstrate the value added by design not only in money terms (e.g., efficiency, improved service) but also in terms of all the nonmoney values that the public sector champions. Design is a powerful and unique way to demonstrate a vision that links, or integrates, a range of sustainability concerns in the practical way that public agencies need. Take architecture, for example. A good example of public initiatives in "green building" comes from the Pacific Northwest. Environmentally sensitive building improves water quality, cuts down on solid waste, preserves and sometimes enhances soil quality, and can contribute to the preservation of urban endangered species such as salmon. Studies show that healthy buildings lead to happier employees and increased productivity, as well as potentially increased profitability. But individual public agencies responsible for one resource, such as water, won't necessarily see this big picture. The agency responsible for economic development may not see environmental building as a productivity booster, and so on. Design adds value to the public sector by presenting this integrated vision that includes a wide range of values (including nonmonetary ones) and showing their interrelationships. This integrated vision allows for better leveraging of resources across public sector agencies.

Design is a natural way to find linkages across public agencies that traditionally managed resources separately

Air

Water

Land

DESIGN
FOR A CAUSE

FOR THOSE DESIGNERS WHO WANT TO PIONEER new ways to organize the practice of design, working in the third sector or social economy is another possibility, by forming or joining an nonprofit organization. The number of nonprofit organizations has grown dramatically over the past fifty years, and that alone is one sign that the private and public sectors are not addressing society's concerns.[67] Working within the nonprofit sector gives you leeway to organize your time differently. You might be able to put more time into learning about the invisibility of a given material (see part 2) before you begin a design project. The nonprofit sector offers the potential to develop projects with nontraditional clients, and if necessary, it allows you to give things away for free—things such as your knowledge and skill, possibly also your artifacts.

Designers who work on sustainability issues find that many people come to them seeking free or low-cost information on sustainability. A frequent refrain from these potential clients is, "it's for a good cause." And so it is. A nonprofit structure allows you to make doing-things-for-a-good-cause your bottom line, freeing you from the profit-making and economic growth requirements of the private sector. Nonprofit organizations can focus on a particular charitable cause rather than be generally accountable to all citizens through tax funding.

Within a nonprofit structure, designers might pursue sustainability in a variety of ways. Designers might focus on research into materials and processes, the way that the Eternally Yours Foundation researched plastic in their Proud Plastics project. They might provide this information or even design tools to other professionals.

The nonprofit form also can be used as a basis for offering training and education about sustainability to other designers. Or designers might find public and private sector sponsors for demonstration projects that highlight new design approaches and then attempt to measure their potential for success. Alternatively, designers might use a nonprofit form as a basis for researching, analyzing, and critiquing current design practices and trends and suggesting better approaches.

In each of these cases, the nonprofit form makes it possible for designers to find funding for activities that don't fit comfortably within the market. This is not to say that a nonprofit organization is without economic concerns. In fact, the opposite is true. In the life of a nonprofit, the designer's race for clients is replaced with the race for funding. Since funders typically have specific criteria for making grants, few of which will specifically involve design, designers must think more broadly about their clients and be extremely creative in identifying areas of design opportunity. Rather than being given a brief by a client who wants a specific piece of design work (such as a new design for a mobile phone), you can develop a project idea and then seek funding to support it. Competition for funds is fierce, and fundraising can be very hard work.

Contrary to what the name suggests, a nonprofit company can earn profits, but the profits are not distributed back to those who control the company (shareholders). Rather, the profits are used to fund the organization's cause. Those who control the nonprofit company and its employees typically earn a modest salary. In reality, most nonprofits seek a combination of funding. One source is grants, from government, corporate, or foundation organizations. Another source is income, usually for services rendered such as consultancy or research. The other common form of funding is from donations by those who believe in the cause—such as members or "supporters." There is a large body of literature on funding and managing nonprofit organizations; see "further reading."

In answering the question of how we should do the business of design, we can see that there are a variety of options through the private, public, and nonprofit sectors of the economy. But there are two more factors that complicate the picture. The first is globalization. The second is the information, digitally networked economy. The three sectors of the economy discussed in the previous chapters are necessarily located within the context of a single country. Yet increasingly, globalization plays a big role in the economy at all levels. In addition, earlier chapters have assumed an industrial economic model based on the production and sale of physical property. The introduction of global, digital networks requires us to think more in terms of information. The last two chapters in part 3 explore these issues.

TRAVELER'S NOTE: Nonprofit Design

Using the tools of design as a way to explore sustainable development through the nonprofit sector is a relatively new approach, although nonprofit design organizations that work toward the greater good (in some form) have been around for a while. Examples include, Architects/Designers/Planners for Social Responsibility, Australia's Society for Responsible Design, Architecture for Humanity, or the United Kingdom's Scottish Ecological Design Association. Design consultancies and other forms of design activity also can make use of the nonprofit form to enable them to address all those concerns that lie outside the market.

Designers serious about the option of working in the non-profit sector should consider joining an existing nonprofit before starting a new one. Starting a new nonprofit is not unlike starting a new business, since there is a great deal of competition for charitable funding. A new nonprofit needs to clearly define a niche and make plans for likely funding sources and so forth, not unlike a business plan. The main difference from a business plan is that you must clearly explain how the organization is "charitable," being explicit about how your goals address social needs neglected by the market (and perhaps underserved by the public sector).

One form of nonprofit that designers have been able to utilize effectively is academic institutions. Universities and colleges, whether publicly or privately funded, almost always are organized as nonprofits. Within academia, there is typically broad scope for research and exploration of ideas in search of understanding and knowledge. For example, in the United Kingdom academic and foundation nonprofits sponsored the 5 Ways project, that generated, among other things, the "No Wash" Shirt. Since the energy needed to wash your favorite garment is about six times that needed to make it, the No Wash project developed a shirt designed so that it is never laundered.[68] Academic structures present their own challenges to designers but offer unique opportunities in return.

NO WASH: This shirt is designed so that it is never laundered—the energy needed to wash a shirt is about 6 times the energy needed to make it.

GOING GLOBAL

"THEY LIKE IT IN BEIJING!" is the latest feedback on your design for the new-model bauble-o-meter. And that's good news because Bauble Inc. has stagnant U.S. markets. The global expansion of markets is necessary to feed continuous economic growth, and designers are increasingly being asked to design for both global production and global consumption. The work environment is becoming more global, and individuals frequently design things for places they've never been and for people whose culture they may not understand. The global media, through advertising and marketing, is also training people around the world to want the same things, including your bauble-o-meter.

As global economic activity increases, individual countries are no longer the main focus of economic activity. In global markets, with the absence of a world government, multinational global corporations wield perhaps more power than they do on any given national economic stage. Digital technologies have enhanced this power, allowing corporations to freely and instantly move money around the globe, out of the view of nation-states or the public.[69]

Freer trade conditions help companies make and sell consumer goods internationally. The quest to continually maximize monetary return by cutting costs drives producers to seek the cheapest labor and materials suppliers, wherever they are in the world. Investors want to be able to move their money anywhere that they can get the best return on investment, so they also demand free international movement of money through global trade and finance.[70]

Free trade was supposed to speed up the development process in third world countries. But free trade has not resulted in the real benefits from increased trade that many developing countries expected. The trade system assumes a group of

 LANDSCAPE FEATURE: Free Trade

It's at the international level that the struggle between democracy and business comes into focus, prompting a range of criticisms of free trade. Truly "free" international trade circumvents the democratic process within individual countries. For example, the World Trade Organization rules say countries must treat all cotton shirts as equal, regardless of how they are produced (such as using child labor or destructive agricultural practices)—even if the citizens of the country don't want to treat all shirts equally. Under this rule of free trade, national governments and their populations frequently cannot choose the sustainable options.[71]

Free trade: The struggle between democracy and business.

DEFINITION: World Trade Organization

The international body that governs global trade, the World Trade Organization regulates international trade on the basis of negotiated rules. Countries that belong to the WTO participate in the negotiation of these rules, but it is not a democratic process in which each member gets a vote on each rule. Instead the rules reflect the balance of power among members, and major trading parties, namely the industrialized, or developed, countries hold much of the decision-making power. The rules, as a result of negotiation and an imbalance of power among WTO members, do not reflect "free" trade for all products. For example, developed (industrialized) countries have protected their agriculture and textile industries—two of few industries where developing countries actually have a competitive advantage.[73]

countries all more or less at the same point in development with the same capacities. But many developing countries don't have the same capacities as industrialized countries and face significant disadvantages by having to take on the same types of obligations as developed countries. For example, developing countries with "infant" industries are not allowed to raise tariffs to help establish the new industry, even though in the past many industrialized countries benefited from just such "protectionism" to establish industries within their own countries.

The arbiter of global trade is an international body called the World Trade Organization (WTO). Because the WTO asks developing countries to increase imports without being able to expand exports (especially due to lowering prices for raw materials), many developing countries have increasing trade deficits. These deficits add to already mounting third world debt. In addition,

WTO rules "constrain the use of subsidies for local industries, prohibit investment measures favouring the use of local components, and make it difficult or costly for local industries to make use of technology that is subjected to intellectual property protection." Under these conditions it is difficult for developing countries to help their local companies compete successfully in the world market for modern industrial products. [72]

With the free movement of corporate business, and the search for lower and lower labor costs, some companies take advantage of lax labor laws and weak regulations found in developing countries. Under these conditions, abuses such as child labor, substandard working conditions, discrimination based on gender, and unfair wages (wages too low to live on) persist. On these matters companies are rarely accountable because neither the consumers of the products nor the governments of the countries in which the company operates can find out about these practices. Even people within the large companies who would not approve of the abuses don't know about them, because they are remote from most other company operations. For those who are concerned about trade issues, there is a range of constructive reactions, which we examine in the next chapter.

TRAVELER'S NOTE: Economic Inequality

As long as vast economic inequality persists at an international level, there will be constant downward pressure on wages in industrialized countries as workers in developing countries accept extremely low wages.[74] With the advent of telecommuting and networks, this is becoming as true for professions such as design and medicine as it has been for factory workers. Despite international efforts to grow capitalism in all countries—part of an effort to expand markets—many countries have not reacted well to having free market capitalism and Western-style democracy thrust onto them without any period of adjustment and without the social safety net (such as unemployment benefits, national health insurance, or retirement benefits) that industrialized countries had and still enjoy.[75]

FAIR TRADE

FEW DESIGNERS WOULD WANT THEIR ARTIFACTS PRODUCED BY EXPLOITATIVE CHILD LABOR or through means of irreversible environmental destruction, but when these things happen on the other side of the world, they are hard to monitor. Because globalization has led to such abuses, a growing movement of individuals, nongovernmental organizations, and nonprofits have formed what is essentially an antiglobalization movement, also referred to as the "global anticorporate network." The network's activities, in support of measures such as fair trade, microeconomics, and local currencies, affect design in several ways.

The fair trade movement is aimed at consumers and, for our purposes, designers, who are concerned about exploitative global trade. Fair trade links concerned consumers with small-scale producers in developing countries to facilitate trade on a basis of fairness and to ensure that large-scale exploitation is avoided. It has been largely nonprofits that initiate fair trade schemes, although a growing number of companies (such as the Body Shop or Starbucks Coffee Company) have incorporated fair trade products into their lines.

There also is a movement toward microeconomics, which enables lenders to support small-scale community initiatives. Large-scale global trade has tended to squeeze out local communities and small traders. Microlenders and community banks rectify this situation by offering small-scale loans to help community members get started in small-scale production.

 LANDSCAPE FEATURE: Globalization

Those concerned about globalization don't form one coherent movement, but rather, their concerns arise from many different issues. For example, some groups are most concerned about the environmental effects of free trade, other groups are concerned about workers' rights and sweatshops, and still others are worried about mounting third world debt and how it is aggravated by WTO rules. A coalition of nonprofit groups and activists with these various interests seemed to emerge most clearly as a "movement" in 1999 at the WTO meeting in Seattle. The movement's general aim is to curb the often exploitative power of global trade and finance while also restoring the vitality and viability of local economies.[76]

Fair trade: Addressing concerns about exploitative global trade.

At the same time, examples have demonstrated that large-scale needs can be met through self-coordinated, small-scale production. In Denmark, for example, industrial networks, groups of small-scale furniture designers, woodworkers, and individual interior designers have banded together to design convention centers and other large projects. After all, to the extent you have a vibrant local economy and are self-reliant, you won't be exploiting others elsewhere.[77] Micro lending started in developing countries but is increasingly seen to have relevance to developed countries because it can help overcome the exclusionary aspects of finance.

Another approach to strengthening local economies is to use local currencies. Local currencies circulate only within one region, such as a city or a neighborhood. By keeping money locally relevant, communities can avoid the transfer of most of their community's savings to richer countries or communities. It also means that local communities are not forced to compete on a global level, dollar against dollar. Local currencies, which could be set up by local governments or other organizations, could be used for whatever transactions were deemed appropriate. Banks could operate accounts in several currencies. Some proposals suggest that local currencies would be interest free.[78]

There are a number of examples of local currencies that are currently in operation. One of the more well-known examples is LETS, or local employment and trading scheme. LETS is usually set up as a nonprofit organization run by and for its members, who are individuals. It doesn't replace the official currency but only supplements it. LETS is operating successfully all over the world, especially in English-speaking countries such as Canada, where it was pioneered in the early 1980s. Other examples include currencies used by local businesses, such as Toronto Dollars and Tucson Traders. Some schemes, such as

Friendly Favors, are based entirely on moral obligation—they do not measure wealth but goodwill. Members voluntarily give as much discount as they can afford to other members, who then offer discounts back to others as a way of saying thank you. There also are commercial barter or trade exchanges. Local currencies could be particularly applicable to designers working either on small local scales or those involved in community development and fair trade initiatives.

Globalization increasingly influences the economic climate for design, in many cases making sustainable options more challenging in the face of the urgent global flow of money. The antiglobalization movement presents some approaches that designers can consider to counter free trade and globalization pressures. The rise of the Internet and the digital economy is another economic factor for designers that poses both problems and opportunities.

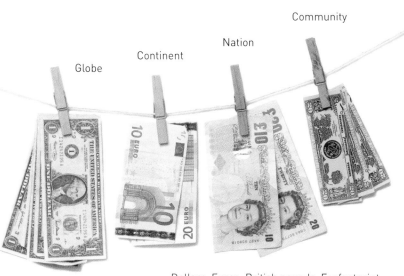

Dollars, Euros, British pounds, Ecofootprint notes. Community currencies avoid the transfer of savings to richer places.

CONNECTED
AND DIGITAL

IN THE DIGITAL ERA it's possible for design ideas to take on a life of their own, as they pass from point to point on a digital network, but there's no longer any certainty that the idea will take a physical form—in that case it's necessary for designers to rethink the value of what they do, as well as how the information economy might allow for ways to capture some of the sustainability values neglected by the physical property market.

Physical property's value is based on its tangible features as well as its scarcity. This is the underlying law of supply and demand. Digital information, on the other hand, is not scarce and can be copied easily and freely. Before the digital era we used to talk about "intellectual property" as the ideas behind physical property, but this concept was based on the owner's ability to put the idea into a physical form—either a "final" publication that wouldn't be altered (such as a book) or a three-dimensional form such as a machine.

But in the digital era we can't be sure that someone somewhere will always give the design physical form by making it or printing it. In addition, we can't always be sure of the authorship of digital ideas. Each point on the global information network is a point of both production and consumption. As digital information circulates freely,

LANDSCAPE FEATURE: Design Is Not Form

Design is about providing form, a physical expression. Or is it? Just as I argued counterintuitively in part 2 that materials are invisible, here I will argue that what designers produce is information and not form. In this age when many companies do not produce their own goods, designers are increasingly in the business of providing information about form and not the physical form itself. The information and ideas that designers produce are very different in nature than "hard products," (physical, three-dimensional property, such as land, buildings, or machines).[79]

globally, and quickly, it is easy for the information to be modified at almost any network node. It becomes difficult to distinguish between "versions" and who has contributed what and how. In the information economy, transmission is more like it was in an oral tradition, each teller passing it on differently. Information leaves a trail of itself wherever it goes, and it constantly mutates, evolves, and adapts, much like a life-form.

The value of information is determined by how recipients of the information can interpret, or get meaning out of, it. For example, do recipients understand your language? Do they have software that can handle your data? Most reception at present is mediated by the monetary economy—much of the interpretation of information is driven by money and the attempt to increase growth in money. This can obscure design's potential holistic value.

There are other features of the value of information that differ from physical property. Familiarity has value because, unless people are familiar with your information stream and its value, there won't be much demand for any new information you produce. In that sense, what people find valuable about information is a trusted point of view that reliably provides meaning. In addition, if this reliability and meaning are of the right nature, people may find it valuable to have exclusive access to information. Information is also more likely than physical property to have time value so that information "at the source" has more value than information removed in time.

Finally, information provides its own satisfaction. Many people find value in learning and the relationships that information entails. In addition, as many of the things we "buy" are not for survival, it becomes apparent that getting information by exchanging it for other information may be easier than converting our interactions to money. Sharing and exchanging information is the reward behind much of the "volunteer" activity that currently drives user groups and mail lists on the Internet, for example.

To the extent that designers produce ideas about form rather than physical form itself, they will need to consider two important issues. The first is how the notion of authorship might be diminished by the mutating nature of information, and the second is the new ways that people might value "information work." It seems likely that the digital economy offers some opportunities for designers to capture important human values that the market leaves behind. We will explore some of these opportunities in terms of human well-being in part 4.

 LANDSCAPE FEATURE: Digital Markets

The new networked, digital market behaves very differently than the traditional markets of the private sector that are based largely on the scarcity of physical property. Thanks to the digital revolution, information is not scarce; it is easy and cheap to copy, store, and transfer large amounts of digital information. When information is transferred, it doesn't have to leave the possession of the original owner, so it often leaves a trail of itself. For example, I can tell you the results of my research but still know the results myself.

CONCLUSION

HOW SHOULD WE DO THE BUSINESS OF DESIGN? That is one of the central economic questions for sustainable design. The market and the for-profit private sector are dominant features in our society, but their current emphasis on monetary growth presents several obstacles to sustainable design. Many important values are ignored. In addition, the features of the economy that concentrate wealth compromise the idea of an economic democracy. The inequality that results is bad for our health, as well as bad for the general economic landscape—including the market and

In the ways we choose to mix, separate, or blend our citizen and market actor roles, we have an important range of economic approaches to sustainable design.

opportunities for design. The central institution of the private sector, the corporation, has gained a great deal of power in the context of prioritizing growth in money, but this power comes with little responsibility to all those who contribute to the corporation's value, such as employees, communities, and local environments. For these reasons, it is generally a mistake to assume that "letting the market decide" is a viable route to sustainable development.

In this part we've considered that the private sector, although dominant in economic decision making, is only one of three main sectors of the economy, which also includes the public and nonprofit sectors. Each sector has differing financial objectives. We've seen that design activities such as research, practice, and education can occur in any of the three sectors. For example, design research could be in the R&D department of a corporation, at a nonprofit think tank, or part of a government agency. The public, private, and nonprofit sectors each offer design a distinctly different opportunity for addressing sustainability through the economy; each has limitations. The backdrop for these approaches is an increasingly global economy and the rising importance of a digital, networked information economy.

As far as sustainability is concerned, the "business" of design is only one of two important economic questions. The second question is about economic literacy and shaping the framework of the economy through the public sector. As both citizens and market actors (consumers and producers), we have the opportunity to take small, incremental steps toward change or to consider larger, more radical changes that we would like to pursue. In the ways we choose to mix, separate, or blend our citizen and market actor roles, we have an important range of economic approaches to sustainable design.

The economy represents a key component of sustainable development because it is a social condition that affects human well-being. Armed with economic literacy, we can begin to address how our work could contribute to economic conditions that promote human well-being indefinitely.

FURTHER READING

Business Case for Sustainability and Corporate Social Responsibility

A large body of literature is available on corporate social responsibility and making a business case for sustainable design. A few starting points include the following:

Cannibals with Forks: Triple Bottom Line of 21st Century Business by John Elkington (Oxford: Capstone, 1997)

The Corporate Responsibility Code Book by Deborah Leipziger (Sheffield, UK: Greenleaf, 2003)

The Sustainability Advantage: Seven Business Case Benefits of a Triple Bottom Line by Bob Willard (Gabriola Island, BC: New Society, 2002)

When Good Companies Do Bad Things: Responsibility and Risk in an Age of Globalization by Peter Schwartz and Blair Gibb (New York: John Wiley and Sons, 1999)

Critiques of the Economy

Beyond Growth: The Economics of Sustainable Development by Herman E. Daly (Boston: Beacon Press, 1997)

Butterfly Economics: A New General Theory of Social and Economic Behavior by Paul Omerod (New York: Basic Books, 2001)

One Market Under God: Extreme Capitalism, Market Populism and the End of Economic Democracy by Thomas Frank (London: Vintage Books, 2000)

Tax Shift: How to Help the Economy, Improve the Environment, and Get the Tax Man Off Our Backs, New Report, No. 7, by Alan Durning and Yoram Bauman (Seattle: Northwest Environment Watch, 1998)

Socially Responsible Investing/Shareholder Activism

The Emperor's Nightingale: Restoring the Integrity of the Corporation in the Age of Shareholder Activism by Robert A. G. Monks (Oxford: Capstone, 1998)

Investing with Your Values: Making Money and Making a Difference by Hal Brill, Jack A. Brill, and Cliff Feigenbaum (Princeton, NJ: Bloomberg Press, 1999)

Morals, Markets and Money: The Case of Ethical Investing by Alan Lewis with contributions from John Cullis

and Philip Jones (London: Financial Times/Prentice Hall, 2002)

Globalization/Free Trade

A large body of literature is available on globalization and trade. A few starting points include the following:

The Travels of a T-Shirt in the Global Economy: An Economist Examines the Markets, Power and Politics of World Trade by Pietra Rivoli (Hoboken, NJ: John Wiley and Sons, 2005)

Fair Trade: Market-Driven Ethical Consumption by Alex Nicholls and Charlotte Opal (London: Sage, 2004)

Rethinking Globalization: Critical Issues and Policy Choices, Global Issues Series, by Martin Khor (London: Zed Books, 2001)

Nonprofit Funding and Management

Demystifying Grant Seeking: What You Really Need to Do to Get Grants by Larissa Golden Brown and Martin John Brown (San Francisco: Jossey-Bass, 2001)

Starting and Building A Nonprofit: A Practical Guide by Peri Pakroo (Berkeley, CA: NOLO, 2005)

Digital Economy and Digital Design

Digital Ground: Architecture, Pervasive Computing, and Environmental Knowing by Malcolm McCullough (Cambridge, MA: MIT Press, 2004)

E-Topia by William Mitchell (Cambridge, MA: MIT Press, 2000) and other works by this author.

Fab: The Coming Revolution on Your Desktop—From Personal Computers to Personal Fabrication by Neil Gershenfeld (New York: Basic Books, 2005)

Free Culture: How Big Media Uses Technology and the Law to Lock Down Culture and Control Creativity by Lawrence Lessig (London: Penguin Books, 2004) and other works by this author.

Hybrid Space: New Forms in Digital Architecture by Peter Zellner (London Thames and Hudson, 2000)

New Rules for the New Economy: Ten Radical Strategies for a Connected World by Kevin Kelly (London: Fourth Estate, 1998) and other works by this author.

Shaping Things by Bruce Sterling (Cambridge, MA: MIT Press, 2005)

SUMMARY MAP of the LANDSCAPE FEATURES for
ECONOMY

When we look at design within the landscape of economy, these features are critical to understanding sustainability.

1 THREE SECTORS

Private
Private individuals and companies whose financial aim is to generate profit for themselves through the mechanism of the marketplace.

Public
Public governments (e.g., cities, counties, states, countries) with the financial aim of collecting public resources to provide collective public services (e.g., military defense, education, legal systems).

Nonprofit
Nonprofit organizations that are neither businesse[s] nor governments. Their financial aim is to better meet social needs, such as the environment, children's welfare, or religion, that tend to be passed over or are underserved b[y] the market and government.

2 GROWTH PRESSURES

Our debt-based economy and our economic measurement tool for national well-being (GDP) are two of the main reasons why economic growth is so important. The economy must expand or collapse under the weight of debt. At the same time, our reliance on growth-in-money to indicate well-being has focused society on generating higher and higher levels of material wealth and money.

3 LOST VALUES

Many important values and resources, such as breathable air, healthy children, or diverse languages, are difficult or impossible to price in the marketplace. The result is that in money terms it is as though they have no value. When these resources are damaged (e.g., air pollution), the market can't measure the damages either. It's difficult for individual designers to overcome this failure of the market.

4 BORROWING FROM THE FUTURE (DISCOUNTING).

The market assumes that everything, from money to materials, will have less value in the future than it does in the present. This is based on the idea that future generations will have more money than we have today. But we cannot assume that future generations will have more old-growth forests than we have today, so it may be wrong to make today's desig[n] decisions based on the assumption that old-growth forest or other natural and social resources will have less value in the future.

5 THE MARKET DECIDES

$1 = 1 vote

Smith theorized possible economic democracy by way of the "invisible hand."

Rich people get more votes.

Marx claimed economic democracy was canceled by the concentration of wealth.

6 THE DYNAMIC ECONOMY

We choose. The market and the larger economy of which it is part are things that most of us tend to take as a given or not see at all. We have not chosen this system; it has accumulated over time. How many of us would choose the extreme concentration of wealth that excludes most of us? Or choose to ignore values that have no market price? Yet the market, as a human artifact, is not a given. By our active involvement in the economy, we can change it.

7 FOR PROFIT

The market's brutally financial approach to people and communities—all to generate money for shareholders—makes it very difficult to capture a wide range of human values in the design process of the private sector. Yet all businesses, including corporations, are made up of people who, in their private lives at least, probably already hold a wide range of human values. The "good" corporation tries to act on these, including in ways that relate, however indirectly, to design.

8 FOR CITIZENS

The public sector is responsible for protecting those things that fall outside the market. But fragmentation among public

agencies creates challenges to pursuing sustainable development. Design can help overcome these by finding linkages among economic, cultural, and ecological issues through the lens of an artifact, whether it be a building or a product.

9 FOR A CAUSE

A nonprofit structure allows you to make doing-things-for-a-good-cause your bottom line, freeing you from the profit-making and economic growth requirements of the private sector. And unlike the public sector, nonprofit organizations can focus on a particular charitable cause rather than be generally accountable to all citizens through public funding.

10 GLOBALIZATION

As global economic activity increases, individual countries are less the focus of economic activity than global corporations. With the free movement of corporate business, and the search for ever lower costs, some companies take advantage of vulnerable developing countries. Few designers would probably want their artifacts produced by exploitative child labor or through means of irreversible environmental destruction, but when these abuses happen on the other side of the world, they are hard to monitor. Fair trade, microeconomics, an local currencies are some of the tools available to counter globalization pressures.

11 DIFFERENCE IN DIGITAL

Design is less about providing form, a physical expression, than it is about providing ideas and information about forms. In such an *information* economy, markets are different. For example, information is not scarce in the way that physical goods can be. Information that is transferred doesn't have to leave the possession of the original owner. Authorship is less clear. There's no certainty that design information will ever take a physical form. These differences will affect design.

PART 4

CULTURE

HUMAN BEINGS ARE ANIMALS, like any other animal, so why isn't culture just a part of nature? What distinguishes a bird's nest from an architect's design for a home? What distinguishes a colorful display of finery in nature, such as a peacock's tail, from something similar in human society, such as a designer gown?

A major distinction between human systems and ecosystems is the fact that, unlike other ecosystems that are governed by dimensions of time and space, human systems are governed by time, space, *and* symbols (including language).[1] The symbolic dimension of human systems allows us to detach from local environments because we can think and communicate with abstract ideas. This thinking allows us to reflect on our own situation and also to embody our knowledge in technology and tools. For example, an architect thinks of a design for a house, draws it for the client, revises it, and adjusts it to suit the site with desired materials and technologies. And in the end, the architect knows she will make a cultural statement with her building.

Another important distinction of human systems is scale. Humans are not just the dominant species; we have substantially altered natural sys-

tems, in some cases irreversibly changing the conditions for all other life on Earth. Our use of symbols and abstract ideas is the very thing that allows us to have impacts over such a large scale. We've made medical and social improvements that in turn help us to survive and live longer. Our ability to harvest energy and use technology causes us to have far greater impact for our numbers than any other species does.

Because humans are fundamentally different from other species, it is important to explore the human, or cultural, aspect of sustainable development. From our history of human activity— such as language, technology, beliefs, and values—what do we want to sustain over the long term? In some ways it's easier to identify things we don't want to maintain—wars, injustice, poverty, racism, and disease are a few examples. Let's suggest that cultural sustainability seeks to create and maintain general human well-being. A particular part of our question concerns the role of design within cultural sustainability. Given their functional, aesthetic, and symbolic roles, what can artifacts and designers contribute to human well-being? These are the ideas explored in this part of the atlas.

Our human pursuits: Language, technology beliefs, and values—What do we want to sustain over the long term?

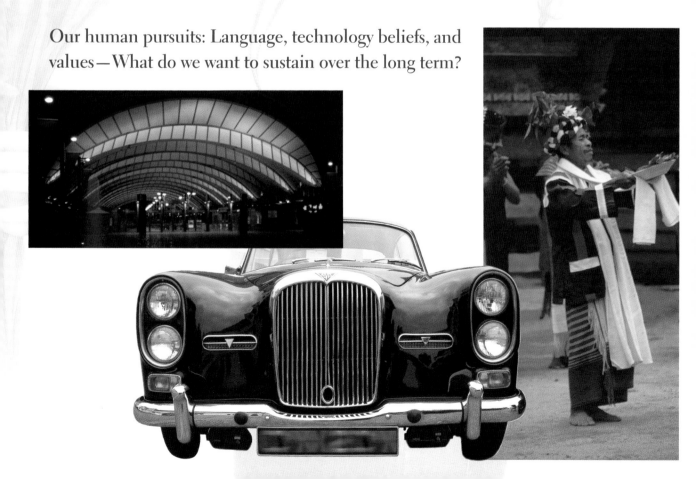

HAPPY PEOPLE

THROUGHOUT TIME human design has sought to satisfy people's emotional and practical needs. In functional terms, designers address accessibility, efficiency, speed, and portability, among others. In emotional terms, designers seek to provide pleasure both in sensual form such as visual beauty and in intellectual form such as wit or charm. Any design problem is ultimately a challenge of balancing the functional and emotional elements of the solution and a struggle to resolve the tension between needs and desires.

> Although we are all different, human beings have a common set of needs that we must meet to achieve well-being.

When it comes to human well-being, what is the distinction between needs and desires? What constitutes human well-being? This seems an impossible question given there are more than six billion people on the planet. How can we come up with a general idea of "well-being" that applies to them all?

By examining some universal motivational forces that all humans experience, there are ways to generalize human well-being. These universal forces include things such as physical survival, communicating with others, creating things, and having a sense of self. There is, in fact, a whole body of work known as "needs theory" that has attempted to map out what we all, as humans, need.[2] What differs among us, of course, is how we choose to meet these needs and how well our choices meet our actual needs.

Among the many different categorizations of human needs, a representative list includes subsistence, protection, affection, understanding, participation, leisure, creation, identity, and freedom.[3] Moreover, these needs have several dimensions. For example, under subsistence we need not only to be healthy but also to have food and shelter. We need to do things such as eat, rest, and occupy ourselves. Finally, there is also always a context for what we do that requires interaction with what is around us, since we are never in a vacuum. These dimensions exist for each need as being, having, doing, and interacting.

Human well-being occurs when these underlying needs are successfully and constructively satisfied. Of the nine needs on the list, the first seven have been with us throughout human existence, but the last two arrived later on the scene.

There are several interesting aspects to human needs. First, needs cannot be prioritized easily. Although it is tempting to say that subsistence needs must come first, in fact there are instances when individuals sacrifice their own survival for other values. People go on hunger strikes, fight wars, or otherwise jeopardize their own well-being for a larger cause. They do this because of their spiritual or intellectual belief in principles that they deem so important as to be worth dying for.

A second interesting feature of these needs is that they describe only underlying human motivations, but they don't describe how the need should be met.[4] For example, the need for sustenance includes the need to eat but makes no distinction between eating junk food or health food. Methods of satisfying needs vary widely over time and across cultures.

A third issue concerning needs is time. Since the needs outlined above are framed in terms of individual well-being, they suggest the time frame of a human life. On the face of it, they may appear to neglect a link to the past and the future that lie beyond the individual's own life. However, a universal motivational force within humans does include connections across time—from ancestors and to offspring. In this way participation, creation, and understanding all might have dimensions that cross generations.

Another important aspect of needs with respect to time relates to our expectations about how quickly needs can be met. Satisfying a need for understanding, for example, requires a large time commitment and can even be a lifelong process. Similarly, building meaningful connections among people takes time and experience. As I will explore in upcoming sections, the time dimension to human well-being has taken on increasing importance in our century.

Although we can outline nine universal human needs, the meeting of which may lead to improved well-being, what can we say in general about successful ways to meet these needs? What role does design play?

 LANDSCAPE FEATURE: Human Needs

Research suggests that, although we are all different, human beings have a common set of needs that we must meet to achieve well-being. If cultural sustainability means establishing and maintaining human well-being, then successfully meeting these needs becomes central to sustainability. Design's task is to help meet these needs well.

Subsistence: Sustenance, health, physical, capability.

Protection: Shelter, safety, security.

Affection: Self-respect/ self-esteem, loving relationships, respect, tolerance.

Understanding: Curiosity, knowing, exploration, conscience, rationality, intuition.

Participation: Solidarity, sense of belonging, responsibility, sharing, connectedness.

Leisure: Rest, play, relaxation, idleness, fantasy.

Creation: Invention, design, composition, interpretation, expression.

Identity: Competence, self-esteem, memory, self-knowledge, authenticity.
Freedom: Autonomy, tolerance, rights, choice, self-direction.

MEET MY NEED

MOST OF THE NINE NEEDS ARE EMOTIONAL OR INTELLECTUAL IN NATURE and are frequently best satisfied by looking inside oneself to develop abilities to pursue meaningful relationships and personal growth. Studies show that the more people look outside themselves as a way of satisfying needs, by seeking money, material wealth, or the good opinion of others, the less likely they are to have their actual needs met. Beyond acquiring food and shelter, wealth contributes little to actual well-being.[5] This is one of the important conclusions of needs theory: not all methods of meeting needs are successful. Internal means of meeting needs work better than external means. When needs are not successfully satisfied, the result can be negative feelings such as depression, anxiety, low energy, or loneliness.[6]

During the past century we have increasingly shifted to external methods of meeting needs, making our century "odd" relative to centuries that came before. This part of the atlas explores design's role as a key supplier of external images and artifacts that we use to meet needs and also examines how design might help people return to a more internal, and more successful, means of meeting their needs. This exploration has four main themes—communication, artifacts, time and nature. I preview these themes briefly below.

Nature

Time

LANDSCAPE FEATURE: The Odd Century

Many of us take for granted the fast-paced, information-rich, and materialistic way of life in the early twenty-first century. But our slice of life, the last one hundred years or so, represents an oddity in many ways.[7] In our century we have fundamentally changed the ways that we try to meet our human needs. Historically, people relied on internal methods (those from within themselves), such as reflection or creativity, to meet needs. In our century there has been a major shift to external methods, such as watching television or buying lots of things. Research suggests that these external methods are much less successful at meeting human needs.

Materialism: A twentieth-century way of meeting needs.

The first theme is communication. Communication underpins many of the nine needs, particularly affection, understanding, and participation—it also is directly associated with creating community and fostering interaction. In our odd century, we have seen a transition away from a rich texture of interpersonal and local communication, which took place through a range of participatory media like live performance, song, community gatherings, poems, religious ceremonies, and personal letters. We have shifted toward one-way broadcast communication, typically at the national or global level. These media are largely visual and passive, such as television, film, and photo magazines.

Designers generate the imagery that keeps the media going. Broadcast media not only shift emphasis away from local communities and toward individuals, but they also shift us away from traditional sources of meaning within a community and toward commercially generated meaning, something we'll return to later.

Can design help people more successfully meet needs? We investigate four themes:

Artifacts

Communication

TRAVELER'S NOTE: Design's Central Role

In the transition from using internal methods of meeting human needs to using external ones (such as images and material goods), design's central role has been to supply images for our viewing and to style objects for us to own. Designers generate the imagery that keeps the media going, from seductive graphics in an advertisement to the interface of a video game, and from home furnishings shown in a television show to the layout of a glossy celebrity magazine. As far as material artifacts go, design makes key contributions to these objects in terms of their visual and functional consumer appeal. Although design is currently a key supplier of external images and artifacts that we use to meet needs, could it help people return to more internal, and more successful, means of meeting their needs?

The second theme we'll use to explore design and well-being is artifacts, which have gone from being on the sidelines throughout most of human history to taking a central role in the last one hundred years. We've become a culture of materialism, going from few personal possessions and general scarcity of material goods in the past to our current situation of plentiful goods and Western-style consumerism based on individual desire rather than need. Our relationship to material artifacts has grown ever more dense and complex. Not only has the number of artifacts increased, the range of materials from which we make them also has grown.[8] Here again, design supplies us with our multitude of material goods, from clothing, buildings, and electronics to sports gear, automobiles, and furnishings, which are all being continually modified and updated.

The third theme for exploring well-being and design is time. In addition to reducing our focus, from the community down to the individual, we have reduced our time horizons. Impatience characterizes the citizens of our century. We seek quicker and easier routes to well-being and expect our individual needs to be satisfied instantaneously or in the immediate future (next week at the latest). Whereas in the past we used to consider the best interests of the community over the long term, our contemporary focus centers on the short-term individual: Me, Right Now![9] Speed and short-termism—these are the two key dimensions of time we will explore in terms of design and well-being.

A fourth theme is nature, but not in the functional and more scientific sense that we examined in part 2. Instead we look at nature as an aspect of culture. Despite our human distinctiveness from the rest of nature, we are still a part of it, and our basic connection with nature appears to be a central part of our well-being. Yet over the last one hundred years we have accelerated our disconnection from nature, immersing ourselves in cities of ever-increasing size; by the end of the twentieth century, more people lived in urban areas than rural ones for the first time in history.[10] In addition, we now want not only to conquer nature through huge infrastructure projects (such as large dams), but also to control and engineer it at the genetic level. Nature-as-culture has typically been expressed in the aesthetics of design—borrowing forms from nature. But can design find a more substantial cultural connection with nature, something that fosters and sustains well-being?

The next chapter provides a brief historical context that sets the stage for future chapters.

DEFINITION: Broadcast Media

To "broadcast" means to scatter over a wide area, but in our media age it also is an expression for transmitting television or radio programs. These are scattered over wider and wider areas. Another key element in any broadcast medium is the way it transmits from one (the broadcaster) to many (the audience, increasingly viewed as consumers). Broadcasting, with some possible exceptions for the Internet, requires a passive audience; there is little, if any, real interaction. It also has a tendency to be commercially driven.

NO GOING BACK

IT IS USEFUL HERE TO BRIEFLY CONSIDER HISTORY, first because this process helps us consider what it is about human life we might want to sustain. Of course, it is fruitless to suggest going back to the way things "used to be" (indeed, many of the old ways we gratefully leave behind), but there are elements from the past, long-standing human approaches, that may be useful to us today. Second, history is useful because it gives us perspective on the way life is now—how and why it may have come into being, where it might go next, and where design has played and will play a role.

Let's consider two of our themes, communication and artifacts. How have they evolved? How do these themes play out in our century compared to how they played out in prior human history?

Using two examples, writing and home furnishings, we find they confirm that the past century presents a real substantive break from previous history in terms of pace, scale, and materials. These changes have helped shift us from internal to external means of meeting needs. The following brief historical exploration focuses largely on Western civilization, in keeping with the development context established for this atlas in part 1.

Writing

Writing appears to have been introduced in Sumaria around 3500 BCE Earliest forms used imprints or carving on clay tablets, wax, or metal. Writing on paper-like surfaces began with scrolls of papyrus (around 3000 BCE) and reed

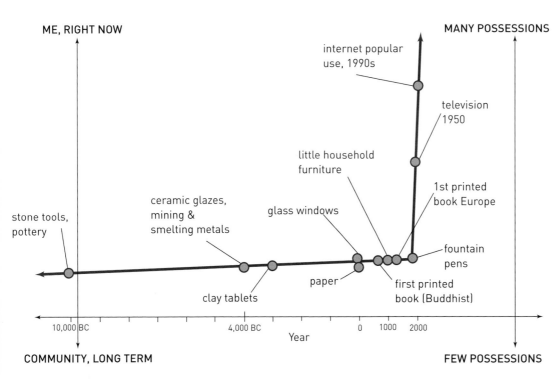

ME, RIGHT NOW

MANY POSSESSIONS

internet popular use, 1990s

television 1950

little household furniture

1st printed book Europe

ceramic glazes, mining & smelting metals

glass windows

stone tools, pottery

fountain pens

paper

first printed book (Buddhist)

clay tablets

10,000 BC   4,000 BC   0   1000   2000

Year

COMMUNITY, LONG TERM

FEW POSSESSIONS

This chart shows the histor transition from our focus community in the long term our focus on the individua the short term. In parallel graph shows the transition from few personal possessi (the norm throughout hur history) to many perso possessions (a phenome emerging in the past hund years). Shown graphically, transition is sudden and sta The graph highlights two themes: communication artifacts, particularly arti for the home.

pens dipped into ink. This format lasted for several thousand years until the codex, or book form, was invented and gained acceptance around the fourth century CE. Books made it easy to access written information: You could write on both sides of the page, and the pages were protected by a binding. Books were also easier than scrolls to label (on the spine) and to organize in a library.

Around the time books became common, many people began reproducing books in Europe. Monks switched from papyrus to parchment and vellum, made from animal skin, as a more readily available and durable writing surface. It would be another few hundred years before quill pens were introduced around 700 CE and these would dominate writing for a thousand years until a workable fountain pen was introduced in the late 1880s. Books were costly and time consuming to produce; religious documents were among the few deemed worthy of reproducing and illuminating. The printing press was introduced in Europe in the 1400s, making written communication more widely available at the same time that plant fiber–based paper was becoming more common. The tools and materials for writing original documents, as opposed to the printing process for reproducing them, were still relatively expensive and scarce.

Paper became common in Europe only after the thirteenth century or so, although it was a luxury item until industrial pulping machines came along in the 1800s. At that point cheap wood-based paper and better pens made books and writing more accessible, improving literacy rates and the flow of information during the Industrial Revolution.

After thousands of years of scrolls and handwritten books penned with feather quills, faster forms of visual and audio media such as telephones, photography, and radio came on the scene only recently, around a hundred years ago. Audiovisual broadcasting (film and television) were even later. Within the past decades these media have been joined by even faster forms such as faxes, the Internet and other emerging electronic forms of communication.[11] We've moved from relatively slow, largely interpersonal communication limited by the pace at which people could write by hand to relatively fast, largely visual communication accelerated by "instant" digital technologies.

Home Furnishings

Furniture existed in the ancient world (e.g., the ancient Greeks invented chairs), but it was primitive and relatively scarce. Possessions were lightweight, portable, and adaptable since they often had to be moved. For example, in the Middle Ages (about 1000 CE) everything that went on at home did so in one room, and furniture had to adjust throughout the day. Chests were very important pieces of furniture because they were the only place to house valuables, such as clothing or money. No permanent shelves, drawers, or closets existed. Books, and even paper, were rare, and there was no need to store them. The evolution of furniture design was slow because pieces lasted such a long time, frequently staying

in families for generations before being replaced out of need. Early wills (1200 CE) reveal that even wealthy households had little furniture or possessions. Chairs, reserved for the master of the house, were uncommon and often so heavy that they could not be moved. Noblemen and even religious men would often merely recline on their beds to receive important visitors. Candles and lamps were also expensive and not widely used. Material possessions mostly addressed basic needs for sustenance and protection.[12]

During the Renaissance (roughly 1400–1700), the arrival of books and papers, along with other developments, made households more crowded with furniture—bookshelves were invented. Cupboards were used to store cups and plates. Houses transitioned very gradually from being public gathering places to private areas with separate rooms for separate functions. Around this time fireplaces and stoves also became much more efficient and provided homes with better heating. Women took on a greater influence in the home and in the fashions of private life. Possessions in the home became more plentiful and more important, and there was a growing interest in fashions, with styles such as baroque and rococo. Fashion, which previously had been reserved for clothing, jewelry, and armor, came to furniture. This period saw the emergence of furniture designers Thomas Chippendale (1718–1779) and George Hepplewhite (d. 1786). They popularized furniture designs in their fashionable design books and helped standardize the craftsman's practice. Fashion had a broader reach into society through objects as diverse as Wedgwood plates, Franklin stoves, and Georgian houses. A measured role for materialism emerged during this period.[13] As

machine production of goods arose in the 1800s and delivered true mass production in the late 1800 and early 1900s, our material culture took off. After thousands of years of sparse furnishings and few possessions, our materialistic lifestyle emerged in the 1880s and grew phenomenally in the last hundred years.

Our brief history of communication and furnishings demonstrates not only the rapid changes in the past century but also the interplay between material artifacts and some central cultural forces. Historically, religion has been a key force, particularly the world's major religions such as Buddhism, Judaism, Christianity, and Islam and the values they espouse. Religious orders often produced furniture and written texts as well as creating churches, monasteries, or temples. Ethnicity, including language and local traditions, also has been a major cultural force expressed through vernacular architecture, indigenous dress, and craft. Science and technology have a significant part in our culture, reflecting our understanding of the world and our place in it, historically typified by clocks, compasses, and scale models and more recently typified by computers and biotechnology.

Modern values, such as freedom of expression or equality of opportunity, also shape societies and artifacts. A contemporary artifactual example of these pressures is design for

RELIGION

**AGE, GENDER,
AND RACE**

Artifacts express the
forces that influence
culture.

ETHNICITY

SCIENCE & TECHNOLOGY

compliance with the Americans with Disabilities Act, ensuring equal physical access to people of all physical abilities. Social pressures based on race, gender, class, age, and other variations among people have also influenced individuals and social units, such as families, across time.

The balance of these forces is continually shifting, and within the last two hundred years or so, traditional cultural pressures have been joined by purely monetary ones, such as the pressure for continuous economic growth as we saw in part 3. During our odd century we've seen the emergence of two key external means of meeting needs: watching and owning. These two represent our first two themes, communication and artifacts, in our exploration of design and human well-being.

In the following chapters we begin with some background on watching and owning. We then look at several concepts that may help designers approach communication and artifacts to restore some of our internal means of meeting needs. Finally, we move on to our remaining themes of time and nature.

WATCHING

AFTER CENTURIES of relatively active forms of communication, we have now become a passive "watching" culture. I call this "visuality" because as yet, it isn't really a virtual reality that one can enter. It is a visual reality that pervades our lives, from advertising on bus stops to television, and from Web pages to video games. Perhaps even more important, much of what we see in visuality looks real but isn't, creating physically unobtainable ideals. Design has a substantial role in shaping the objects and images in visuality, so it is important for us to consider its dominance as a form of communication as well as how it helps and hinders our well-being.

 LANDSCAPE FEATURE: Visuality

"Visuality" is my term for the dominance of visual images in our lives and the one-way direction those images tend to flow. Images surround us and invade every conceivable place, largely through advertising. One way of gauging how important visuality has become in meeting needs is to measure the amount of time we spend with the media. We tend to think of television as the central culprit in our watching culture, and it is, but it is not alone. Television watching is on the rise, mainly through hundreds of cable and "pay" stations, but it is now joined by a heap of other broadcast media, including digital radio, specialized magazines, video games, personal digital assistants, mobile phones and, of course, the Internet. When we consider all major media sources combined, studies reveal that people spend an average of eleven hours per day with the media.[14] Although these media are called communication "channels," they might better be labeled "streams," because they overwhelmingly flow one-way from the broadcaster to the consumer audience. We are largely a passive audience, and our children are inheriting this passive role.

Just because there's a lot of it, we can't assume visuality is all bad. Visuality can provide valuable information and entertainment. The global dominance of visual imagery means we are quickly connected to places and issues that might otherwise remain remote. Through pictures we can better comprehend and be moved by hardships such as war or famine or by accomplishments like the landing of humans on the moon. In this way visuality helps meet our need for understanding and connection. The fictional stories of film, video games, and television provide release, escape, fantasy, and perhaps even insight into the self, among other things. These features of visuality help meet our needs for leisure, understanding, and identity.

But to the extent that visuality dominates, it keeps us focused on external and largely material sources of satisfying our needs and squeezes out other, internal methods for satisfying them. In addition, visuality often acts as a pseudosatisfier, providing a short-term sense of satisfaction that is fleeting and leaves dissatisfaction in its wake.

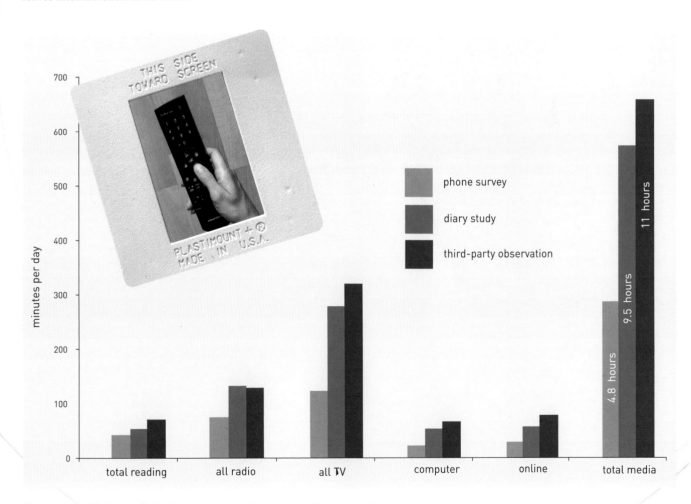

Time spent with the media by day: our perceptions vs. actual consumption.

Images surround us, largely through advertising, and invade every conceivable place.

The false reality shown in visuality illustrates how this dissatisfaction arises. We routinely strive to achieve the impossible that is shown to us as convincingly real. Artificial images create a discrepancy between what we see presented as ideals (material goods and personal appearances) to achieve and what we can actually achieve. We become dissatisfied with our own selves, reducing our well-being in terms of identity.[15] In addition, the inhabitants of visuality, such as Hollywood movie characters, news presenters, or actors in advertisements, are typically young, able-bodied white people (and often men) who are relatively wealthy. The majority of real people—racially diverse, relatively poor, more than 50% female, and in industrialized countries, older than thirty-five—are underrepresented in most of visuality.[16] Because visuality doesn't reflect the real population, it also weakens our sense of connectedness.

We begin to dismiss the value of our own reality, which isn't validated by the imagery we see in visuality, and instead we adopt what is shown as a "reverse" validation. This process detracts from fulfilling our need for authentic identity and creation. The activity of watching in itself takes away from opportunities for us to satisfy needs actively and innovatively. Visuality reduces much of life to the two dimensions of sex and violence, appealing to viewers' fantasies, further limiting satisfaction in the real world and arguably interfering with the need for affection (caring, respect, and loving relationships).

Visuality is related to materialism not least because it is the primary means of delivering commercial messages—messages that urge us to buy material goods and suggest that material wealth and the right appearance will bring us happiness. Indeed, studies have shown that people who have high materialistic values tend to watch a lot of television.[17] The next chapter examines materialism.

OWNING

LET'S SAY your desire is to answer the question, "Who am I?" by saying, "I am a rugged outdoorsman with survival skills, strength, and endurance." In this case acquiring rugged outdoor gear for activities that require strength and endurance might make your answer appear legitimate to the outside world. You could get a four-wheel-drive vehicle and many other technical gadgets, along with high-performance clothing. You could even acquire a mountain cabin. You can acquire these artifacts quickly, but learning to use them with skill takes time. Yet unless you actually build strength, skills, and endurance, your "Who-am-I?" answer is not honest and won't contribute to building your identity; on the contrary, it only generates a sense of inauthenticity. In contrast, we might argue that those who are confident in their internal resources—actual survival skills, strength, and endurance—rely less on the appearance of things.

LANDSCAPE FEATURE: Materialism

"Materialism" is a focus on material wealth. It suggests that you define yourself in terms of your material possessions and your physical appearance, that you place the most importance in life on these. Although it's difficult to pinpoint exactly how much we rely on materialism to fulfill our needs, we do know that it's on the increase, according to studies that ask college students about what is important to them. In the 1960s, about 40% said that it is "very important" or "essential" to "be very well off financially," but by the 1990s, the figure had risen to over 70%.[18]

The twin trends of materialism and visuality pressure us to rely increasingly on things and appearances to try to satisfy our human needs—to use appearance as a substitute for real meaning and experience. Materialism suggests that you can define yourself in terms of your material possessions and your physical appearance, like the would-be rugged outdoorsman from above.

As with visuality, materialism is not intrinsically bad. Material objects, our artifacts, contribute to our well-being *functionally*; for example, houses shelter us and ergonomic chairs support our backs. Availability of material goods has also broadened our functional horizons, making material objects and tools to satisfying other human needs: A microscope can improve understanding, a piano can provide opportunities for creativity, and a museum can inspire reflection. But artifacts also contribute *emotionally* to human well-being, and it is this emotional dimension of artifacts that has changed the most over time.

Historically, the emotional and cultural meaning behind material objects originated with the community. Individuals were more closely involved in making all the items they needed in order to survive as well as creating what they wanted for entertainment and leisure. In this sense, making and using artifacts was more important than buying and owning them.

In earlier times, artifacts held much stronger links to the past and the future, since most material goods were passed from one generation to the next. Artifacts, which were all handcrafted, also held cultural meaning, serving as symbols of community roles or expressions of religious or social values.

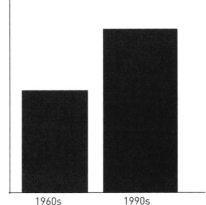

Percentage of college students who say it is "very important" or "essential" to "be very well off financially."

Tools, ceremonial objects, and finery existed but were deployed with care because of their expense and scarcity. Although artifacts contributed to well-being, the community and its activities were the primary source of meaning and experience. Participation in community life, such as rites of passage that mark various life stages, supplied symbolic meaning, discipline, challenge, and motivation that could "carry the human spirit forward."[19] They satisfied needs for connectedness, self-understanding, and creativity.

In our century we are largely lacking the commonly accepted social rituals (such as rites of passage or religious ceremonies) and other social markers (such as family place or profession) that historically supported personal identity, cultural meaning, and community coherence.[20] These lost social elements, sometimes called "symbolic resources," also tended to promote a longer term perspective. Having lost appropriate social symbolic resources, we have turned to material goods to provide some of our social-marking services. This works to some extent because the things we own project an identity for others to see—whether that identity is real or just an appearance (like the would-be rugged outdoorsman). In this sense the owning and displaying of artifacts allows us to construct and reconstruct individual identity, social relationships, and meaning in a fast-changing world.[21] We may even select a brand as a way of joining a social group, so artifacts can also be seen as a way of creating, or at least articulating, relationships.

Even though materialism has some positive aspects, as a dominant approach to meeting human needs, it's worrying. Research suggests that materialistic values emerge in people who have not had their needs for security and identity effectively met. Even worse, pursuing materialistic values won't

Materialism suggests that you define yourself in terms of your material possessions and your physcial appearence.

DEFINITION: Symbolic Resources

Material goods play important symbolic roles in our lives. Although most material goods have some functionality, many are even more important for what they signify to ourselves and others. Their symbolic role is to communicate meaning. For example, a car may have the function of getting you to work and back, but a Ferrari symbolizes far more than just a commute to the office. In this sense material goods are "symbolic" resources as well as functional ones.

satisfy these unmet needs; instead, it aggravates unhappiness. Individuals who are focused on materialistic values have both lower psychological health and lower physical well-being. Remarkably consistent research results from across the world suggest that there are four main ways that materialism hurts well-being and decreases happiness, including substituting for security, providing false self-esteem, crowding out meaningful relationships, and reducing self-expression.[22]

An important aspect to both visuality and materialism that may help us understand their weakness in meeting human needs is the role of commerce, or the marketplace. It is these notions of commercialism and consumerism that we examine in the next chapter.

COMMERCE

TODAY WE ARE OVERWHELMED WITH ARTIFACTS and images, each boasting importance for our identity and our potential.[23] "Buy this gadget because it signifies financial success." "Make your hair blond, and you'll attract a boyfriend." In most cases these meanings and messages are commercially generated through advertising and marketing.

How captive are we to commercial messages? To some extent, we do critically view, in fact "decode," commercial messages and then rationally accept or reject these based on our own creative choices.[24] But as emotional beings we engage in desire and fantasy; we have psychological needs for love and acceptance. These are powerful forces in our lives, and it is these forces that advertising usually appeals to. Although we have rational powers to resist advertising, we also are emotionally attuned to it.[25]

We are captive to commercial messages in another way as well, because commercialism is so pervasive in visuality. U.S. television viewers see nearly forty thousand television advertisements per year.[26] But *Business Week* estimates that we each see about three thousand commercial messages per day when we consider all forms of media, from T-shirt logos to bus stop billboards. The amount of money spent on advertising is enormous and growing daily. From 1935 to 1994 U.S. expenditures on media advertising and other promotions grew eightfold from $19 billion to $148 billion.[27] The amount spent on advertising rose by slightly more than 65% to $215 billion, in only nine years, between 1990 and 1999.[28]

But advertising spending figures don't capture the pervasive and intrusive techniques used by advertisers and marketers. A few examples of these techniques include the presentation of advertising as:

- Educational materials, especially in primary education
- Entertainment "infomercials"
- Public services
- Fashion (e.g., logos on clothing, bags, shoes)
- Civic institutions (e.g., names of symphony halls, sports stadiums.)

Routinely, it is commercial interests that are able to produce the best and most sophisticated images in visuality, and just a few very large corporations dominate commercial media interests. In the United States, for example, six companies control most of the media. These companies own publishing companies, television channels, film companies, radio stations, and newspapers. They tightly control their media outlets for the purpose of generating profits. Truly local media outlets

DEFINITION: Commerce and Commercial

"Commerce" describes the buying and selling of goods, particularly on a large scale. The term "commercial" describes things related to commerce, particularly the goal of making money from the buying and selling of goods.

that respond to local issues and concerns are all but extinct.[29] Commercialism is tied to the need for continuous economic expansion.

The rise of commercialism over the past fifty years affects design in two main ways. The first is a pressure to focus narrowly on economic interests. The second is a pressure to simplify many aspects of design and artifacts. Commercial pressure has, arguably, caused design to be increasingly and exclusively defined as an economic tool

US Advertising expenditures continue to grow

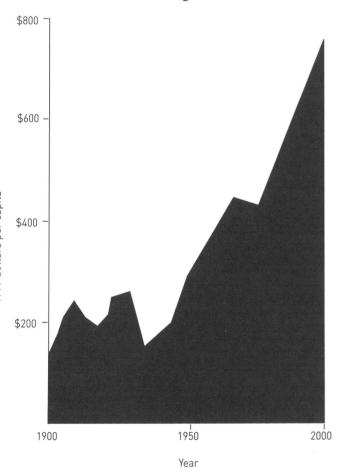

LANDSCAPE FEATURE:
Commercial Culture

We are captive to commercialism in several ways. First, we are emotionally attuned to advertising, even though rationally we know the producer is just trying to sell us something. Second, we are bombarded with thousands of commercial messages every day; they are pervasive in visuality, and there is no escaping them. Third, commercial messages often take camouflaged forms, masquerading as educational materials or public services. Finally, commercial messages are frequently the most captivating and sophisticated images in visuality.

for adding value, expanding markets, or increasing sales. Design is then measured strictly by its commercial success: how well it sold, met marketing objectives, and so forth. As most designers are already aware, this drives the kinds of jobs designers get and makes designers feel powerless to address, in any significant way, a wide range of other, noneconomic concerns. It squeezes out concerns that appear to "cost extra" because the economy doesn't measure them properly. See part 3 for a full discussion of these issues.

The commercial focus also puts pressure on design to aim for bigger spenders as well as bigger markets. From this perspective, the more all consumers are alike, or can be groomed through advertising to be alike, the better it is for selling: They'll all want the same product. Finally, commercial pressure forces designers to build on a company's existing commercial assets, such as existing technologies, rather than consider more efficient or socially desirable solutions.

The pressure to simplify goes beyond

the obvious drive to concentrate heavily on visual appearance of artifacts. In addition, consumer-oriented design is asked to appeal almost exclusively to fantasy and desire rather than address a full spectrum of human need.[30] The pressure to create immediate benefits to consumers forces design to focus on the short term as well as to create artifacts that "de-skill," that is, objects that don't require much skill to use.[31]

De-skilling is a way of moving more and more activities into the mass market because it enables everyone to do them instantly, without learning a craft or skill. At the same time, for this very reason, it takes away from the internal well-being people might get through acquiring a skill.

Catering to fantasy and desire also causes a disconnection from reality—not only physical reality but also social reality and the reality of ideas. The average American recognizes fewer than ten types of plants but recognizes hundreds of corporate logos. As for social reality, what duties do you have to your fellow

Designers are under pressure to "de-skill" artifacts.

Sainsbury's
single use camera
for colour prints with flash

flash

for all round great performance

flash   all weather

Which can you identify and name more quickly—leaves or logos?

consumers? Compare that with your duties to your fellow citizens. As a *consumer*, your sense of community is generally "no bigger than your shopping basket."[32] When fantasy and idealizations become more dominant, more important, and in a sense more real than the places and communities around us, we lose connection to real ideas. By putting our money into individual consumerism instead of into community (through taxes, volunteer time, participation in decisions and discussion), the public domain shrinks and becomes impoverished, opening the door to large private companies that are willing to pay for "community" as long as they control it for commercial gain.[33] In this we lose the idea of democracy.

Finally, designers are forced to work from simplified marketing data about the consumer population, since the one-way stream of communica-

LANDSCAPE FEATURE:
Designers as "Pushers"

Although some "user-centered" design approaches attempt to understand and improve the true well-being of the ultimate users of design, the terminology itself is lacking. For example, we have no constructive, human way to refer to the people on the other end of our designs. Either they are commercial entities—"consumers," "clients," "buyers"—or they are functional, often rational entities—*users*. It's hard to resist the temptation to cast designers as *pushers* because, seen in the light of commerce, it's what they do. They help businesses push more of their products through the market and onto the users—through frequent styling updates, advertising, or that old familiar planned obsolescence.

tion between the media and the viewers does not allow the viewers to provide any substantive feedback. Their feedback comes in one of two forms: either they buy or they don't. Designers have typically tried to overcome the absence of substantive consumer input through techniques such as "user-centered" design. Designers study the needs of the person (or people) who will use the product or building, imagining scenarios that might arise and how the design can respond well to meet various user needs. A related approach is "participatory" design that includes direct observation of user behavior as well as activities that engage the user in collecting or documenting how objects are used.[34] In architectural design an even wider definition of "user" often includes people who will build and maintain the structure.

Commercial pressures on design affect cultural sustainability because they generally push us toward short-term economic gains that rely, in many ways, on superficial style that provides an external means of meeting human needs and meaning. Commercial pressures also appear to make designers into "pushers," helping business push more and more products and images onto consumers. How can design begin to escape?

NO MORE PUSHERS

A BRIEF SUMMARY of the previous few chapters may be useful here before we press on to investigating design concepts that might move designers out of the role of "pushers" and into a role that more substantively supports cultural sustainability, in terms of human well-being.

Previous chapters have shown us that in the past century we have moved rather suddenly from centuries of using mainly internal means of meeting our needs to using mainly external ones. Two of the key external means are visuality and mate-rialism. Although these two mechanisms do meet some human needs, our reliance on them appears to have grown much too large. Research suggests that this reliance has gotten to the point of being destructive. We can confirm this by looking to a broad range of social ills, such as the growing use of antidepressants, increasing reliance on plastic surgery to improve our appearances, rising prison populations, increasing obesity rates, and growing concerns about children's psychological and phys-ical health.

One of design's main cultural roles is to supply the images and artifacts that make up visual-ity and materialism. But, as we've seen, design is not acting alone. Designers become pushers under pressure from commerce—the needs of the market—just as owning and watching have strong commercial origins. Meanwhile, history suggests that something that has served the human family well for centuries in meeting human needs is a reliance on participatory com-

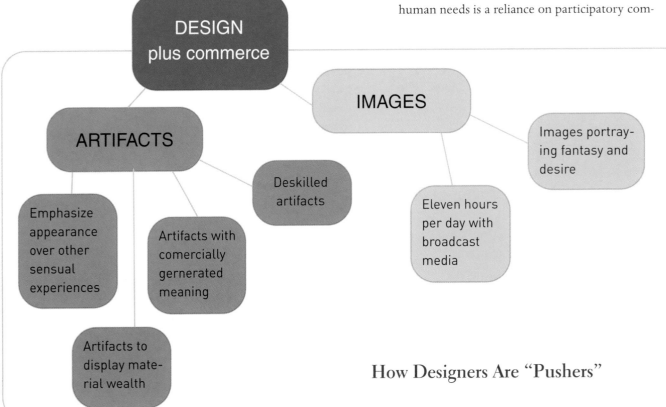

How Designers Are "Pushers"

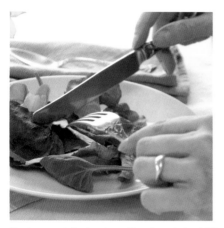  

Design contributes to cultural sustainability by improving connection and engagement

munication within our own communities, where artifacts had an important but limited role. What, then, can designers do to step out of the role of "pusher"?

In the next chapters we'll use the themes of communication and artifacts to explore two key concepts for design. The first is how design can help users engage with or connect to others. A particular emphasis here is on opening up the one-way broadcast stream of visuality and creating (or restoring) richer multidirectional and participatory modes of communication.

The second concept focuses on how artifacts allow for engagement or connection—either to the self or to the world. We might think of these as the engaging or connecting "services" of arti-

facts. For example, silverware connects you to sustenance and your health but also to tradition, ceremony, conversation, and many other aspects of sharing a meal. A particular issue here has to do with the lost symbolic resources—the sources of meaning and identity that used to be provided by community connections but that are now coming to us largely through commercially engineered media and material objects. For designers, a key question is how we can help to provide symbolic resources, but in such a way that they are not so materially intensive and that they are more internally or community driven rather than externally and commercially driven. Let's turn, then, to these concepts of engagement and connection and how designers can use them.

ENGAGE, CONNECT

THINK BACK to the nine human needs we identified earlier and recall that each of these has four dimensions: having, doing, being, and interacting. In some senses the dominance of visuality and materialism—of owning and watching—emphasizes *having* above the other modes of doing, being, and interacting. Yet we might argue that it is not until we meet our needs in all four dimensions that we can really gain well-being. And these four modes of well-being are well summarized by the terms "engagement" and "connection."

Engagement happens when you play the piano, talk with a friend, or cook a gourmet meal. It doesn't happen when you watch TV. Engagement involves real connection on a num-

DEFINITION: Engage and Connect

To "engage" means to attract and hold someone's attention or to engross, absorb, or mesh. It can also mean to involve oneself or become occupied, as in "being in gear." A designer can't simply push things at an engaged user.

"To connect" means to link, unite, or establish communication between.

Engagement: Doing, being, and interacting

ber of levels, like doing, being, and interacting. For the purposes of contributing to cultural sustainability, one task for design is to "make material culture conducive to engagement."35 In turn, we want the person on the other end of design to be not just a consumer or a user but to be an engaged user. Ideally, we'd like to measure the success of design by this ruler instead of purely by sales.

In terms of human well-being, could design help people engage in a more robust range of relationships? Could it help people connect, either to others or by getting in touch with themselves? In the past, rites of passage publicly marked, and in a sense validated, an individual's progress in life. These rites typically involved elaborate roles for community members as well as spiritual tests for the subjects. The rites provided for both private and public engagement.36 As we've lost these traditions we've used materials goods ("my first car") and other economic measures ("my first paycheck") to try to gain this individual validation. Our own communities, now largely anonymous, are often tuned in more completely to the media than to the people around them. Unless we adopt the material goods and appearances we see in visuality, we generally don't gain the individual validation we need.

In what sense can we restore meaningful, community-based, contemporary rites of passage? For example, what symbolic or practical objects could mark the transition to adulthood—in all its dimensions, not just the economic ones? Designing a modern rite of passage is an intrinsically local, tangible process that involves real people, not people from visuality. What other passages would we mark that would constructively engage and connect both individuals and communities?

How else can we open up flow among people, create connection, and break off the one-way stream from visuality? The overwhelming emphasis on individual consumers means that there has been only modest opportunity for designers to consider relationships in the civic, or social, domain. Many of these opportunities lie with

We've lost most formal rights of passage, but design could have a role in marking contemporary passages in ways that engage and connect both individuals and communities.

Artifacts hold cultural meaning through community roles, such as expression of religious or social values.

architects and landscape architects whose work more naturally addresses public spaces with projects such as parks, museums, or schools. But what if design in general were to explicitly include criteria for helping individuals build and maintain a wider range of relationships?

A new set of questions begins to emerge:

- What's civic about a personal stereo system or a personal digital assistant (PDA)?
- What sort of features would a car shared by four families need to have?
- How can a workplace accommodate children?
- And so forth.

These types of questions suggest the possibility of a role for "community designers." Imagine someone who works for a community full-time, purposefully observing, participating in, and facilitating activities and discussion about how material culture can bring engagement. This person might track demographic issues, such as youth and old age, or explore the nesting of material goods, from small, short-life products to big, long-life institutional constructions. This approach suggests a way for design to help negotiate human needs locally.

TRAVELER'S NOTE: Design and Relationships

If design's challenge is indeed to make material culture conducive to engagement, then it is important to examine design's role in supporting relationships among people and breaking down the dominance of one-way visuality. Whether we consider design opportunities in modern rites of passage or a new role for community designers, there is a range of possibilities for design to help people meet their need for meaning (symbolic resources) in a less materially intensive and less commercial way.

The idea of community designers has a precedent in the concept of "stewardship." There are stewards for many major river basins in the Puget Sound watershed of U.S. Pacific Northwest. The river basin steward, who works for a large county, is familiar with the whole basin and helps to negotiate all the concerns of the basin. Guided by laws, principles, and interdisciplinary knowledge, the steward combines personal relationships and observation skills to help meet human and ecological needs.[37]

Or consider the flip side. We might train a much broader range of people in creative and visual design skills. Like volunteer firefighters, these citizen designers might be called upon as the need arises to openly explore local material culture. With the ability to show ideas visually (perhaps in 3-D models) and trained in facilitating discussions about "vision," these citizen designers would be able to translate vision into preliminary tangible form.

These are some ways to consider helping people engage with others, bringing to life those dimensions of human well-being that concern doing, being, and interacting. The result breaks the one-way flow of visuality and allows for a much fuller discussion, at the local level, not only about what the role of materials goods in life is but also about what it should or could be with respect to human well-being. In addition, by connecting people, we find ways to meet their need for meaning (symbolic resources) in a less materially intensive and less commercial way. Whereas commercial interests want to engage consumers only in terms of creating desire for new material goods, design to support cultural sustainability must think about engaged users, real people who are in fact more than just desirous consumers. The following chapters carry on with this exploration of how design can help people connect.

How can design help connect people
and support relationships, and counter
the overwhelming effects of visuality?

SENSUAL

Your footsteps echo down the hallway as you press the soft synthetic button to turn off your mobile phone. The aroma of leather emanates from your jacket, as you remove it to sit at the table. The warmth of the smooth wooden handle greets your fingertips as you open a drawer to reach for the cool steel of your favorite fountain pen. The drawer rolls smoothly closed with a satisfying click. You take off your shoes and stretch the fabric of your socks to pull them up. You feel the stubbly flooring under your toes as you walk over to get yourself a cup of tea. You taste the metal of your steel thermos cup as you put it to your mouth for a sip.

What's unusual about the above scenario is how devoid it is of any visual descriptions. It relies entirely on the other senses: smell, sound, touch, and taste—a series of sensations. Visuality has generally cut us off from these other senses.[38] And this insight suggests another approach to connection: Design can concern itself with reconnecting us to what has been lost as visuality and materialism-as-meaning have taken over.

Let's consider the five senses. Design often neglects actual "materiality"—the physical or sensual qualities of a thing. This may sound strange, but consider that in the past, design concentrated heavily on function, and presently it tends to concentrate on meaning, particularly visual meaning. Design's current focus is on the ideas that artifacts represent, not on the material aspects of the artifacts themselves.[39] In architecture, for example, the approach has been to control indoor environments so that outdoor thermal changes are masked. But a more sensually attuned approach would take advantage of outdoor temperature,

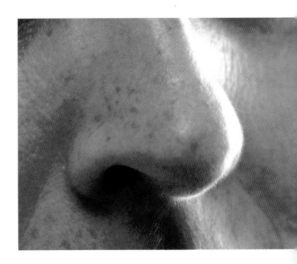

LANDSCAPE FEATURE: Design Neglects Materiality

Even though design seems to be about making things out of materials, designers have increasingly ignored the "materiality"—or the sensuality—of things. Design fails to offer a truly sensual experience, largely because of the reliance on visual forms, which don't offer experiences developed through diverse sensations.[40] There appear to be several reasons for ignoring materiality. The market forces us to select the cheapest materials rather than the most meaningful or appropriate ones. In addition, as we saw in part 2, our industrial system makes the reality of materials—their sources, processing, by-products—invisible to consumers and designers alike, making it less likely that designers actually understand their materials.

Design often neglects "materiality"—the material or sensual qualities of a thing.

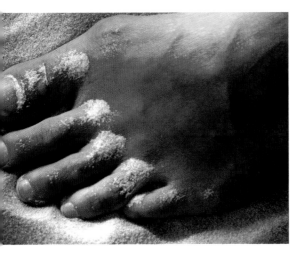

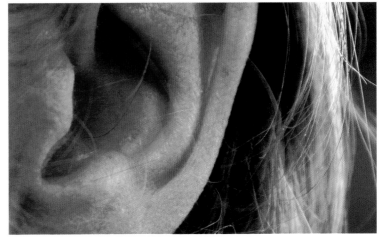

engaging people in their real environment. Consider the way sand dunes are always warm on one side and cool on the other, so we can choose to sit on the warm side in the cool morning air or sit on the cool side during the late afternoon sun.[41]

With increasing social and commercial pressure on the visual, how can we reconnect with other senses? There are techniques that help move beyond the visual. "Prototyping experience" is one of these. Rather than focus on visual elements of a design solution, such as form or visual cues, this technique concentrates on what the task at hand feels like—physically, emotionally, even in terms of smell.[42] An example of this comes from product design company IDEO's prototyping of a new experience for airline travel: sleeping in economy class. By putting a row of chairs together and having people lie next to each other under them and on top of them, the experience immediately engages the senses. You feel the cramped conditions; you hear how close your neighbors are, perhaps even smell their perfume. You are immediately transported into a tangible experience that engages your sense as well as your emotions and intellect.

Computing capability, although currently dependent on screen-based visual indicators, also could offer opportunities to engage with other senses. We have technology that allows us to talk to our computers and they to us—using sound to replace visual cues. Other innovations include creating signals and signs that appear as changes to the ambient environment. For example, instead of seeing a graph showing the latest level of trading on the stock market, you might hear the sound of falling rain, with heavier rain indicating heavier trading. Indeed, one recent design involved making a computer game that relies entirely on tactile and audio interaction—there is no screen.[43]

By consciously bringing back the role of the other senses, we can begin to enrich our sensory

experiences and counter some of visuality's domination. Cultural sustainability, the quest for human well-being, suggests that there are several other aspects of connection that should concern us. The first of these is connection between artifacts and those who use them in a particular place or time, sometimes characterized as "fit." Second is the connection between the designer and the user of the design. We explore these connections in the following chapters.

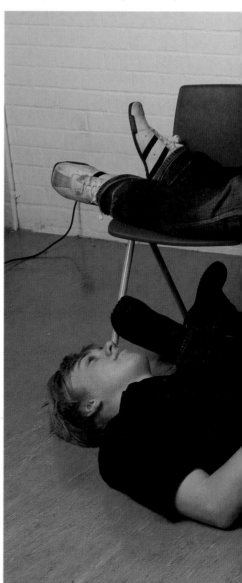

Prototyping experience: What would sleeping in economy class on an airplane really feel like?

With increasing social and commercial pressure on the visual, how can we reconnect with other senses? There are techniques that help move beyond the visual. "Prototyping experience" is one of these.

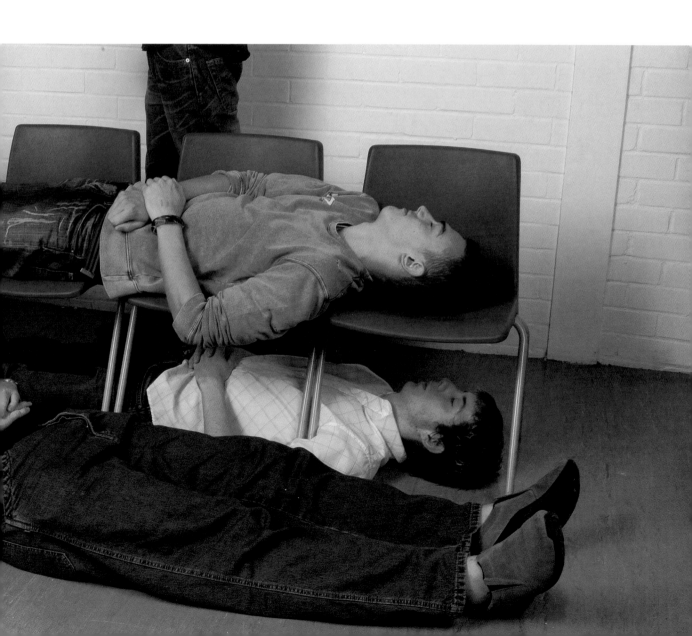

COOKED VERSUS RAW

WHAT IF I DESIGNED FOR YOU HALF OF A HOUSE, or one-third of a computer—a quarter of a car? It would represent the fraction that you need and can afford right now. I would leave room for the other part, ensuring that your artifact could grow with you. Metaphorically, the portion that I design is "cooked," the undesigned part is "raw," available to be shaped as needed. Perhaps you will cook up the rest yourself; perhaps I'll help you. Perhaps it will be a collective process by which a group of people contributes ideas to

🐝 **LANDSCAPE FEATURE: Designer Against Consumer**

With the rise of industrialization and consumerism, the *roles* of designer and user have been clearly divided. I design the thing, then I'm out of the picture; you get the thing and use it, perhaps in frustration because it doesn't do what you want. The *aspirations* of designer and consumer are separate as well. The designer generally has to consider one dimension of an artifact—desirability from the consumer's stand-point or salability—above all else. On the other hand, consumers are concerned with a wide range of dimensions that reflect their real lives, not just fantasies that are typically captured in seductive advertise-ments. In addition, because of the importance of consumer appeal within the context of visuality, designers are often forced to try to com-municate meaning and function entirely through appearance. In con-trast, people—real users—experience objects through a wide variety of sensations, not just appearance. People also assign meaning to objects based on complex social and cultural contexts, in contrast to the sim-plified commercial meaning that designers must try to convey.

"cook" your artifact. There are a variety of ways that this might happen, and they concern the relationship between designer and engaged user as well as the relationship between artifact and context.[44]

It's generally not been possible to follow the cooked/raw format described above because, with the rise of modern industrial con-sumerism, the roles of designer and consumer are so entirely divided. Yet a number of models suggest that people are willing and able to actively engage in design, and each model offers a poten-tially better mechanism for meaning-fully involving people. One model is the do-it-yourself movement, which covers not only self-built homes but also things like self-assembled furniture or do-it-yourself home improvements. A second model has the subversive name of "transgressive" products and build-ings.[45] Unlike the first model in which doing it yourself is intentional, trans-gression occurs in situations in which a completed building or product does not meet needs or expectations so the consumer is forced to modify it. The artifact transgresses its original design. A third model is called "open source," a term used to describe computer code that is developed collaboratively with users in a transparent process rather than by a small team of experts who then keep the code secret. I'll group these approaches under the heading of "open design."

These three models have a few important features in common that support cultural sustainability. They all engage the user beyond simply buying and owning an artifact. An engaged user brings more of the meaning (e.g., the symbolic resources) to the artifact, reducing the role of designers (and advertisers) in inventing ready-made commercial meaning for artifacts. These models begin to release designers and users from the predominance of owning and watching.

If users have a chance to provide more input about themselves and the context for their activities, the result is likely a better "fit," or match, between real human needs (not just fantasies and desires) and artifact. Users can provide input such as ideas, feedback on prototypes, or suggestions for resolving design questions. We're beginning to see a version of this in the form of "mass customization" where consumers, often using Web sites, can customize a car, house, or other item by selecting among a range of components, sizes, features, and colors.[46] Although this is a small step, it does improve an individual's sense of authenticity and engage the person actively rather than passively. It begins to shift meaning away from the thing itself and back to the individual and his or her experiences and knowledge.

A concept similar to engagement is "flow." Flow describes a mode that you get into when you are completely absorbed in something, losing track of time. Flow is a universally sought human experience, central to well-being, that appears in all cultures and all walks of life.[47] Like engagement, flow makes people feel alive and tangibly connected to the world around them, either through ideas or actions. Flow is likely to result from doing activities that are in one's optimal challenge zone—not too easy, not too hard.[48] In the framework of human needs, flow satisfies needs for authenticity, competency, connection, and meaningful activity.

Collaborative or open design processes could result in designs that are not just a better fit but that also result in flow for the participants. Individuals could of course choose their own level of "optimal challenge" in terms of involvement—from open source to mass customization there is already a wide range of choice. The economy has relegated

DEFINITION: Open Design

For the purposes of this discussion, we can define "open design" as a process in which users are involved with designers in the design development of artifacts, although the degree of user participation and its means may vary widely.

many of our creative activities, "hobbies" we might call them, to the sidelines. By becoming involved somewhere along the spectrum from raw to cooked, many people could apply more of their creative selves to the world around them. A small example occurs when people not only assemble their flat-pack furniture but also finish it with paint, color, unique handles, and so on to their liking. Whether an individual thinks up an original approach to such tasks or follows guidance in a paint-by-number approach, by engaging in the activity there is more chance that flow will occur than in simply owning the artifact. It signals a move away from simply watching and owning to doing, being, and interacting.

People also could use their flow experiences to inform the design project. Many designers would

☀ TRAVELER'S NOTE: Meaningful Objects

Open design processes could result in objects that are kept for longer or that even become heirlooms. But the most important aspect of an open process may be that objects that produce better fit, flow, or appropriation are merely better everyday expressions of meaning for people, replacing some of the commercially driven meanings we have now. Open design could help people develop more successful internal methods of meeting needs, improving cultural conditions for human well-being, and contributing to cultural sustainability.

like to generate flow for users, but currently when this occurs it seems to be accomplished more by accident than by anything encoded in the design process.[49] By calling upon a much wider range of people's experiences with flow, designers might better be able to support it. This would counteract a trend to simplify all artifacts so that they offer the appearance of "instant" satisfaction.

In addition to fit and flow, a third opportunity resulting from open design processes is captured in the term "appropriation," which means "making it your own." It can take time for an individual to feel a real connection to an artifact, to feel a strong sense of ownership, or for an artifact to take on any meaning. When one contributes to the design or construction of an artifact, there is an automatic personal investment. At the same time, people delight in discovering things for themselves.[50] When we truly appropriate something as our own, it has genuine meaning for us; we care more about maintaining it and feel more concern about what might happen to it later on. This care could result in longer-lasting, more meaningful objects.

So open design processes seem to have something to offer in terms of creating meaning that is internally or community driven (rather than commercially, externally driven). Open design also appears to help people engage and connect since it gives opportunities for them to do and interact rather than be passive audiences that simply watch, then own. The following chapters explore open processes in more depth.

DEFINITION: Fit, Flow, Appropriation

Fit means to be appropriate or made suitable for the circumstances of a given situation.

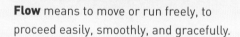

Flow means to move or run freely, to proceed easily, smoothly, and gracefully.

Appropriate means to make your own.

OPEN SESAME

THE OPEN SOURCE
process for developing
computer software is of particular
interest to design. Open source is one
case in which users are also truly designers, and
the open source process allows for rapid, massive feedback on imperfect prototypes. The most prominent
example of this model is the development of the operating system, Linux, which contrasts with the "closed"
and proprietary development of the other operating systems. Almost every problem during the development of
Linux was relatively quickly identified and then fixed,
since the solution was typically obvious to someone.[51]
In this case the contribution of each designer is seen as
an incremental step toward a better solution. By releas-
ing versions early and often, the coordinator of the
Linux effort rewarded his contributors, who
quickly saw their work incorporated in new
and better versions.

Every node on the network is
a point of both production
and consumption.

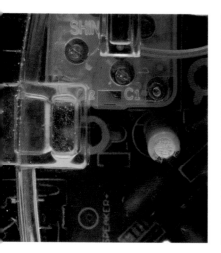

Worldwide computer networks accessible from almost everywhere allowed many people to be involved in the development of Linux. And as that development makes clear, every node on the network is a point of both production and consumption. The freely contributed design improvements to Linux constitute a "gift culture" in which contributions are rewarded not with money but with information and a boost to the ego in seeing your work used and appreciated in a better version of Linux. The lead designer becomes the coordinator and cheerleader for a large collaborative team.

To what extent could the open source revolution apply to buildings, products, or graphic design? Since computer code does not take physical form, it is of course fundamentally different from physical artifacts. But at the same time, more and more designers are engaged in providing information *about* form rather than physical forms themselves (see part 3). For example, graphic design and photography are already experiencing, either formally or informally, the kinds of multiple "contributions" typical of Linux. This takes the form of photographs that get digitally altered, cropped, and otherwise distorted or graphics that get borrowed, rejigged, and issued for further "development" in cyberspace.[52]

The open source framework suggests a few features that a parallel open process in artifact design might have. We already mentioned a mechanism for mass feedback on imperfect prototypes to allow problems to be identified and fixed quickly. We also mentioned frequent release of prototypes that make clear the collaborative improvements. Since open source code is "open" or visible to all for adjustment and modification, a corresponding feature in physical artifacts might be commonly accessible construction and repair information, along with easily available parts and components. These might include aesthetic as well as functional aspects. Moreover, since open source code is "living code," new additions can be easily incorporated.

"Open artifacts" might be visibly or functionally accessible for construction and repair.

For open artifacts, we might expect new features and components to be backward compatible; that is, you don't need to go out and buy a new artifact to get the newest capabilities.

An important question is what types of products/artifacts would benefit from the open source process. One answer might be any artifact that enough people are interested in. Existing networks on the Internet, such as "book crossings," eBay, and Freecycle, suggest that people are willing and able to participate by taking control of interactive channels. But to what degree are users willing or able to create or choose within an open design process? This will be dictated in large part by the balance between convenience and engagement, between "ready-to-hand" devices and focal activities or events. We don't all want to bother with the design of our toothbrushes or paperclips, but a surprising number of people probably have useful input on these artifacts. Each individual's optimal challenge zone and "flow" will also play a role.

Participants in the Linux development were self-selecting and came to the process with specialized knowledge. With other types of design, what is the likelihood that a similar level of expertise will emerge? We can speculate on the value of a wide range of perspectives—the multiway discussion would result in designers having a much better picture of what the design's engagement is all about. This multiway discussion is the one that visuality has largely erased but that our digitally networked society has the potential to restore.

Another challenge is whether open design could actually make fit better for three-dimensional artifacts. We have a fair amount of evidence that closed processes, typical of design competitions, do not produce the best fit. An example comes from the design and construction for the Sydney 2000 Olympics. Although design teams were evaluated specifically on the sustainability aspects of their solutions, the proprietary nature of the solutions meant that no one solution captured all the sustainability benefits that were represented across all the design bids. In addition, because design teams kept confidential what they had learned from each construction project (hoping to use it to advantage in upcoming bids), little collective knowledge about what works and what doesn't emerged from the process.

The idea of private property, either physical goods or proprietary information, is a long-standing one. And when it comes to design, more than proprietary information for competitive advantage is at stake with open design. The notion of "authorship" is also challenged. Examples from the open design experience suggest that there is a role for lead designers in instigating and coordinating the design process, even for making judgments about how the pieces fit together. But an open process challenges the notion of one vision, handed down from a "great man," the type of vision typically sought in the world of design competitions that tend to feature individual designers as stars.

It may be easier to honor a designer-as-stylist who puts a coherent shape on a complex piece of engineering, but an open design process more accurately acknowledges the cooperative work of a much bigger team that includes users as well as other professionals such as engineers. In leading an open design process it is perhaps even more important to be able to recognize brilliant design ideas contributed by others than it is to generate brilliant design ideas yourself. An open design process suggests a sort of self-organizing pattern based on networks of relationships and shared knowledge. It also suggests a potential role for designers as keepers of collective knowledge about the work of design.

The idea of giving up unique authorship, or artistic control, can be an uncomfortable one for designers. The thought of many people trying to shape an artifact is appalling to some designers who view it as "design by committee" that can only result in ugly, compromised solutions.[53] In a top-down, or closed design process, "a single stylist can draw a line around the communal and complicated efforts of the engineering input and present a single, unified image to the world of the consumer."[54] This brings us back to the question of visuality. Just because dominance of the visual causes some problems in terms of sustainability, it does not mean that we should neglect the importance of visual aesthetic in the design process. Yet there is a fundamental tension between the designer as artist (design as artistic expression) and the designer as "satisfier," or one who is subservient to the needs of others—human users, manufacturers, ecology, or commerce. And this issue of artistry generally doesn't arise in the design of computer code, making the open source model again different from design.

Although creative insight is a critical aspect of successful design, it is not the same as "self-expression" that results from a craftperson's work.[55] Yet on an individual level, the designer does express him- or herself through artifacts, even though that self-expression in the end becomes only one small part of a much larger team effort.[56] The consumerist need for nearly continual restyling does, on some level, appeal to the designer's eagerness for opportunities of expression. What we can conclude is that the importance of stylistic expression is perhaps disproportionately high and needs to be balanced against other concerns. This rebalancing, such as through an open design process, doesn't remove designers from stylistic expression but makes it more challenging in light of real communication rather than engineered meaning that is broadcast uniformly to all.

The open design process gives designers a role as "connector" that helps relieve the one-way nature of broadcast visuality. In addition, information about the meaning of artifacts (the symbolic resources they offer) is collected from real people rather than commerce. Finally, these processes involve the user actively, creating connection among people as well as within the individual through dynamics such as flow.

Open design collides with design "authorship," where a single designer hands down a vision and becomes known as a celebrity.

TOWARD TIME

BEFORE WE MOVE ON to our third theme within cultural sustainability—time—it is useful to summarize the results from exploring our first two themes, communication and artifacts, which have focused on the predominance of external means of meeting needs. Much of our community-based, active communication has been replaced by national and global media that are broadcast to us in a one-way, largely visual stream, for which we are a passive audience. At the same time, artifacts that used to have a rich range of community meanings are now imbued with meaning by advertisers and marketers, with the help of designers. Rather than have any active involvement in the creation or meaning of artifacts, we passively own them. The situation casts designers in the role of "pushers," pushing more and more commercially devised artifacts and images onto consumers.

The past few chapters have reviewed some concepts, including reconnecting to the senses, reviving the idea of rites of passage, and considering the potential role of community designers, that would allow design to move out of the role of pusher. Open design also looks promising for shifting the generation

Now we are always connected. Expectations of speed increase, and hurried frenzy obstructs long-term perspective.

of meaning away from commerce and toward individuals and communities. Global digital networks are making the open design process viable because each point on the network is a point of production and consumption. Yet it is this very digital network that also pressures us to speed up, and this introduces our third theme of time.

Once we are always connected—always on— expectations of speed increase, and the resulting frenzy obstructs our long-term perspective, keeping us focused on the short term. Consider communication: the national and global broadcast media are fast, whereas a real discussion among members of a community, collecting and expressing thoughtful input, tends to be slower. In terms of artifacts, we expect them to bring immediate

satisfaction, and simply owning something is faster and easier than actually developing new knowledge and skills.

It is rare for us to reflect on the broader effect of these time pressures that become an obstacle to cultural sustainability. But many of the activities (such as knowledge, public participation, caring, meditation) that promote well-being, although not priced or valued by the market, do cost us in terms of time. To the extent that our concepts of time are now closely related to money—"Time is money," as the saying goes—it is appropriate to explore the dimension of time in more detail here.

The next chapters explore the issue of time, first in terms of speed, then in terms our time horizon—the short view versus the long view of time.

FAST

EVERYTHING ABOUT DESIGN IS SPEEDING UP. In the "old" days, artifacts were made at the pace of the craftsperson. Large or complex projects could take decades, even centuries. Machinery accelerated the making process so that it might take only several years to develop a product, create the appropriate machinery and tools, source the materials, produce, and market. But computers are speeding the process up even further. Now the product development process can take a year or less. Similarly, grand architectural statements that used innovative technology of the time—cathedrals—took hundreds of years to build, whereas the same level of grand architectural statement today takes a decade or less. We see the same trends in two-dimensional design, where computers allow nearly instant design and production—and distribution through the Internet.

 LANDSCAPE FEATURE: Acceleration

One of the main characteristics of time over the last fifty years has been how it has sped up. The biggest driver of this speed has been the pace of technological change. Technological changes have brought with them a worldwide network that is always on, flooding us with more information than we can digest, creating higher expectations for how fast work can be done, and taking away any time for reflection. Such acceleration causes disconnection—from real places, from our internal thoughts, and from long-term considerations—and weakens cultural sustainability.

Over the last fifty years time has seemed to speed up. The biggest driver of this speed has been the pace of technological change. The pace was initially set by the rapid improvements in computer chip capability. There's been a mind-boggling 137 billionfold increase in capability in the last fifty-six years. The exponential increases are even expected to continue until 2015, possibly beyond. There is no precedent in history for this pace of technological change. Similarly, there have been rapid changes in the power of networking (the Internet) and biotechnology (the ability to identify and use genetic information).[57]

Computers have brought with them a global network that is always on. We can be connected all the time. We also have access to more information than ever before, and our inability to keep up with information enhances our feeling of not having enough time, leading to a state of perpetual distraction. We are always multitasking—whether with a cell phone or a split-screen television. The potential for twenty-four-hour activity pushes us faster than our natural pace, resulting in a crisis orientation. A sense of urgency is also portrayed frequently throughout the global media, which competes to deliver information the fastest, resulting in broadcasts of short information fragments, well suited to commercial breaks and stock price reporting.[58] Whether on Web pages or the nightly news, information is in smaller and smaller pieces to compete for our ever more thinly spread attention.

Speed is an obstacle to cultural sustainability because it disconnects us. For example, it disconnects us from reflection. In business or political matters there is rarely a diplomatic "pause for thought." In fact, we now have "instant" public opinion polls, suggesting that there can be a public opinion without any time for public discussion or debate.[59] Speed also disconnects us from our investments. People used to keep money invested for years, if not decades, in businesses they knew and respected. Now investors seek short-term gain, holding stocks in companies they don't know for as little as a few days, hours, or even minutes. The crisis orientation caused by speed also disconnects us from ourselves.

The speed of design: large, complex projects that would have taken decades, or centuries, now take a few years.

Psychological disconnection thwarts security and identity. Our frantic pace of life reduces the resilience of our cultural systems: There is little left to maintain long-term stability or memory. In previous chapters, we discussed the loss in natural systems due to the tremendous speed of change. An important example of cultural loss associated with speed is the loss of diverse languages and the knowledge bases they represent.

Commerce hurries us to communicate more quickly, dispensing with more and more languages in favor of English. Language experts fear that roughly half of the world's six thousand languages will be extinct within one hundred years.[60] Currently, thousands of languages and cultures are threatened. As these languages are lost, it's arguable that the sum of human knowledge may be decreasing for the first time in history.[61] The "size" of civilization so far, about ten thousand years, is only about four hundred generations (twenty-five years each, four per hundred years). It's taken these four hundred generations to develop the thousands of languages that we now seem destined to loose within the span of three generations, leaving us with fewer ways to meet our needs for authenticity and reducing our knowledge and understanding.

Speed can take on the sense of an activity in and of itself, since constant novelty disguises boredom or loneliness. But speed only offers the illusion of novelty. It actually requires that things be more similar. One-size-fits-all is much faster than a tailored fit. We see this in entertainment, fashion, products, and even housing. Economic speed requires us to give up the local in favor of the global. Chain stores replace local businesses. Speed is seen as good, although aging is seen as bad, whether for products, information, or people.[62]

How fast can we go? Where will it end? Techno futurists say it will end at "the convergence," the point at which technological progress becomes so radical (innovations in minutes rather than months or even days) and so integrated (e.g., biotechnology with computer networks) that it represents the end of the world as we know it. The convergence is sometimes also referred to as the singularity after the unknown contents of a black hole. Beyond the "singularity," our ability to predict the future breaks down. Some futurists have even put a date on the convergence of around 2035.

Thoughts vary on what might trigger the convergence. Some think the trigger will be nanotechnology, also known as molecular manufacturing; others think it will happen when machine intelligence surpasses human intelligence. The very possibility of a technological singularity makes the future, as we know it, look shorter. This is perhaps the largest disconnect generated by the increasing pace of life—disconnection from the future because it ceases to exist in terms we understand.[63] Are there any alternatives?

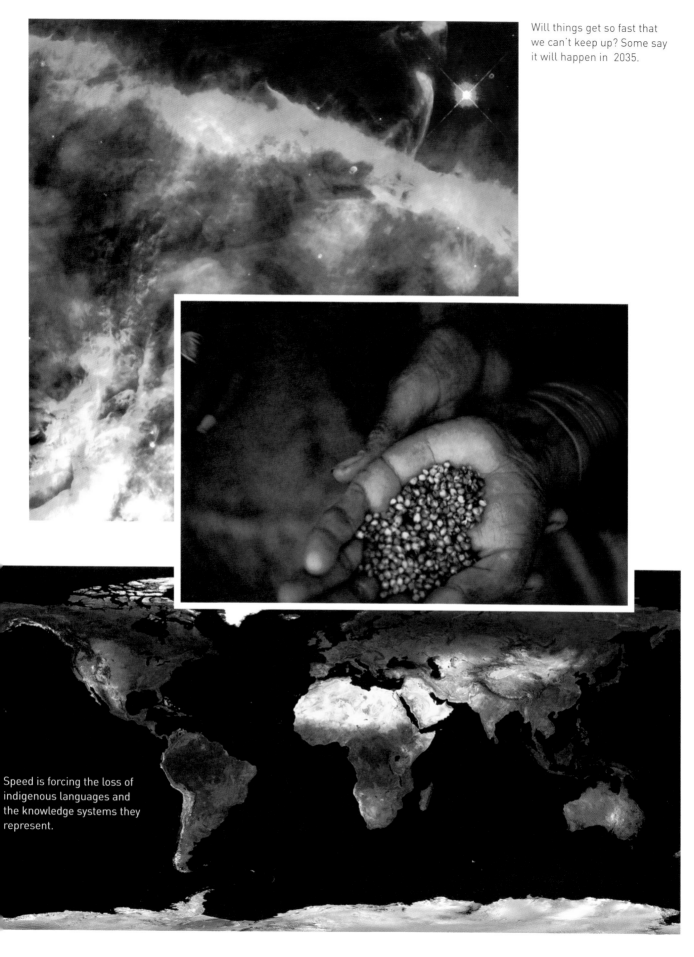

Will things get so fast that we can't keep up? Some say it will happen in 2035.

Speed is forcing the loss of indigenous languages and the knowledge systems they represent.

SLOW

ARE YOU DRINKING YOUR COFFEE FROM A FAST CUP or a slow cup? The fast cup is disposable, made of paper. The slow cup is a handmade ceramic mug. The artifacts themselves, in their materials, life spans, function, and even the way they look, tell us whether they are fast or slow. We could make the same distinction in a lot of other artifacts—buildings, cars, toys.

 LANDSCAPE FEATURE: Fast vs. Slow

Fast knowledge is characterized by being technological, profit oriented, hierarchical, competitive, universally applied. Slow knowledge is characterized by being shared and multidisciplinary, unowned, shaped to particular cultural and geographical context.[64] We can look at a range of things around us, from ownership patterns to communication techniques and from our food to our money, and for each of these find fast and slow alternatives.

Some have suggested that there is fast knowledge and slow knowledge. We can even characterize human activities in terms of whether they are underpinned by universal, one-size-fits-all, fast knowledge or customized, respect-for-differences, cooperative, slow knowledge. We saw that in ecosystems, nature uses fast and slow systems to create resiliency and respond to shocks (see part 2). Could a resilient human civilization use a similar concept of fast and slow layers of activity to balance our range of values? After all, some artifacts actually do need to be fast.

One suggestion is for six levels of pace and size so that when the whole system is balanced, it "combines learning with continuity."[65] From fast to slow the layers are art/fashion, commerce, infrastructure, governance, culture, and nature.

The fastest layers of art/fashion and commerce innovate, while the slowest layers of culture and nature maintain stability and provide long-term supporting structure.[66] Culture in this sense includes such features as religion and language. The system works when each layer respects the pace of the others. Our Western civilization has lost the balance among its layers as the commerce

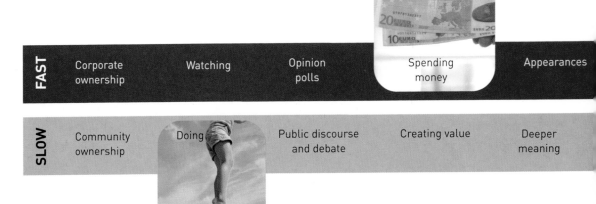

| FAST | Corporate ownership | Watching | Opinion polls | Spending money | Appearances |
| SLOW | Community ownership | Doing | Public discourse and debate | Creating value | Deeper meaning |

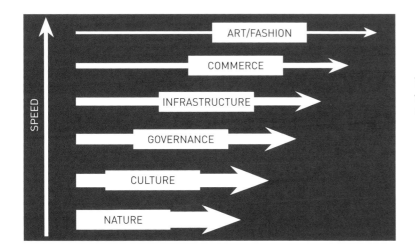

The fastest layers innovate, while the slower layers maintain stability.

layer (resting firmly on technological change) has assumed a dominant role (see part 3), driving nearly all other layers to exist at its pace. This is leading to the loss of slower layers, including nature (as we saw in part 2) and culture. Can resilience using size and rate of change be better built into products or product systems? Can artifacts be designed to learn or adapt?

Whether we call it "slowing down" or "reconnecting," it is clear that cultural sustainability has an important dimension related to time if we aim to create meaning from internal or community processes and not from global commerce. Satisfying human needs well is primarily a slow process, not a fast one. What role can design play? I believe that design offers ways of translating or transitioning between fast and slow knowledge and fast and slow layers of society. Indeed, ideas such as engagement and connection are inherently slower than standard, mainstream approaches. Community ownership of a car, for example, suggests a very different design solution than individual ownership. Artifacts that involve the use of

Broadcasting   Disposability   One size fits all, standardization   Making by machine   Buying food

Interpersonal communication   Durability, multiple lives   Diversity, suit local needs   Making by hand   Growing food

> The slow food movement is concerned with the pace of life and how large-scale standardization and mechanization are erasing many time-honored, artisan techniques.

skills, rather than passive watching or consuming, are more likely to meet human needs than simply spending money to buy something. By addressing these types of design issues, design can actually slow things down.

Another model for designers to consider is the "slow food" movement, which is concerned with the pace of life and how large-scale standardization and mechanization are erasing many time-honored, artisan techniques and diverse local foods. Under the label "ecogastronomy," the slow food organization has launched an "ark of taste" in an effort to preserve small-scale quality food production and the diversity of local varieties of food. The slow food movement aims to preserve

traditional crop varieties and food traditions and even bring back lost ones. Beer provides an example. In the early 1900s there were forty-eight breweries in Brooklyn, some brewing slow beer that took months to mature rather than weeks. Now there is only one, but it is represented in the ark of taste that has brought back some of the earlier brewing traditions.[67]

In the end, on both personal and professional levels, a key element in freeing us from temporal fatigue and crisis orientation is *finesse*, which is restraint, refinement, or delicacy.[69] Whether it's the technological singularity or a day at the office, finesse means not doing everything that is possible to do. Rather, finesse means resisting the force of speed by being sensitive, skillful, and strategic.

 TRAVELER'S NOTE: Slow Food

What sort of ideas can designers take from the slow food movement? Perhaps most important, the slow food movement celebrates slowness and the diversity that results from it. Explicitly addressing the issue of speed is the first step. Looking to historical or traditional ways of satisfying human needs is another idea, one that we've explored in the notion of rights of passage. Among many other ideas is one to examine more consciously the pauses that can be generated by design and the purposes they serve, the rhythm between activity and inactivity. This rhythm always occurs in nature but does not occur with machines.[68] Pauses play a role in the balance between the slow-moving, stabilizing layers of society and the fast-moving, innovative ones.

There were 48 breweries in Brooklyn; now there is only one.

THE LONG VIEW

IS THERE ANY FORCE that exerts upon designers to think about the long-term consequences of their work, consequences that might occur two hundred years in the future? What about two thousand years in the future? I am aware of few forces aside from personal motivation, such as wanting to build a lasting reputation. Aside from these personal agendas, what is the longest time frame a designer would normally consider? A building should be designed for three hundred years but rarely is.[70] People who design equipment for a mission to explore outer space or for storage of nuclear waste that will persist for thousands of years have to think further out into the future. Although furniture used to last for generations, we might expect a modern piece of low-cost furniture to last a few years. More important, there are many forces today that cause us to give up furniture well before it is functionally dead.

You might wonder why it is useful to have such a long-term perspective. One answer is that our species' long-term sustainability relies on six different time scales:[71]

1. Years—individual
2. Decades—family
3. Centuries—tribe or nation
4. Millennia—civilization
5. Tens of millennia—species
6. Eons—whole web of life on our planet

LANDSCAPE FEATURE: Short Termism

Another time dimension to sustainability is our time horizon. Indeed, we define sustainability as something that carries on indefinitely, in other words, for the very long term. Yet our culture is dominated by short termism. We don't think very far into the future, and the fast pace of life, speed, tends to shorten our time horizon.

OUTERSPACE

In modern terms, an outerspace mission is one of few activities that necessitates long-term thinking. Yet for many native cultures, as well as ancient religions, moral or spiritual duties required extremely long time horizons.

ANCIENT CULTURES AND RELIGIONS

Native Americans, who made major decisions only after considering the implications for seven generations into the future, were at least mindful of centuries—nearly two centuries for each major decision.[72] For many native cultures, as well as ancient religions, moral or spiritual duties crossed time periods that were far longer than the span of a human life. For example, some Zen Buddhists proclaim infinite gratitude for the past, infinite service to the present, and infinite responsibility to the future.[73] Historically, people had more natural connections to the past and future—not only through their artifacts such as furniture and timbers that were handed down but also through social networks that had a stronger focus on family and community.

It's fair to say that current societal decision makers, our politicians and our business leaders, use much, much shorter time frames. In general, we see political decisions based on reelection campaigns (two to four years) and business decisions based on quarterly earnings reports (three months). There is so much pressure to show results quickly that anything in the future, especially far off in the future, is often ignored. This short termism weakens cultural sustainability because it doesn't respect the past or the future. We have a harder time locating ourselves within a tradition or assigning meaning to our place in time. Without a bigger sense of time, we don't gain a connection to the people before us or those after us. There will be many more people alive after us than ever lived before us or are alive now; the population throughout time is asymmetrical. The majority of people affected by our decisions are always yet to come.[74] Future generations, who have no input to our decisions, will experience the cumulative effect of all our very short-term decisions.

Our current population of about six billion is expanding by ten thousand people per hour. The population is expected to level out at about twelve billion people. These yet-to-live people are our descendants and heirs. Some of them are in our family, many are in our tribe, and all will be in our

civilization and species. Yet our current system makes it nearly impossible for us to consider them in the things we do today. It appears that the long-term future—decades, centuries, or millennia—has become a cultural blind spot.

In terms of design or craft, we might compare a Web page designer of today to a cathedral builder of centuries ago. Many people who built the cathedrals knew they would never see the structures completed in their lifetimes, but they had a vision beyond their own lifetimes.[75] As for the Web page designer, well, it's hard to do anything for the long-term online. We have more *online* thinkers every day. There is an argument that we need more *cathedral* thinkers. These thinkers would be concerned with creating human well-being by meeting our need for connection across time: to the past, the present, and much longer term—decades and even centuries into the future. The following two chapters explore how designers might approach cathedral thinking.

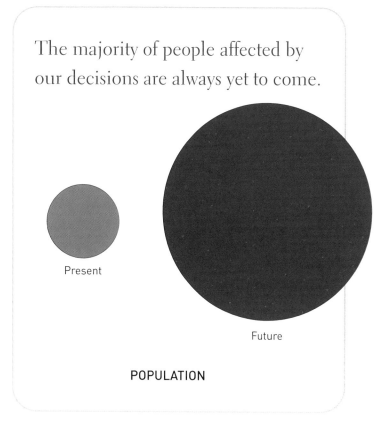

The majority of people affected by our decisions are always yet to come.

Present

Future

POPULATION

EVOLVING ARTIFACTS

Where a product has traveled, who has used it and how

THE RECENT RELEASE OF UPDATED CLASSIC CARS, such as the VW Bug and the Cooper Mini, is one indicator that we want design that is "new" but also capable of remembering. So far this hasn't gone much beyond the visual, with retro styles or stylistic updates.[76] Similarly, efforts to extend the life span of artifacts have typically concentrated on the functional, such as making products more durable, repairable, or upgradable. What other ways could design help connect us to the past while also being mindful of the future?

We can answer this question by following three avenues of thought. The first concerns stories from the past and collective knowledge. The second considers maintenance and wear, and the third examines scenarios, or stories of the future. Stories are a way of making sense, or making meaning, out of actions and events, and they draw us in emotionally. Artifacts from the past embodied stories because of the way they were handed down. Where this handing down has now all but disappeared, some designers are proposing a new way that artifacts can tell stories the way that heirlooms used to.

A product, for example, can tell of where it has traveled, who has used it, and how it had been a part of people's lives. An old example of this is the piece of luggage with stickers showing all the places that luggage had been. A modern example is a tote bag made from an old sail. The label tells you the sail's "story" in terms of the sail type (e.g., mainsail, spinnaker, jib), the boat type (e.g., racing yacht, sailing cruiser), and the waters sailed (e.g., North Sea, Mediterranean

TRAVELER'S NOTE: Artifacts Connect Us

Artifacts can help us get beyond short termism connecting us across time. We can then avoid favoring the present too heavily. Designers can use tools such as making artifacts wear well, blending old and new, and creating stories around artifacts to bridge the past and the future. A fairly good literature exists on this topic (see the "further reading" section).

"Storybooks" about a building's collective experience.

Sea, Indian Ocean). As a side story, objects could also tell us how they have been maintained and pass along tips on performance. In a digital era, a lot of information can be monitored and implanted on very small electronic media.

This idea has also been proposed for buildings. Much the way ships have complete and accurate records of all that is done to them, when and by whom, buildings could come with their own "storybooks" about the collective experiences—maintenance, remodels, tenants' experiences, babies born in the building, and so on—books that could give a full picture of the building's "life." This involves a shift "from a hotel room aesthetic to a mountain hut aesthetic."[77] In the mountain hut, you find a visitors book where everyone who stops there can report on the hut as well as their experiences, leaving entertainment and information for all who come after. In the hotel room, all traces of previous occupancy are erased daily, wiping out any connection among people. The mountain hut method represents connective design.

Somewhat naturally, the maintenance and wear of an artifact provide another opportunity for its evolution. Consider how materials wear. Wood and leather age well, as does denim. The materials become more friendly and lustrous with age. Synthetic materials—industrial materials—are typically the opposite. For example, a smooth shiny plastic surface will scratch easily. But there are ways to help synthetic materials age more gracefully. A textured plastic surface may wear better. By using layered finishes, a designer can create a more interesting and appealing aging process for a synthetic surface, allowing it to evolve. For example, new colors might be revealed as top layers wear off, similar to the way blue jeans fade. The Swatch watch company produced some watches that were covered in a rubber that wore off to reveal an underlying design on the band and face.[78]

Helping materials age gracefully.

TRAVELER'S NOTE: Design Scenarios

Scenarios are stories about the future, and "design scenarios" help designers avoid the trap of favoring the present too heavily. Scenario planning was developed several decades ago in military strategy, then migrated to corporations like Shell Oil, who found that traditional forecasting methods were no longer useful. Scenario planning applies to design because, to paraphrase a leading thinker in this area, "all artifacts are predictions. All predictions are wrong." [81]

By thoughtfully creating several plausible scenarios about the future and devising a strategy that addresses all of them, designers can avoid the trap of short termism. Designers can still have a favorite prediction; they can still think of their building or artifact as a hero and script out a long and eventful life. But this activity invariably overrepresents current needs and users, optimizing for the present while underrepresenting different future users, or even the same ones whose needs change in the future.

Scenarios stem from key issues or decisions facing the designer. Should we base a new product line on analog or digital technology? Do we actually need to offer a new line? How can our artifact help elderly people? After identifying the issues, the design team has to explore the driving forces that will shape the future. Driving forces for architecture might include the local community, tenants, and local economy. Ironically for smaller artifacts, driving forces probably include some elements that are more global, such as production and distribution. But they could also include lifestyles, technology, and regional economies.

Of the two to five future scenarios that emerge, one should represent the future that is most expected (digital technology remains prevalent, we can expand our market only through new product offerings, the elderly population stays at home watching TV). But the goal is to develop scenarios that are plausible and surprising, even shocking. The design team, or team that includes designers, can imagine a wide range of horrible or wonderful things that might happen. From these will emerge the basic plot lines for the scenarios, ideally with vivid names—"advertising backlash," "supply chain ethics," or "gray-haired raves"—that are shorthand descriptions. Once the basic details of these various futures are described, the group can go back to the key issues to be decided. The challenge is to develop a design strategy that works for all, or most, of the scenarios described.

Approaches to creating a robust strategy might include technology decisions, such as not locking in a particular technology too soon, or looking at questions in a larger context, such as "better understanding the aging process" rather than "targeting elderly people." As a closing activity, the team can pick a few indicators that it will monitor to find out which future is actually unfolding.

The result of successful scenario planning is an object or building that is both conservative (you don't stake everything on one future) and innovative. The process helps preserve the continuity of the artifact while also giving it adaptive capability for the future.

Just as a material surface might reveal new layers as it wears, buildings could better evolve by giving people a way to see what is under the surface. Where are the service cables, the structural supports, and so forth? Photo documentation of the building before it is finished allows anyone who comes along afterward to understand how it might be remodeled. The log of collective knowledge and maintenance suggested above, along with a set of drawings showing how the building was actually built (as-built drawings), would also contribute to this evolution.[79]

Other ideas for helping artifacts evolve include blending the new and the old, so that a product is no longer either "new" or "old" but a combination of new and used parts, all of high quality. Even some of these parts could tell stories. A log of the product's experiences could also help people get more use out of it. Two examples of these backward-compatible and story-laden products come from Denmark. Both Lego building bricks and Bang and Olufsen stereo equipment retain their compatibility across versions, allowing for stories to be built up around older parts of the system while welcoming innovation in the new parts.[80]

Another strategy proposed for helping products evolve is a lifetime guarantee. It represents the dedication to maintaining and supporting the artifact, and not forgetting what the ones from ten, fifty, or one hundred years ago are like. Part of the task is to maintain records, collective knowledge, and tools that can work backward in the artifact's life as well as forward.

Helping artifacts evolve is one way design can connect us across time.

The QWERTY keyboard purposefully slowed typists so the keys wouldn't jam. It's permanence is an example of how design overemphasizes the needs of the present and shortchanges the future.

EMBODYING TIME

IMAGINE A FUNCTIONAL OBJECT that is useful now but that will also last and be useful for thousands of years. Like the Native Americans considering the results of their decisions down through seven generations, designers for this type of artifact would have to think about the very long term. This kind of thinking is rare, especially considering how few clients there are for this type of project. Imagine how discounting (see part 3) would affect the decisions made for several thousand years in the future! There are probably few, if any, for-profit companies that would do it.

But to reconnect with our past and our future, to restore connections that have been lost gradually in the "Me, Right Now" century, design needs to think about ways to embody time both on a societal level, where broad cultural issues frame the design projects, and on a personal level, where we connect more closely with our own past and future.

The Long Now Foundation envisions a societal scenario for their Rosetta Disk, which takes its name from the Rosetta Stone, a carved stone tablet that carries the same text in three different languages (ancient Greek, Demotic, and hieroglyphs) that helped historians decipher hieroglyphic writing.[82] The modern disk stores one thousand languages using the same method—it shows one piece of text written in one thousand different languages. Although this information is available now in paper and electronic format, the long-term form of the Rosetta Disk is a microetched nickel disk that is expected to last two thousand years. As an artifact the disk has functional and aesthetic considerations as well.[83]

The disk is contained in a 4-inch sphere that

The Rosetta Disk embodies time: A functional object that is useful now but will also last and be useful more than 1,000 years from now.

protects it but also magnifies it through a top half made of optical glass. The text appears in rings around a central earth map, to which the languages are linked through numbers. The external band of text, in eight major world languages, starts at eye-readable scale and then tapers down to a microscale, so that there are twenty-seven pages of text for each language on the 3-inch disk.

An optical cover gives viewers a deeper view into the text rings while also suggesting to the viewer that more powerful magnification will reveal more text. The eight major world languages increase the chance that someone picking up the disk will be able to read something immediately. The disk will be widely distributed under the principle that "lots of copies keep stuff safe." There is also a place in the bottom, stainless-steel half of the spherical holder for keepers of the disc to add their own mark—such as name, location, and date.

On a personal level, there are other mechanisms for embodying time. For example, "design for our future selves" suggests that we think about our own futures as a way of connecting to the third age.[84] The "third age" is a recent demographic phenomenon that describes people living for eighty or ninety years or more, easily twenty-five to thirty years past the retirement age of sixty-five. Most designers are far from understanding the physical and psychological condition of these ages.

Physical accessories, such as goggles that distort vision or braces that curtail movement, can simulate the physical abilities of older adults. But their emotional, creative, and connective capacity has been overlooked, particularly in our society that focuses on youth and prefers to warehouse the elderly. Young designers can imagine their own old age as one step to connecting with their elders.

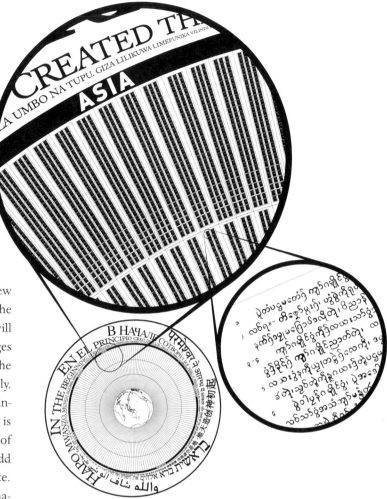

The text appears in the rings around a central earth map, to which the languages are linked through numbers. The external band of text, in 8 major world languages, starts at eye-readable scale and then tapers down to a micro scale.

Before moving on to our last theme, we can recap the discussion regarding time and cultural sustainability. Speed and short termism are the two interconnected cultural elements of time that appear to be obstacles to sustainability. Design has several options for overcoming these. In the case of speed, our alternative is to study the characteristics of slow and try to incorporate them more consciously.

In the case of short termism, design has the task of thinking about how artifacts can evolve as well as how they can embody time, making connection across the past, present, and future. The final theme of this part is presented in the next chapter on how nature is a part of culture.

NATURE AS CULTURE

NATURE MAKES ITS WAY INTO CULTURE in many ways, and it is often expressed through design. A wooden building with exposed, rough-hewn beams and skylights says "back to nature." Even a high-tech electronic gadget in jellybean colors may have an organic shape, recalling the sensuality of nature. Although the majority of the world's population now lives in cities, "wild" nature continues to influence us.

Seen in the light of healthy psychological development, our lack of connection to nature does not support well-being. Indeed, some have noted that our rapid destruction of natural resources is a source of psychological pain to most people who, overwhelmed by a feeling of powerlessness, simply deny this pain.[86] Some have also characterized our current state as one of "addiction" to materialism and visuality, an addiction that has resulted from the failure to meet our basic needs, particularly for connection to nature, which provides some element of our identity. This view is underpinned by the notion that out of about four hundred generations of humans, only five or six generations have lived in technological culture, which has arisen quickly. Technological culture has not only removed us physically from nature but, as we have seen, has also removed many of the traditional rights of passage and other social mecha-

nisms that allowed us to progress from adolescence and private life to a larger, ordered society.[87]

In terms of cultural sustainability, we then need to rethink our connection to nature—the way in which nature is in fact part of culture as it shapes us on a psychological as well as a physical level. Ecological awareness and respect, in this context, are not just nice ideas; they are an essential part of human development. Rebuilding this personal and cultural connection to nature can occur on several levels from societal to personal.

On a societal level, we can look back and see that the simple necessities of rural life required a strong connection to nature. More formal rites of passage and ceremonies also often included offerings to nature. For example, the assignment of animal totems to children was meant to embody the child's link with the natural world.[88] Although many of these early approaches were not necessarily based on a scientific understanding of nature, they connected people to natural forces in a personal way.

Is there a way for designers to regain this connection to natural forces in a personal way? Ecopsychology suggests one approach. We have to overcome our repressed feelings about the destruction of nature before we can move forward to make positive changes.[89] There are many

Organic shapes and natural materials: design expressing nature as culture.

reasons why we repress our feelings about what is happening to life on Earth. We fear feeling the full impact of despair and how that might wipe out any sense of purpose or meaning we've tried to establish for our lives. We're afraid of exposing our ignorance about the facts and figures related to ecological decline. We're not comfortable trusting our own judgment about it. We also might fear that by expressing our concerns we will distress others—our families and friends. This goes against a general societal pressure to keep up appearances of success and happiness. Since we are conditioned to consider primarily our individual needs and wants, it seems difficult to believe that we could feel suffering on behalf of society or nature itself. But as ecopsychology suggests, such feelings are a valid part of our human mind. Finally, we also feel powerless, or more precisely, we fear experiencing the feeling of powerlessness—the feeling that we do not really have full control over our lives.

 LANDSCAPE FEATURE:
Nature as Mental Health

A connection with nature appears to be a central part of our mental and physical health. Formative psychologists, such as Sigmund Freud and Carl Jung, understood human beings largely in terms of the individual psyche, or the relationships among individual family members. This framework of understanding generally ignored any influences from the natural world. These influences might come from, for example, a rural upbringing, childhood summer camp, or simply the landscape of your hometown. New theories of ecopsychology suggest there is an important ecological dimension to the human personality—a dimension that is both natural and universal. According to these theories, we are influenced in identity and basic development by the natural world, as well as the social world.[85]

DEFINITION: Ecological Literacy

Ecological literacy is sometimes called "ecoliteracy." You are ecologically literate when you have a solid understanding of not only the general workings of the ecosphere but also a general ecological knowledge of your local bioregion. This knowledge should include aspects of the urban ecologies of your region—for example, do you know:[90]

> The path of your drinking water from precipitation to the tap?
>
> The predominant soils where you live?
>
> Five native plants in your region including an edible one?
>
> The length of the outdoor growing season in your region?
>
> Your region's average annual precipitation and what constitutes a drought?
>
> The names of five birds found in your region and which are migratory?
>
> How the land in your region has been used by humans over the last two centuries?
>
> The final destination of your garbage?
>
> The primary geological events or processes that shaped the land in your region?
>
> The spring wildflowers that are first to bloom each year?
>
> Some of the vital ecological interactions that occur in your region to maintain its viability as an ecosystem?
>
> When your region's moon was last full and how many days until the next full moon?
>
> Where your energy comes from?
>
> The primary sources of pollution in your region?
>
> The predominate natural sounds in your region, by season?

By recognizing an ecological self that does mourn the destruction of life on Earth up to this point, we can then begin to move forward with the knowledge that we can play a positive role in the web of life of which we are part. This is a very personal aspect of nature as culture. Although there are many spiritual and social dimensions to this approach, they are beyond the scope of this book. But there are some ideas offered in the "further reading" section. Without entirely leaving behind the more spiritual frame of mind we can explore below some of the more practical ways that designers might improve their personal connection to natural forces, particularly through ecological literacy.

Ecological literacy is a way of describing a solid understanding of the ecosphere. But for our purposes, I think it also means a more acute awareness of your corner of the ecosphere. For example, you know your own zip code, but do you know what watershed you live in? A "watershed" is a region that drains into a certain river or

Techno-cities disconnect us from nature. Notions such as animal totems and eco-literacy are ways of connecting.

body of water. Similarly, you can probably identify hundreds of corporate logos and brands, but can you identify ten kinds of plants and animals that are native to your bioregion?

Do you have a mental picture of the bioregion you live in—its boundaries and key characteristics? In the past most materials were of local origin. Not only did this make it easier to match materials in repair or replacement, but being near the source gave better understanding and appreciation of it as well. This appreciation diluted purely economic considerations. If you are accustomed to walking through a local wood, you may have qualms about clear-cutting it to produce your line of furniture.

And what about urban ecology? How do resources flow through your town or city? If your design work touches upon other regions, for example, through overseas production, you may want to develop some ecoliteracy about these other regions as well. It can be relevant to the design process itself and to your health.

Nature is the last of our themes, and in some ways the most personal, or spiritual. Contrasting sharply with previous discussions, in parts 2 and 3, about the largely functional and service value of nature, this cultural dimension of nature provides an important element of cultural sustainability.

CONCLUSION

ALTHOUGH THE FINDINGS OF ECOPSYCHOLOGY suggest that nature provides an intrinsic element in our social development, humans are fundamentally different from other species, requiring a consideration of cultural sustainability. Cultural patterns related to time, communication, artifacts, and nature have changed dramatically over the last century in particular. The relatively passive endeavors of visuality and materialism have replaced many of our previous, more engaging ways of meeting human needs. Yet critically, visuality and materialism combine to provide symbolic resources that do meet some human needs.

We've seen that tying symbolic resources or social meaning to material goods is often a poor way of meeting human needs. Since design, along with commercialism, plays an important role in conveying symbolic resources, we have investigated how design might begin to detach visuality and materialism from our notions of well-being. In particular, we've considered engagement, sensuality, time and history, open design, and the acceptance of nature as part of culture. Within each of these categories, there are small steps (such as simply developing an awareness of the issues or improving your ecological literacy) to large steps (such as open design).

Many of the concepts supporting cultural sustainability appear impractical when seen in the light of commercial pressures, making it important to consider these notions in conjunction with the discussion about the economy. Indeed, cultural and economic aspects together make up the "social conditions" that are part of our definition of sustainable development. The discussion of the economy showed that many important values are not priced in the all-important free market, and our discussion of culture shows that most successful methods for achieving human well-being lie entirely outside the market. Design must struggle with how to shed its role as "pusher" (in a sense, trying to push consumers into market-based methods of well-being) and contribute to social conditions that support true human well-being indefinitely.

In the last part we'll explore the interplay among the three landscapes of sustainability.

FURTHER READING

The books and articles that served as sources for culture part of the atlas are cited in the endnotes. The following books provide more information on some of the topics discussed in this part.

Human Well-being

Flow: The Psychology of Optimal Experience by Mihaly Csikszentmihalyi (London: Rider, 1992, 2002)

Happiness: Lessons from a New Science by Richard Layard (London: Allen Lane, 2005)

Rites of Passage

Crossroads: The Quest for Contemporary Rites of Passage by Louise Carus Mahdi, ed. (Peru, IL: Open Court, 1996)

The Rites of Passage by Arnold van Gennep, Monika B. Vizedom, and Gabrielle L. Caffee (translators) (London: Routledge and Kegan Paul, 1960)

Rites of Passage: Celebrating Life's Changes by Kathleen Wall and Gary Ferguson (Hillsboro, OR: Beyond Words, 1998)

Connection, the Senses, and Time

Emotionally Durable Design: Objects, Experiences and Empathy by Jonathan Chapman (London: Earthscan, 2005)

Health: Co-Creating Services by Hilary Cottam and Charles Leadbeater (London: Design Council, November 2004)

In the Bubble by John Thackara (Cambridge, MA: MIT Press, 2005)

In Praise of Slow: How a Worldwide Movement Is Challenging the Cult of Speed by Carl Honore (London: Orion, 2004)

The Meaning of Things: Domestic Symbols and the Self by Mihaly Csikszentmihalyi and Eugene Rochberg-Halton (Cambridge: Cambridge University Press, 1981)

Wabi-Sabi: For Artists, Designers, Poets and Philosophers by Leonard Koren (Berkeley: Stonebridge Press, 1994)

Open Processes and Digital Design

See "Digital Economy and Digital Design" in the "further reading" section in part 3.

Nature and Spirit/Mind

The Dream of the Earth by Thomas Berry (San Francisco: Sierra Club Books, 1990)

Soulcraft: Crossing into the Mysteries of Nature and Psyche by Bill Poltkin (Novato, CA: New World Library, 2003)

SUMMARY MAP of the LANDSCAPE FEATURES for

CULTURE

When we look at design within the landscape of culture, these features are critical to understanding sustainability.

1 UNIVERSAL HUMAN NEEDS

There are ways to generalize human well-being, particularly by examining some universal motivational forces that all humans experience, such as physical survival, participating and communicating with others, creating things, and having a sense of self. Human well-being occurs when these needs are successfully and constructively satisfied in their fullest dimensions. What differs among us is how we try to meet these needs.

2 THE ODD CENTURY

Historically, people relied on internal methods, such as prayer, cultivation of skills (music, painting, or writing), or personal relationships, to meet needs. In the twentieth century there was a major shift to external methods, such as watching the media or owning lots of materials goods. Research suggests that external methods are much less successful than internal methods for satisfying human needs.

3 VISUALITY

"Visuality" is a visual reality that pervades our lives, primarily through the media, from advertising on bus stops to television, and from Web pages to

video games. Studies reveal that people spend an average of nearly twelve hours per day with the media. Much of what we see in visuality looks real but isn't, and design has a substantial role in shaping visuality's objects, images, and meanings.

4 MATERIALISM

"Materialism" suggests that you define yourself in terms of your material possessions and your physical appearance, placing more importance on material wealth than

other aspects of life. The unfortunate result is that we use appearance as a substitute for real meaning and experience. Design has a central role in shaping appearances to convey commercially generated meaning.

5 COMMERCIAL CULTURE

Visuality and materialism are closely tied to commercial culture. Artifacts and images overwhelm us, each claiming to have important meaning

for us about our identity and potential. In most cases these messages are commercially generated through advertising and marketing and play on our insecurities. Commercial culture pressures designers to focus narrowly on economic interests and to simplify many aspects of design and artifacts.

6 PUSHERS

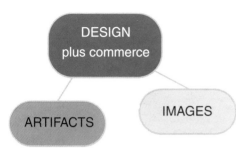

The people for whom we design are either commercial entities—consumers, clients, buyers—or functional, rational entities—users. It's tempting to cast designers as "pushers" because, seen in the light of commerce, it's what they do. They help businesses push more artifacts through the market and into the user's possessions.

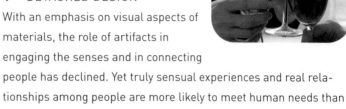

7 DETACHED DESIGN

With an emphasis on visual aspects of materials, the role of artifacts in engaging the senses and in connecting people has declined. Yet truly sensual experiences and real relationships among people are more likely to meet human needs than viewing images and owning objects.

8 DESIGNER AGAINST CONSUMER

The roles of designer and consumer as well as their aspirations are separate. The designer considers one dimension of an artifact—its salability—above all else. Yet people (let's not call them consumers) are concerned with a wide range of things that reflect their real lives, not just the fantasies of seductive advertisements or sleek trendy styling. "Open design" suggests a way for people to participate in making everyday objects better expressions of meaning and help replace some of the commercial "meaning" that we're sold.

9 FAST AND SLOW

One of the main characteristics of time over the last fifty years has been how it has speeded up, and design is no exception. Yet the very suggestion that today we are dominated by "fast" suggests that there is an alternative in "slow." We can even characterize human activities and artifacts in terms of whether they are underpinned by universal, one-size-fits-all, fast knowledge or customized, respect-for-differences, cooperative, slow knowledge.

10 SHORT-TERMISM

Sustainability carries on indefinitely, for the very long term. Yet our culture is dominated by "short termism." Designers rarely think about the long-term consequences—two hundred or even two thousand years in the future—of their work. More important, commercial forces push us to focus increasingly on the needs of the present, to the exclusion of the needs of the future.

11 NATURE IN CULTURE

New theories suggest there is an important ecological dimension to the human personality—that the natural world influences our identity and basic development. Ecological awareness and respect, in this context, are not just nice ideas; they are an essential part of human development. For designers, rebuilding this connection to nature can occur on several levels from personal to societal.

PART 5

FRONTIERS

THE THREE PREVIOUS PARTS have highlighted for designers some important elements in the landscape of sustainability. In some ways this landscape presents a frontier, where there are not necessarily any "right answers" available. Your challenge is to navigate this landscape based on the constraints, criteria, and priorities for your actual projects. Where do the opportunities and pitfalls for sustainable design lie? We'll begin addressing this question after a brief recap of the previous three parts.

Part 2 on ecology highlighted the key issue of human systems overwhelming nature's systems and examined ways that design can help harmonize human and natural systems, such as learning to see invisible connections and using nature's own techniques (biomimicry). The process of human design takes materials, frequently from the lithosphere, and distributes them, in a relatively useless form, in all the other spheres. An important conclusion from this part is that every artifact is part of human and natural systems, and only a holistic approach will enable us to successfully address these systems.

Part 3 on economy framed the key issue as our market system failing to capture important values, many of which are at the core of sustainability. This part examined the economy as a whole, not only the private sector (or free market) where design has traditionally been positioned, but also the public and nonprofit sectors of the economy. In general, it has been a mistake to think that the market is the best decision maker when it comes to sustainable development—the two other sectors of the economy are also important. This part noted how important it is that designers have some degree of economic literacy and that they consider opportunities for organizing projects or their whole practice outside the private sector, in the public or nonprofit ones.

Part 4 on culture presented the key issue of understanding cultural sustainability in terms of human well-being and how design can support it. This part used four main themes—communication, artifacts, time, and nature—to explore how design might better support human well-being. The last century has seen the increasing use of external mechanisms (such as materialism and visuality) to meet our needs, although these are less effective than internal ones. Design's role has been as a supplier of images and artifacts, largely to support commerce. In fact, commercial pressures have fashioned designers into pushers, a role they need to break out of in order to support sustainable development. Speed and short termism contribute to poorly met needs, as does our lack of connection to nature.

Reflecting on the three landscapes of sustainability together, we can now consider, in this part, some of their main interconnections. We can also look at the key theme of change, which arises in each landscape. To achieve sustainability, we need to make changes. These changes have many dimensions, including personal and professional choices. Some changes challenge our notions of what design is and others challenge our systems.

Mapmakers in earlier days used to signal the end of known territories with pictures of dragons and other terrible beasts. People believed it was possible to fall off the edge of the world. In some ways, this is the same position in which we find ourselves now. There are potentially promising unknown trails out there through the landscapes of sustainable design, but how do we get there from here, and what sort of dragons must we face?

What unknown challenges and opportunities lie ahead for sustainable design?

LANDSCAPE CONNECTIONS

DESIGN'S THREE LANDSCAPES OF SUSTAINABILITY are connected. We touched on some of these connections throughout the book, but in this chapter we can bring them into sharper focus.

Looking first at economy and culture, we can now see more clearly that the drive for economic expansion pushes much of our commercial culture. In addition, it becomes very clear that the bulk of human well-being lies entirely outside the market. Both the aspects of our health that rely on a healthy ecology and many aspects of our human needs (such as understanding, creativity, or identity) cannot be valued in monetary terms by the free market. They are really captured only in the public and nonprofit sectors of the economy. This has serious implications for how designers choose to organize the activity of design. Although the market (private sector) does offer some opportunities to pursue sustainable design, many of the social and environmental conditions that will support human well-being indefinitely simply cannot be captured by the market as it currently works and perhaps never should be captured by the market. Many of the ecological and cultural approaches to sustainable design will not be occurring in the private sector, meaning that designers who want to try them will need to consider the other two sectors of the economy and how to work with them, if not in them.

We can also see that the market's pace, with pressure for more money now, rather than in the future, puts pressure on cultural aspects of time, too. We are pressured to take short-term approaches that do not bode well for sustainability. An example of this is the increasing use of disposability—in products and buildings. In addition, the pressure to move more and more of our traditionally "nonmoney" activities into the market reduces our opportunities for flow, engagement, and appropriation. For example, if we buy clothes instead of make them, buy meals instead of cook them, or pay nannies instead of look after our own children, we loose opportunities for enhancing human well-being by cultivating understanding, creativity, and caring relationships. If we continue to let the market be the arbiter of society, we are unlikely to cultivate the social conditions that support human well-being indefinitely.

When we consider the landscapes of ecology and culture together, we can see several important links. There is a high ecological cost to using materialism as a means of meeting human needs. As we've seen, materialism meets most human needs quite badly, so there appears to be a win–win opportunity available for both ecology and culture if designers can find less materially intensive and more successful ways to meet human needs.

In addition, we can see that ecology has a central role not only in our physical well-being (for sustenance and shelter) but also in our psychological well-being. The theories of ecopsychology suggest that a connection to nature is central to our healthy development. This finding implies another potential win–win opportunity. A stronger connection to nature could lead to greater appreciation of its intrinsic value and the "free" services (breathable air) it provides, creating a stronger motivation to sustain the planet's ecological health.

In considering the link between the landscapes of ecology and economy, we can reiterate the point that most of ecology's value lies outside the free market. Given the dominance of the free market, we currently put ecological sustainability at the mercy of altruism. The pace of the market and the concentration of wealth and power tend to speed up ecological destruction. Unless we want to set up artificial markets and use artificial prices, we need to look at mechanisms in the public or nonprofit sector (such as democratic processes) to capture these values.

When we consider some of the design approaches that arose in each of the three landscapes of sustainability, we find some synergies among these design approaches and also some conflicts. For example, extending the life of products and buildings may contribute to cultural sustainability by connecting people to the past and the future. It could also save some resources by eliminating the need for new versions. But some of these artifacts will lock in old technology that wastes energy and contains undesirable materials. From an ecological point of view, it might be better to update to efficient technology and cleaner materials.

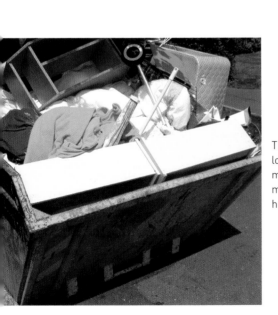

There is a high ecological cost to using materialism as a means of meeting human needs.

In another example, our ecological review suggests that under an organic/technical nutrient system, the "life story" of any given material would be fairly tightly scripted, especially for technical nutrients. Products and even buildings might be designed for easy disassembly and reuse; large-scale collection systems would prefer standardized product types. Yet in our survey of cultural sustainability, the discussion of open design and the "cooked-vs.-raw" approach argues for just the opposite. The open design process is free and unscripted and could possibly result in completely unique artifacts, assembled in a way that is like no other. On a global scale this looks a difficult problem, but could it be more easily resolved if we had locally or regionally based economies?

Similarly, in arguments for ecological efficiency we seek to get more use out of each artifact. A corporate parking lot doubles as a skateboard park on weekends or a set of tools is shared among people in a neighborhood. This doing-more-with-less approach contrasts with the idea of appropriation, a potential outcome of open design when a unique artifact is truly owned by its user, who also participated in making it. Where is the balance between appropriation, making it your own, and sharing, to get more community use out of artifacts? Is it possible for each individual in a group to appropriate a shared artifact? Some examples of this exist for favorite landmarks, for example. But the notion of sharing also struggles against the concept of private property, which remains at the heart of a market economy.

In terms of time, we can see that not only does the fast pace of commerce and the resulting short termism undercut ecosystem survival, but they also create obstacles to our movement away from commercial sources of meaning. Participating in open design or otherwise creating individual- or community-based meaning takes more time than buying ready-made commercial messages that are broadcast nationally and internationally for easy comprehension by all consumers. Despite these challenges, the reward for swimming against the commercial time tide is more authentic human well-being grounded in real communities and human relationships.

Indeed, as far as the role of communities is concerned, the more local your approach, the more likely you are to be able to negotiate solutions that fit the context. The importance of local diversity and adaptation is critical to ecological sustainability. Diversity presents options for how to solve problems or innovate, and diversity allows adaptation—essentially a better fit. We are also seeing that lack of diversity in our methods of satisfying human needs causes cultural sustainability to suffer. "Think globally, act locally" has been one of the slogans of the sustainable development movement. The relationship between local and global has been a central tension for development in general and for sustainability in particular.

I've highlighted some of the more challenging aspects of the relationships among the landscapes of sustainability to illustrate the complexities that sustainable design holds. There are no easy answers. Devising design solutions that move us toward sustainability requires that we look more closely at the notion of change and how design can bring about changes. To carry out this discussion, I characterize change as having three dimensions.

The first dimension is systems. We can think of systems as the larger structures and patterns in society, such as the technologies we use, the policies we choose, and the cultural behaviors we enact. The second dimension is professional and relates to choices we make as designers and to our view of what design is or does. The third dimension is personal, concerning the choices we make in our own lives. The following chapters examine these different dimensions of change.

LANDSCAPE FEATURE: Design's Three Landscapes

Design's three landscapes of sustainability are connected. We can see important linkages among ecology, economy, and culture, such as how economic pressures affect ecology or how materialism as a way of meeting human needs has a high ecological cost. In addition, when we look across the range of design approaches that arise in each landscape, we note that there are some interesting synergies and also some conflicts. For example, if we build strong emotional connections to artifacts and want to keep them, we may be locking in old (and ecologically wasteful) technology. Similarly, the approach of doing more with less, or maximizing the use of a given artifact, conflicts with the idea of individual appropriation of an artifact that could result from open design. This range of synergies and conflicts highlights the fact that the landscape of sustainable design is complex and that there are no easy answers.

Organic material cycle

Does a tightly scripted material cycle clash with the potentially wide range of unique results from open design?

Open design includes individual users.

THREE SYSTEMS OF CHANGE

HOW DO OUR SYSTEMS HELP OR HINDER change? In one scenario, change is a cultural response in which people find an advantage in changing behaviors. For example, with the arrival of the Internet, people began to download individual songs that they liked instead of buying a whole CD. Consumers who used to want a portable CD player now want a digital player that can store thousands of personally selected songs.

But is this really about changing behavior, or is it about responding to technological change? New behaviors are merely making use of new technology. But what about cost? It's cheaper to buy the one song that you want instead of paying for a whole album that contains only one song you really want. People change their behavior and adopt new technology when there's an economic advantage. When musicians and record producers agree to the policy of selling songs individually, then designs that capture this economic advantage promote the change.

When it comes to discussions of how we will move toward sustainable development, these three systems—technology, policy, and behavior—intersect.[1] It's important to note that the system of "policy" is very closely tied to *pricing*. As we saw in

> Why switch from CD player to digital player? For better performance, to be more fashionable. To have more flexible purchasing policies.

the economy section, the public sector, which sets policy, creates a consistent set of operating conditions for the market. When public policy changes, there is frequently an effect on pricing. For this reason, we need to think about policy as a dominant force in sending the right price signals to the market. We might think of these three areas—technology, policy, and behavior—as forming three points on a "triangle" of change.

Which of these systems is the most powerful? It depends on whom you ask. Our review of ecology suggests that some good technical solutions may exist, such as borrowing the metabolism idea from nature and creating an organic and technical nutrient system. Yet our review of the economy indicates that under current economic policies, ecology has zero price and so it has zero market value. In this policy and pricing climate, few business people will be motivated to develop and implement a material metabolism.

At the same time, we saw that democratic processes could change policies, such as regulation

Technology

3 Systems
of Change

Policy

Behavior

and taxation, for how we solve the zero-price problem and capture values that escape the market. For example, government could, through democratic participation of citizens, create a material metabolism framework within which the market is required to operate. Our review of cultural systems offers hope in that we can see our current system is not actually meeting human needs very robustly. If better ways to meet human needs emerge, people might change their cultural behavior patterns.

Often there are arguments about whether technology, policy, or culture is most effective or how fast each results in change. Sometimes the issue is portrayed as a "choice." For example, should we try to get people to change their behavior, or should we let them keep doing what they have always done but give them a better (cleaner) technology?

In reality, of course, we need all three of these systems working together. Behavioral change typically requires leadership from the social or political arena—from policymakers or other recognized public figures. As we've seen, policy changes require participation (a behavior) in the democratic process. Technology requires users to behave in certain ways. It is impossible, really, to separate these systems, but the "triangle" may help us think about where to target our work.

Also, we can see that in this triangle, the designer has a role in each system. Designers explore, invent, or apply new technologies, whether in buildings, fashion, or products. Designers can also seek out, suggest, or experiment with technologies that seem to contribute to sustainability. In this way they can demonstrate the potential of new technical approaches.

Since design is largely about communication, designers have a role in helping people chose how to behave. In fact, a really good design tells the user what to do—a handle says "Pull here," a panel cover says "Don't touch *that*," a festive interior says "Smile!" Design can contribute to the way that certain behaviors become fashionable or unfashionable. We've also seen a variety of ways designers might engage people to begin changing the one-way watching and owning dynamic that currently exists in the marketplace for design. Finally, designers are economic "actors" who shape and respond to policies.

Regardless of where and how it happens, change is always challenging. And big, well-established things, such as these three large systems, are especially hard to change. But change does happen all the time. People adopt new technologies like personal computers. They give up smoking in public buildings or in the workplace to comply with policy changes. They save bottles and cans when there is an opportunity for recycling.

Designers are entwined with these larger systems of change, but the profession itself has some struggles ahead to carry out changes that sustainability suggests. The next chapter begins our look at the professional dimension of change by examining professional codes of practice.

Design and Change

Policy

Designers are economic "actors" that shape and respond to policies.

Behavior

Good design tells the user what to do—a handle says "Grab."

Technology

Designers explore, invent, or apply new technologies, such as organic cotton.

CRACKING THE CODE

THE DESIGN PROFESSIONS HAVE EMERGED largely as a response to commercial pressures, and they are heavily engaged with the issues of commerce. It's hard to imagine that a wider engagement, one that would go beyond commerce and the visual, is possible in the face of so much economic pressure. We've seen that structuring design work in nontraditional forms, such as nonprofit organizations, might help. Could the ethical codes or principles of professional design associations also provide some support?

Ethical codes or codes of practice embody our moral obligations as professionals. These codes stem from a central idea in modern society that in exchange for freedom to determine our own direction in life, we accept some degree of responsibility in our relationships with others. We follow certain moral or ethical codes appropriate to the relationship, in this case, work relationships.

Historically, design codes of practice have covered the business aspects of work, leaving both personal and broader social issues aside. This is the general pattern that emerges from a review of a range of codes of ethics and codes of practice from design

societies covering disciplines such as interior design, graphic design, industrial design, and architecture.[2] Most codes of ethics have detailed sections pertaining to client responsibilities and business practices, particularly the treatment of peers and colleagues, including issues such as

- Competence and not misrepresenting competence
- Fair practice with regard to other designers
- Public health and safety
- Discretion and confidentiality of client information
- Taking credit for work fairly
- Intellectual property

Most organizations enforce little of their code not related to business practices. Beyond these commerce-related responsibilities, the practice of design is much more fluid than some other professions. For example, doctors swear to do no harm to their patients, lawyers swear to protect confidentiality, other professions have competency

TRAVELER'S NOTE: Professional Codes of Practice

We might characterize four stages in the evolution of design's professional codes of practice toward sustainability. The first three stages entail market, ecological, and cultural concerns. The last entails broader economic concerns that capture values and resources that fall outside the private sector, or market. Most professional codes of practice/ethics appear to be at the second or third stage. The first stage concerns business (or market) practices and ethics. The second stage contains the first but adds environmental impacts. The third stage contains the first two but adds preliminary cultural aspects of sustainability, such as nondiscrimination and human rights. The fourth stage would fully address economic, ecological, and cultural aspects of sustainability. It will be difficult to reach this stage if design continues to be viewed solely as a private sector activity.

	1st Stage	2nd Stage	3rd Stage	4th Stage
Economic concerns	🛒	🛒	🛒	🛒🍁✋
Ecological concerns		🍁	🍁	🍁
Cultural concerns			✋	✋

licensing schemes, and so forth. These professions subscribe to strict and legally acknowledged codes of ethics. But design has an important expressive and emotional role that does not easily lend itself to ethical codes. This might be why much of the existing codes of practice and ethics are voluntary, or aspirational. But the far-reaching, significant effects of design throughout society suggest that some more clearly agreed notion of responsibility

> The tension between design freedom and responsibility is a central issue for sustainability.

is appropriate. For example, in addition to his or her client, a designer's responsibility could extend to the users of the design, to the environment, to those who make the artifact, or to broader society.

Designers, such as Victor Papanek, who call for a more ethical focus in design, have been criticized for being "too serious" or taking themselves too seriously. Some also claim that specialist professions, such as those that follow strict codes of ethics, are paternalistic, doing things "to you" rather than

"with you."[3] The tension between design freedom and responsibility is a central issue for sustainability. Addressing this tension may be a job for design's professional associations and may offer ways to temper the dominance of economic values in design. Somewhere on a spectrum from reckless freedom to rigidly prescribed morals is a balancing point that design needs to find.

Many professional design organizations are beginning to address the ecological aspects of sustainability, and a few address cultural aspects. Cultural sustainability is generally addressed only in terms of human rights and nondiscrimination. A few mention cultural and environmental heritage, which is the only real mention of the aspect of time in sustainability. These ecological and cultural principles are phrased generally; for example, designers should "thoughtfully consider the social and environmental impact of their professional activities."[4] One code suggests that members pursue public interest projects and undertake civic responsibility as citizens and professionals.[5]

It is good to see that professional design societies are beginning to cover at least some elements in all three landscapes of sustainable development. But what would it look like if they went further? A comprehensive treatment of the sustainability landscape would have to entail a broader discussion of economic challenges, including matters such as work–life balance and all the many values that the economy doesn't capture. We would also expect a cultural discussion more grounded in terms of human well-being. In addition to examining the role of design in visuality and materialism, we might see the code address issues such as time, engagement, and connection.

The absence of these more comprehensive professional agendas for sustainability has led some groups of designers to develop their own independent statements. For example, graphic designers assembled the "First Things First Manifesto" in 2000 (for graphic and visual design). The manifesto, although not explicitly addressing sustainable development, touches upon many key issues. For example, one excerpt expresses the following:

> The profession's time and energy is used up manufacturing demand for things that are inessential at best.
>
> We propose a reversal of priorities in favor of more useful, lasting, and democratic forms of communication— a mindshift away from product marketing and toward the exploration and production of a new kind of meaning. The scope of debate is shrinking; it must expand. Consumerism is running uncontested; it must be challenged by other perspectives expressed, in part, through the visual languages and resources of design.[6]

Interestingly, this manifesto is a reissue of an earlier manifesto from 1964 in which graphic designers were already calling for more worthwhile pursuits for their profession. Another example of a code of ethics comes from the

> Somewhere on a spectrum from reckless freedom to rigidly prescribed morals is a balancing point that design needs to find.

International Council of Societies of Industrial Design 2001 Seoul Industrial Designers' Declaration, which includes the following sections:

> Benefit the Client
> Benefit the User
> Protect the Ecosystem
> Enrich Cultural Identity
> Benefit the Profession

A final example is the 1992 Hannover Principles that the city of Hannover, Germany, commissioned from William McDonough to address sustainable design specifically. These principles discuss issues such as interdependence, relationships, human well-being, and sharing of knowledge.

Although these agendas are admirable, they do tend to underestimate, or perhaps underplay, the challenges of economic sustainability while simplifying cultural sustainability. Nevertheless, they provide an excellent starting point. Going beyond these formal codes of practice, we can examine the broader concept of design and how we might revise it in light of new perspectives that sustainability yields.

DESIGN
IN A NEW LIGHT

THE LANDSCAPE OF SUSTAINABILITY has shown us design in a new light, one that illuminates ecological, economic, and cultural aspects that we might not have seen before. In particular, the agenda of the marketplace, of economic growth, colors many of the opportunities and challenges for sustainable design. A key question emerges whether we can somehow separate design from the industrial economy's growth engines. This sort of "decoupling" has occurred for society's

energy use, for example. It used to be the case that economic growth necessarily required increased energy use. Now with improved technologies, lifestyle changes, and stronger energy efficiency policies, there is no longer a direct tie between economic growth and increase in energy use.

It seems clear that as long as we continue to view design primarily as a tool of the market, or of the private sector, we will have trouble envisioning

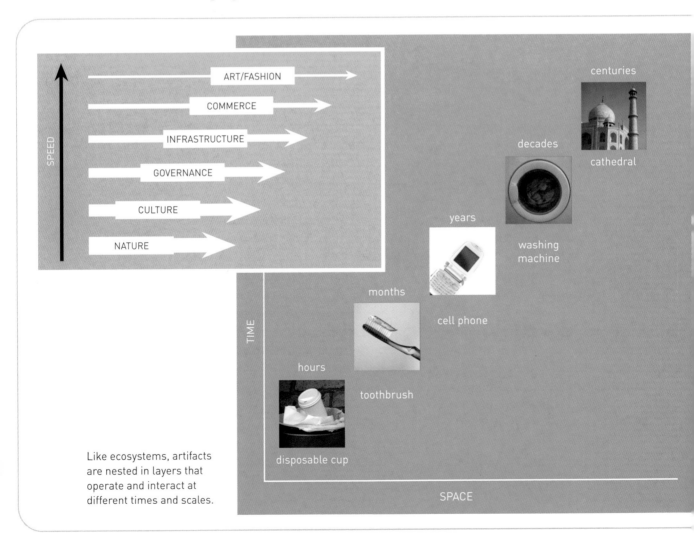

Like ecosystems, artifacts are nested in layers that operate and interact at different times and scales.

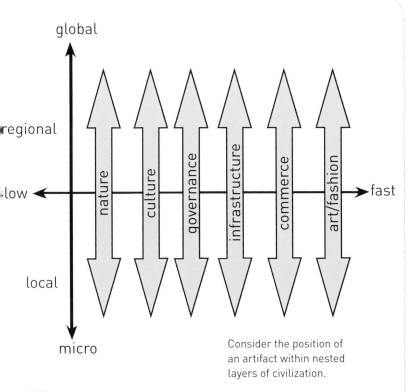

Consider the position of an artifact within nested layers of civilization.

TRAVELER'S NOTE: Pacing and Nesting

Combining the idea of different-paced layers of society with the ecological pattern of nested ecosystems suggests a possible view of design acting in dimensions of time and space, as well as across society's layers. The chart shows our layers, from slowest to fastest. Although nature has some mechanisms that are fast, the overall pattern in nature—even the fast parts—are typically retained for much longer than the overall patterns in, say, art/fashion or commerce. The vertical axis of the diagram shows the dimension of space (or size). For each layer of society, we also have activity from the microscale up to the global scale. It is within this framework, or something like it, that it might be possible to roughly classify artifacts in certain nesting layers that would dictate at least some of the priorities for their sustainable design. In this nested system, small, fast layers would experiment and invent. The big, slow layers would continue the system's stability.

how to decouple it from economic growth. But when we consider the scope for design in the two other sectors of the economy, a few ideas start to emerge.

The first idea is to characterize design in terms of how deep it goes. Surface styling would be in a different category than design that attempted to address issues of engagement, skill, time, or ecological metabolism. A useful way to think about this is in terms of the layers of civilization outlined in part 4. Is the designer working largely in the fast-paced, visuality-based fashion layer or wading more deeply into the layers of culture and nature?

Similarly, we could revisit the nested ecosystem pattern in nature. Would it be possible to establish a similar nesting for individual artifacts with regard to both time and distance scales. For example, disposable packaging has a short life and often a short travel distance during its useful life. A building typically has a long life. It doesn't move through space, but the geographic range it touches might be large; for example, people from all over the world visit the Empire State Building. Although matters of distribution and use would complicate matters, by looking at how these nested layers interact, it might be possible to roughly classify artifacts in certain nesting layers that would dictate at least some of the priorities for their sustainable design. Then people who work on/with those objects would respond suitably to the needs of

Truly local work is
typically deep and slow

the layers. It wouldn't matter if you were trained as an architect or a textile designer, what would matter is which nested layer you're working on. In this scenario, one aim could be to ensure that the small, fast layers absorb shocks to the system and that they invent and experiment but that they not rob the big, slow layers of the ability to maintain long-term stability and continuity. Another way of looking at the notion of design is in terms of how local or global its emphasis is. In some ways, this approach parallels the notion of "depth" or "speed," since truly local work is typically deep and slow.

Much of design is trapped in "mass commerce" mentality. In contrast, when we peruse most books or catalogs showing sustainable design examples, many of the good ideas are tested only as prototypes or student projects. These designs never make it into mass commerce because they are slow, engaging, and connective; sometimes they're relevant only to a small local population—not suitable for "commerce as we know it." Those designs that do reach commercial production typically stay in production for only a brief period before being ousted by the next wave of consumer-appeal artifacts.

There appears to be room for a new layer of commerce, one that captures a broader range of values than just growth in money and one that operates on a smaller scale. This system would reflect not mass production but appropriate production. Microloans, local currencies, and some of the other elements from the antiglobalization movement hint at this approach. This type of system might be found by combining digital, networked technology, local currencies, and ecosphere understanding. It would mean a shift away from measuring how good a design is by how well it sells.

Along with this revision of design's commerce, we might consider redefining the notion of authorship and intellectual property, something we began

exploring in part 4. This might require that designers, starting with their education onward, loosen up on the ownership of design ideas and find their recognition within a team structure. An important skill in this scenario is recognizing really good ideas contributed by others, not just having good ideas yourself. The idea of partnerships and collaborations might extend beyond traditional design teams or even beyond partnerships among designers and engaged users. It might extend to associated, even adversarial professions—for example, pairing architects with building inspectors or product designers with consumer safety advocates. Even limited exposure to the perspective of these other professions provides a completely different angle on the problem of artifacts.

A final idea relates again to the exposure of design to other professions and other perspectives. In part 3 we examined the nonprofit sector as one that allows pursuit of criteria other than "growth in money." In the years since sustainable design has emerged, there has been a fair amount of effort to bring "sustainability" into the field of design. Another approach would be to bring design, as a profession, into the field of sustainable development, for example, into nonprofit organizations, governments, and educational institutions. These are all the groups that usually work on sustainable development, but typically they lack the tools that designers have to assess and combine human factors, technology, style, and function into an appealing package.

Each of these approaches that could delink design from economic growth would require substantial movement in each of the three dimensions of change.

As we leave this chapter, we turn our attention to the fact that all designers are also people, not cogs in a great machine. For this reason, it is important to consider personal dimensions of change.

DESIGNERS AS PEOPLE

ARE YOU HAPPY? What makes you tick? As individuals, we each have to negotiate personal and professional lives. Many of the issues confronting us in the landscape of sustainability are those that feel more personal than professional, for example, your connection to nature, your politics as a citizen, or your willingness to put your personal resources toward ecological sustainability.

You are probably also faced with the question of balancing your own lifestyle decisions and approaches against the kinds of lifestyle choices and approaches your designs recommend to others. If you don't live a totally sustainable lifestyle, are you disqualified from practicing sustainable design? Certainly not, and for several reasons. First, given our current system, it is near impossible to live a

There are a number of questions that require personal answers before you make professional decisions about how to pursue sustainability.

totally sustainable lifestyle. The important thing is to make some effort, and this helps not only sustainability, but also your ability to bring sustainability issues into the design process in a productive way. Second, no one is perfect. Third, when it comes to measuring your life by a sustainability ruler, we have to think beyond how much you recycle and whether or not you eat organic food.

Although environmental measurements are useful, we also have to consider human needs as well as the economic picture. For example, do you vote or participate in public policy discussions related to the economy? Perhaps you are an employer and choose to share profits or otherwise address the concentration of wealth. You may place your design business within the private sector but seek out public and nonprofit clients, allowing you to pursue a broader range of values within design projects. You may organize your design activity within the nonprofit sector but seek out private companies to help them find ways of expanding the range of values they consider in their own designs. How do you use your own income? How much do you rely on external methods of visuality and materialism to meet your human needs instead of using more internal, and effective, methods? These, among others, are also relevant to measuring your contributions to sustainability.

These personal questions lead to another question—about the tone of sustainability. It is difficult to be put in the position of a doomsday prophet, preaching the end of the world due to unsustainable practices. It is equally difficult to be put in the position of a saint, with the expectation that you must save the world every minute of every day. In the current climate these are often the roles one is cast into when entering the pursuit of sustainability.[7] We can cast off the doomsayer role when we see the big picture, all the dynamics in play, and we have a more holistic perspective of the opportunities for sustainability and the versatility of the human spirit to carry us forward through a range of problems.

Equally, the role of saint is impractical: Nobody is perfect, and none of us can do it alone. When confronted with the very difficult issues of third world development, it is easy to question the value of what we might be doing in our own, industrialized context. But we must start from what we know and where we are. Nine months living in India made it clear to me that my effectiveness is much greater at home, and that is one of the main reasons this book doesn't deal with third world development issues. I want to support others on the sustainability team there—and worldwide—but work largely within my own cultural context.

There are other questions that require personal answers before you make professional decisions. Consider some of the central debates surrounding sustainable design. For example, who do you believe is responsible for sustainability? Should sustainable design look different from other design? Is incremental change good enough, or do we need to do something radical to get on track for sustainability? How can you balance your own local and global roles?

TRAVELER'S NOTE: Personal

Many of the issues confronting us in the landscape of sustainability are issues that feel more personal than professional. We may often end up with conflicts between our personal lifestyle decisions on one hand and lifestyle approaches that our designs recommend to others. We may end up feeling disqualified from practicing sustainable design if we don't live a totally sustainable lifestyle, but we shouldn't. Not only does our current industrial system make it very difficult to live a totally sustainable lifestyle, but as we have seen there are many measures of sustainability that span not only environmental issues (such as waste and recycling) but also economic issues (such as concentration of wealth) or cultural issues (such as using materialism as a way to meet human needs). Similarly, designers, like others involved in sustainable development, must avoid being cast as either doomsayers or saints.

TRAVELER'S NOTE: The Central Debates

Who is responsible for sustainable design? The current answer is no one. It should be every-one. From a design perspective there are perhaps four distinct groups that have specific roles: designers, clients (typically companies), governments, and consumers. Yet each points the finger at the other as being the one who should take the lead. The client should ask for it. The designer should offer it as an option. The government should require it. The consumer should ask for it from both companies and governments.

But the client doesn't know too much about it and doesn't ask for it. The designer, if knowl-edgeable about it, doesn't want to upset the client relationship by bringing up what could be a con-frontational subject to a client who hasn't demonstrated interest in it. If the designer doesn't know, then he or she typically can't afford the time to find out. They often turn to government agencies and nonprofit groups to get quick information (for free). The government could have more regula-tions that call for sustainability, but only if citizens, also known as consumers, ask for it. Many citizens, busy with their own lives or perhaps daunted by the complexity of sustainability, hope or assume that government is already doing its job of protecting them. Others hope that watch-dog nonprofit organizations will keep governments and corporations in line, making sure noth-ing "too bad" happens. As with the question of change, the answer to questions about who is responsible for sustainable design must be—everyone. The point is, what kind of responsibility can you take from within your sector of the economy and from within your personal choices?

How much change do we need, and when do we need it? In terms of pace, can we achieve a sustainable society through incremental design improvements, such as energy efficiency and recyclable materials? Or do we need radical change that calls upon designers for fundamen-tal reinvention? Whether you feel more comfortable in the fast, radical innovation lane or the slow, stability lane, it is important to recognize the value of those traveling at other speeds. As we've seen, a fundamental principle of nature's resiliency, or sustainability, is the ability to conserve while also being able to innovate—maintaining adaptive capability for the future. The capacity for sustainability requires some fast-moving and some slow-moving layers.

How should sustainable design look? Historically, a society's concept of nature has served as a behavioral constraint on society's actions affecting the ecosphere. For example, if your culture believes that the earth is a living, sacred being, then your culture will respect nature in a different way than a more scientifically oriented culture.[8] Concepts of nature, in turn, have been generated and maintained by imagery and representation of nature in the "creative industries" throughout time (e.g., paintings, ceremonial objects, tools, architecture, advertising). Sustainability has proven a very complex concept that is difficult to represent. In design terms, how far should design go toward expressing a cultural concept of sustainability? Should sustainable design look a certain way? And if it looks the same as all the rest, then how will the consumer know to choose it?

What's the appropriate balance between local and global? Sustainable development is commonly seen as development that is extremely well suited to local conditions (e.g., materials, climate, ecosystems) following the principle of natural adaptation. But we now have a global economy. Many people question whether global companies and the global economy can effectively respond to local needs without destroying local diversity. Designers now have a world of materials, production facilities, and consumers available to them—is it realistic for them to commit themselves to local economies? Similarly, we've seen that by using microlending, local currencies, and cooperative structures among small businesses, it may be possible for small and even "micro" businesses to meet mass market demands without compromising local diversity. Where does the balance lie?

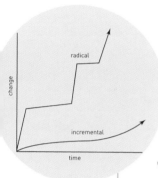

HOW FAST?
Do we need incremental
or radical change?

WHO'S RESPONSIBLE?
Who is responsible for,
or has the power over,
sustainable design—designer,
consumer, producer, or government?

Central Debates

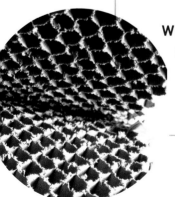

WHAT APPEARANCE?
How should
sustainable
design look?

HOW LOCAL OR GLOBAL?
Can global companies
address local needs and
vice versa?

DESIGN FOR CHANGE

HAVING REVIEWED SEVERAL DIMENSIONS OF CHANGE, it's now useful to briefly consider how these notions of change might revolve around a specific design project.

As a starting point, designers can and must think broadly about their design problem—beyond the artifact's features to consider that it is part of a system. To use a holistic approach, we can ask how the problem area or artifact is connected to the different landscapes of sustainability. Most likely there will be issues around harmonizing human systems with nature's systems, including invisible materials. There will be the question of each stakeholder's position within the economy—public, private, or nonprofit entities. And what about cultural dimensions—internal and external (largely commercial) means of meeting needs?

Along these lines, we also can consider the spectrum from incremental to radical. Although I mentioned this above as a central debate, it is a practical problem for many designers. Parts 2, 3, and 4 offered ideas that ranged from small steps, such as trying to do a better job with recycling, to larger steps, such as reinventing our material cycles. Within the economic landscape there are smaller steps, such as looking for opportunities within your private sector job, to more radical ideas such as organizing as a nonprofit group. As far as cultural sustainability goes, we saw that just being aware of the issues, such as speed, is an important first step. Awareness will, in time, lead to opportunities to act.

Designers also have the larger systems to consider. In each design case the systems of technology, policy, and behavior may be more or less important or useful. They can serve as brainstorming points. For example, let's say you're a fashion designer working in men's wear. For your next project you've highlighted parenthood and the roles of fathers as an area of social systems that you'd like to address through your work. You explore what kind of changes are likely to support fatherhood, such as more time spent with children, flexible work environments, and so forth. You also explore what fatherhood means to different people and at different children's ages. Using the three areas of change to inspire your work, you might consider

- *Policy changes:* Subsidized clothing for fathers who work less than full-time to participate more fully in parenting .

- *Behavioral changes:* Clothing that makes a statement about your role as father, such as a black necktie with the word "father" in large, bold white letters, prompting more discussions in the workplace about fatherhood and the work–life balance.

PERSONAL
Personal feelings about the central debates of sustainable design.

CHANGE

PROFESSIONAL
Professional codes of practice, notions of design.

SYSTEM
Technology, policy, and behavior.

• *Technology:* Clothing that has built-in "shields" against drool and so on so that fathers in work clothes can hold and play with small children.

This is a small, partially developed example, but it illustrates how very different solutions emerge across these systems.

In considering personal and professional dimensions of change, specific projects, or sets of projects, may serve as turning points, either within a profession or within your personal life. For example, some designers find that a given project or client provides them with the opportunity to build up essential experience in sustainable design work. In other cases a set of exciting projects can bring sustainability to the next frontier in discussions at the professional level. Through personal and professional experience you may find that sometimes you need to start toward change from within the design process itself; other times you need to start from the standpoint of how to organize a particular design project, or the whole design practice, within the economy.

Surveying the three landscapes for sustainability, the potential design opportunities and challenges they offer, as well as the dynamics of change, yields a complex picture with many potential "travel routes." The aim of this atlas is not to resolve which is the best route—but rather to chart the complexities in such a way as to help you navigate various routes through the landscape of sustainability.

TRAVEL ROUTES

Landscapes for Sustainability

ECOLOGY

Landscape Features:

Nature's Resiliency

Human designs overwhelm nature through

- Speed of resource use
- Magnitude of resource use
- Location (redistribution of materials from lithosphere to other spheres).

TRAVELER'S NOTE:

Learn to see invisible materials, borrow from nature (e.g., biomimicry).

ECONOMY

Landscape Features:

Three sectors: public, private (the market), and nonprofit

Letting the market decide weakness sustainability through

- Need for constant economic expansion
- Uncaptured values (human values that have no price)
- Concentration of wealth.

TRAVELER'S NOTE:

Look outside the market to organize design activities, gain economic literacy.

CULTURE

Landscape Features:

Human well-being; nine universal needs

Shift from internal to external means of meeting needs weakens sustainability through

- Communication—watching
- Artifacts—owning
- Time—speed and short termism
- Nature—techno-cities.

TRAVELER'S NOTE:

Help individuals and communities bring own meaning to artifacts, break out of one-way visuality.

CONCLUSION

IN THIS FINAL PART OF THE ATLAS, we've taken the opportunity to begin integrating the three landscapes of sustainable design. This integration has illustrated that there are some synergies as well as some conflicts among the landscapes. The complex, interwoven patterns of synergy and conflict also play out in terms of the types of changes that might move us toward sustainability. We've seen that many of these issues manifest themselves in a series of "central debates" about sustainable design.

We examined three dimensions of change at the levels of system, profession, and individual. Together these suggest that there is no right answer, no one-size-fits-all design solution. This realization is perhaps simultaneously freeing and daunting, requiring us each to navigate a complex landscape.

I'm often tempted to see the economic system as the most powerful in terms of thwarting sustainable design, but in the end it is human beings who create the systems that constrain and motivate them. Ironically, these same humans then lose the sense that they've created the systems in the first place. They start accepting them as "given" or part of the natural order of things. Yet these systems are social products. And in order to carry on they have to be continually "re-created" in social action, the way that ecosystems continually reproduce themselves.[9] Change comes when people don't carry on what was done before and transcend the boundaries of the social systems they've created.

As designers we can break from what was done before in many ways. Overall, we must consider human well-being in terms of environmental, economic, and cultural conditions and consider whether our contributions to those conditions truly support well-being and support it indefinitely. That support is what defines and enables sustainable design.

People create change by looking at the past to find better ways of doing things in the future: by transcending the boundaries of the social systems they've created.

ENDNOTES

PART 1 ENDNOTES

1. The phrase "freedom to design is based on other more profound freedoms" is a reworking of Anita Roddick's phrase describing the freedom to do business. She says, "It seems absolutely fundamental to me that our freedom to do business rests on other, more profound freedoms" in "Fair Trade: The Real Bottom Line" from *Globalization: Take It Personally*, Anita Roddick, editor (London: HarperCollins, 2001), 98.

2. Chris Park, *Tropical Rainforests* (London: Routledge, 1992), 10.

3. World Commission on Environment and Development, *Our Common Future* (Oxford: Oxford University Press, 1987), 8.

4. Julian D. Marshall and Michael W. Toffel provide a useful overview of the "definitional chaos" that has plagued sustainable development in "Framing the Elusive Concept of Sustainability: A Sustainability Hierarchy," *Environmental Science and Technology* 39, no. 3 (2005): 673–682. Their discussion includes an assessment of the weaknesses in the commission's definition as well as observations about quality-of-life indicators, and reflections on what, in fact, we want to "sustain."

5. A. J. McMichael, C. D. Butler, and C. Folke, "New Visions for Addressing Sustainability," *Science* 12 (December 2003): vol. 302: 1919–1920.

6. John Heskett notes this as a separation of decorative concerns from function in *Toothpicks and Logos: Design in Everyday Life* (Oxford: Oxford University Press, 2002). Stuart Ewen notes that by the 1830s design had evolved into "the superficial application of decoration to the form and surface of a product" in *All Consuming Images: The Politics of Style in Contemporary Culture* (New York: Basic Books, HarperCollins 1988), 33. The separation of form from substance became the defining characteristic of design in the eighteenth century.

7. This expression originates with architect Louis Sullivan, who wrote "form ever follows function" in an 1896 essay entitled "'Tall Office Buildings Artistically Considered," cited in Heskett, *Toothpicks and Logos*, 36.

8. Most famously said by architect Mies van der Rohe (1886–1968), cited in Alan Powers, *Nature in Design: The Shapes, Colours and Forms That Have Inspired Visual Invention* (London: Conran Octopus, 1999.)

9. Functionalism is well covered in the literature of design history; for example, see Heskett, *Toothpicks and Logos* 27–39; and Peter Dormer, *Design Since 1945* (London: Thames and Hudson, 1993), 55–60.

10. Dormer, *Design Since 1945*, 24.

11. Heskett, *Toothpicks and Logos*, 33.

12. For example, see Nigel Whiteley, *Design for Society* (London: Reaktion Books, 1993), chap. 1; and Heskett, *Toothpicks and Logos*, 57–60.

13. For example, see Heskett, *Toothpicks and Logos*, 103–104.

PART 2 ENDNOTES

1. Peter H. Raven and Linda R. Berg explain the effect of lost calcium on bird's eggshells in *Environment*, 3rd ed. (New York: Harcourt College, 2001), 505. Lester Brown documents waste from iron mining and damage from mining activities in *Eco-Economy: Building an Economy for the Earth* (New York: W. W. Norton, 2001), 123, 127–130. John McNeill profiles specific examples of environmental devastation in *Something New Under the Sun: An Environmental History of the Twentieth Century* (London: Penguin Books, 2000), 27–35.

2. Paul Hawken, Amory Lovins, and L. Hunter Lovins cite an article from the journal *Nature* in which all biomes studied are in decline in terms of area, productivity, and viability in *Natural Capitalism: Creating the Next Industrial Revolution* (New York: Little, Brown, 1999), 156.

3. Jonathan Loh and Mathis Wackernagel, eds., *Living Planet Report 2004* (Gland, Switzerland: World Wildlife Fund, 2004), 1–2. The report was developed in partnership with United Nations Environment Programme and the Global Footprint Network.

4. McNeill develops this idea in *Something New Under the Sun*, 192–193.

5. Helen Lewis and John Gertsakis, *Design + Environment: A Global Guide to Designing Greener Goods* (Sheffield, UK: Greenleaf, 2001), 131.

6. Edwin Datschefski provides a brief review of material choices, including cotton, in *The Total Beauty of Sustainable*

Products (Hove, UK: Rotovision, 2001), 161. Riikamaria Paakkunainen provides a very comprehensive overview of environmental impacts of each stage of textile production, including finishing, in *Textiles and the Environment* (Eindhoven, the Netherlands: European Design Centre, July 1995), 24–27.

7. United Nations Development Programme et al., *A Guide to World Resources 2000–2001: People and Ecosystems, the Fraying Web of Life* (Washington, DC: World Resources Institute, 2000), 3.

8. Chris Park, *Tropical Rainforests* (London: Routledge, 1992), 10.

9. Kevin T. Pickering and Lewis A. Owen develop the concept of the spheres in *Global Environmental Issues*, 2nd Edition (London: Routledge, 1994); and John McNeill also uses the concept of the spheres as an organizing framework for his book *Something New Under the Sun* (2000).

10. Tim Jackson, *Material Concerns: Pollution, Profit and Quality of Life* (London: Routledge, 1996), 14.

11. McNeill, *Something New Under the Sun*, 2000, 15.

12. S. D. Frey, Dr. D. J. Harrison, Prof. E. H. Billett, "Environmental Assessment of Electronic Products Using LCA and Ecological Footprint" in the proceedings from the Joint International Congress and Exhibition. Electronics Goes Green 2000, Berlin,Germany, 11–13 September 2000, 253–258.

13. Country-specific ecofootprint data from Jonathan Loh and Mathis Wackernagel, eds., *Living Planet Report 2004*, 24–31. For a general discussion of the ecological footprint concept and how it was developed, see Mathis Wackernagel and William Rees, *Our Ecological Footprint: Reducing Human Impact on Earth* (Gabriola Island, BC: New Society, 1996), particularly chap. 1.

14. Jackson, *Material Concerns: Pollution, Profit and Quality of Life*, 29.

15. Lewis and Gertsakis. *Design + Environment*, 13.

16. Karl-Henrik Robèrt et al. discuss the redistribution of materials in "A Compass for Sustainable Development," March 26, 1997, 8–13.

17. Theo Colborn, Diane Dumanoski, and John Peterson Myers, *Our Stolen Future: Are We Threatening Our Fertility, Intelligence, and Survival? A Scientific Detective Story* (New York: Plume, 1997), 137–138.

18. Karl-Henrik Robèrt et. al. explain the system conditions and the reasoning behind them in "A Compass for Sustainable Development," 812–15.

19. Commission of the European Communities, *Green Paper: Environmental Issues of PVC* (Brussels: Commission of the European Communities, 2000), 14.

20. Edwin Datschefski, *The Total Beauty of Sustainable Products*, 160.

21. Many public agencies, ranging from the state of California to the U.S. federal government, and some large corporations have green procurement policies.

22. Gary Gardner and Payal Sampat, *Mind over Matter: Recasting the Role of Materials in Our Lives*, Worldwatch Paper 144 (Washington, DC: Worldwatch Institute, 1998), 24–25.

23. Robert Ayres and A. V. Neese cited in William McDonough and Michael Braungart, *Cradle to Cradle: Remaking the Way We Make Things* (New York: North Point Press, 2002), 27.

24. Lester Brown, *Eco-Economy: Building an Economy for the Earth*, 2001, 123, 127–130. Brown notes that we have extracted all of the highest-quality ores, those with the highest concentrations of metal, and now, "Over time, as high-grade ores have been depleted, miners have shifted to lower-grade ores, inflicting progressively more environmental damage with each ton of metal produced."

25. Kevin Carmody cites the statistics of the Silicon Valley Toxics Coalition in "U.S. Scores Poorly on Toxic Report," *Austin American-Statesman* (Austin, TX), November 29, 2001.

26. McDonough and Braungart, *Cradle to Cradle*, 38–39.

27. For examples of tests on electric products, see ibid., 36–38. Good indoor environmental quality, particularly air quality, is associated with higher employee productivity, reduced absenteeism, and improved health, according to a variety of sources such as the U.S. Green Building Council, *LEED Training Workshop*, Seattle, March 3, 2000.

28. James Owens, "Oceans Awash with Microscopic Plastic, Scientists Say," *National Geographic News*, May 6, 2004. Ian Sample reviews the chemical contents of common house dust in "A Sharp Intake of Breath," in *The Guardian* (London), March 22, 2004, special section "Chemical World."

29. These ideas are well developed and explained by Karl-Henrik Robèrt, the founder of The Natural Step. For example, see K.-E. Eriksson and Karl-Henri Robèrt, "From the Big Bang to Sustainable Societies," *Reviews in Oncology* 4, no. 2(1991): 5–14. For a good layperson's explanation of structure and concentration, see Jackson, *Material Concerns*, 1–21.

30. Fran Abrams and James Astill, "Story of the Blues" in *The Guardian* (London) May 29, 2001.

31. This discussion of down-cycling, danger-cycling, and up-cycling is drawn from McDonough and Braungart, *Cradle to Cradle*, 56–58.

32. Ibid., 92–117.

33. Adriaan Beukers and Ed van Hinte, *Lightness: The Inevitable Renaissance of Minimum Energy Structures* (Rotterdam: 010 Publishers, 1998), 70–79. See also Mike Ashby and Kara Johnson, *Materials and Design: The Art and Science of Material Selection in Product Design* (Oxford: Butterworth-Heinemann, 2002), 182–183.

34. Janine Benyus, *Biomimicry: Innovation Inspired by Nature* (New York: Quill William Morrow, 1997), 95–145.

35. Colin Dawson et al., "Heat Transfer through Penguin Feathers," *Journal of Theoretical Biology* (1999): 199, 291–295.

36. T. E. Graedel and B. R. Allenby, *Industrial Ecology* (Englewood Cliffs, NJ: Prentice Hall, 1995), 286–287.

37. The two approaches to biomimicry described for designers here were developed through discussions with Professor George Jeronimidis at the Centre for Biomimetics, Reading University, winter/spring 2002.

38. Carolyn Merchant in *Radical Ecology: The Search for a Livable World* (New York: Routledge, 1992) cites Peter Berg's definition of "bioregion," 218. David M. Olson and Eric Dinerstein in "The Global 200: Priority Ecoregions for Global Conservation" (*Annals of the Missouri Botanical Garden.* 2002, 89: 199–224) describe their work to identify earth's distinct eco regions–assemblages of biological communities and key ecological processes. They propose 30 biomes and 867 terrestrial ecoregions, with an unspecified number of marine and freshwater ecoregions, which are harder to delineate.

39. Fritjof Capra provides a good layperson's explanation of both self-organizing systems and how living systems continually re-create themselves in *The Hidden Connections: A Science for Sustainable Living* (London: HarperCollins, 2002), 8–12.

40. Lance H. Gunderson and C. S. Holling develop the concept of the four-phase ecosystem cycle and the concept of ecosystems having a wide range of functional states in *Panarchy: Understanding Transformations in Human and Natural Systems*, ed. Lance H. Gunderson and C. S. Holling (Washington, DC: Island Press, 2002), 33–40.

41. Stewart Brand uses this forest example to explain how nature is resilient, in *The Clock of the Long Now: Time and Responsibility* (London: Weidenfeld and Nicolson, 1999), 34–35.

42. Lance H. Gunderson, C. S. Holling, and Garry D. Peterson, "Sustainability and Panarchies," in *Panarchy*, 76.

43. Ibid., 74–77.

44. Mathis Wackernagel and William Rees explore the concept of carrying capacity in *Our Ecological Footprint: Reducing Human Impact on Earth* (Gabriola Island, BC: New Society 1996), 48–51.

45. Gunderson and Holling, *Panarchy,* 32, 77.

46. Several authors have covered the concept of holism for the layperson. I have drawn largely from the following: David Korten, *The Post-Corporate World: Life After Capitalism* (West Hartford, CT: Kumarian Press; San Francisco: Berrett-Koehler, 1999), 113–114; Capra, *The Hidden Connections*, 9; and Alan Powers, *Nature in Design: The Shapes, Colours and Forms That Have Inspired Visual Invention* (London: Conran Octopus, 1999), 38–41.

PART 3 ENDNOTES

1. Burton A. Weisbrod examined a three-sector economy composed of public, private, and nonprofit sectors in "Toward a Theory of the Voluntary Non-Profit Sector in a Three-Sector Economy," in *Altruism, Morality and Economic Theory*, ed. Edmond S. Phelps (New York: Russell Sage Foundation, 1975), 171–195. The notion of a third sector, also called the "social economy," and its importance to sustainable development has gained currency. For example, see Real World Coalition, *The Politics of the Real World* (London: Earthscan, 1996), 96–100; and James Robertson, *The New Economics of Sustainable Development: A Briefing for Policy Makers* (Luxembourg: Office for Official Publications of the European Communities; London: Kogan Page, 1999), 8.

2. Two good overviews of private sector objectives are found in David C. Korten, *The Post-Corporate World: Life After Capitalism (*West Hartford, CT: Kumarian Press; San

Francisco: Berrett-Koehler, 1999), 75–79; and Marjorie Kelly, *The Divine Right of Capital: Dethroning the Corporate Aristocracy* (San Francisco: Berrett-Koehler, 2001), 54–58.

3. Mark A. Lutz and Kenneth Lux provide a good review of the public sector role in the economy in *Humanistic Economics: The New Challenge* (New York: Bootstrap Press, 1988), 202–221. For example, they comment that "[t]he market is best seen as a contest or a competitive game with winners and losers....As in any such activity, there need to be rules and a referee. In an economic system these are provided by government."

4. A number of authors develop the theme of an "amoral" market; for example, see Jeff Gates, *Democracy at Risk: Rescuing Main Street from Wall Street* (Cambridge, MA: Perseus, 2000), 3, 88–89; and Lutz and Lux, *Humanistic Economics*, 207.

5. For example, Gates, in *Democracy at Risk*, 167, notes that taxes are optional for the wealthy, although they benefit disproportionately from public infrastructure. Kelley, in *The Divine Right of Capital*, 7, notes that there are relatively few public policy tools for governing corporations in the face of their enormous power. Korten, in *Post-Corporate World*, 46–48, notes how effective corporations are at winning government subsidies for themselves. Lutz and Lux, in *Humanistic Economics*, 214–216, profile the enormous power of corporate lobbying. Michael F. Jacobson and Laurie Ann Mazur provide examples of corporate influence on nonprofit arts and culture groups in *Marketing Madness: A Survival Guide for Consumer Society* (Boulder, CO: Westview Press, 1995), 101–110. In *Money: Understanding and Creating Alternatives to Legal Tender* (White River Junction, VT: Chelsea Green, 2001), 14, Thomas H. Greco Jr. notes that corporations are becoming ever more powerful as the countervailing forces, such as government and other nonprofit society groups, are "neutralized or co-opted," a situation that makes alternative currencies ever more important.

6. Nigel Whiteley develops the theme of a move from "need" to "desire" of material goods in *Design for Society* (London: Reaktion Books, 1993), 15–19. According to *The Economist*, "In the 40 years up to 1997, America's private sector was always a net saver, meaning that the total income of households and firms was greater than their spending." But by 2000 a massive boom in borrowing and spending reversed this, putting the private sector in the

red. Moreover, households have done much less than firms to improve their debt-to-savings ratio. "Special Report: World Economy," June 28, 2003, 27.

7. The theme of how architecture has played a role in economic expansion, or how form follows economic power, has been developed by several authors; for example, see Stuart Ewen, *All Consuming Images: The Politics of Style in Contemporary Culture* (San Francisco: HarperCollins, 1988), 221, 226–230. Ewen comments that "[t]he overwhelming scale of modernist monumentalism was coming under more general attack as a conspicuous symbol of predatory economic power, and of an increasingly dehumanized physical environment." He also profiles the rise of suburban developments from Levittown.

8. James Robertson and Thomas H. Greco Jr. offer interesting perspectives on the creation of new money and how currently the benefits from it accrue to private banks and investors. Robertson, *The New Economics of Sustainable Development: A Briefing for Policy Makers* (Luxembourg: Office of Official Publications of the European Communities; London: Kogan Page, 1999), 102; and Greco, *Money: Understanding and Creating Alternatives to Legal Tender* (White River Junction, VT: Chelsea Green, 2001), 8–9.

9. Richard Layard, *Happiness: Lessons from a New Science* (London: Allen Lane, 2005), ix.

10. Clifford Cobb, Ted Halstead, and Jonathan Rowe provide a detailed look at the weaknesses of the GDP measure in "If the GDP Is Up, Why Is America Down?" *Atlantic Monthly*, October 1995, (26) 4:59–78.

11. Clifford Cobb, Mark Glickman, and Craig Cheslog, *The Genuine Progress Indicator 2000 Update* (Oakland, CA: Redefining Progress, 2001). For examples of other alternative measures of well-being, including the British "Measure of Domestic Progress" produced by the New Economics Foundation and the Index of Sustainable Economic Welfare (ISEW), see UK Sustainable Development Commission, *Progress: Sustainable Development Commission Critique 2004* (London: Sustainable Development Commission.), 6–9.

12. Cobb, Glickman, and Cheslog, *The Genuine Progress Indicator 2000 Update*, 3, table 1.

13. Cobb, Halstead, and Rowe "If the GDP is Up, Why is America Down?"

14. A number of authors have explained the phenomenon of "unpriced goods." For example, see David Burningham and John Davies, *Green Economics*, 2nd ed. (Oxford: Heinemann, 1995), 18–20; and R. Kerry Turner, David Pearce, and Ian Bateman, *Environmental Economics: An Elementary Introduction* (Harlow, UK: Financial Times, Prentice Hall, 1994), 72–78.

15. Paul Hawken, Amory Lovins, and L. Hunter Lovins, *Natural Capitalism* (London: Earthscan, 1999), 5.

16. Burningham and Davies document the use of pollution permit trading in the United States in *Green Economics*, 90–91.

17. John M. Gowdy notes that "extreme bids," such as an infinitely high price or a price of zero, can constitute as much as 25% of responses when people are asked to put theoretical money values on things such as nature. These people may place an absolute value on preserving the environment and so won't accept the idea of trading it for any amount of money. He notes that these extreme bids are often excluded from the economic analysis, and in this way the opinions of a significant number of "bidders" are ignored in favor of a more "conservative" choice. Gowdy notes the trend away from surveys that might result in "unrealistically high answers" and toward surveys that offer a limited range of values to choose from. But overall, he suggests, there has never been any serious assessment or justification of what constitutes "unrealistically high" answers or why a conservative choice is better than an extreme one. In "The Revolution in Welfare Economics and its Implications for Environmental Valuation and Policy," Department of Economics, Rensselaer Polytechnic Institute, Troy, NY, 14–15.

18. Burningham and Davies present government regulatory approaches in Chapter 7, "Environmental Improvement in Theory: Government Action," in *Green Economics*; Turner, Pearce, and Bateman profile a range of government actions in Part IV, "Economic Control of the Environment" in *Environmental Economics;* Tim Jackson provides an accessible overview of regulatory approaches in *Material Concerns: Pollution, Profit and Quality of Life* (London: Routledge, 1996), 148–158.

19. Several authors develop the notion that corporate influence weakens government regulation. For example, see United Nations Development Programme, *Human Development Report 2002: Deepening Democracy in a Fragmented World* (Oxford: Oxford University Press, 2002), 68, box 3.3; and John De Graaf, David Wann, and Thomas H. Naylor *Affluenza: The All-Consuming Epidemic* (San Francisco: Berrett-Koehler, 2001), chap. 20.

20. For example, energy labels are profiled in Helen Lewis and John Gertsakis et al., *Design + Environment: A Global Guide to Designing Greener Goods* (Sheffield, UK: Greenleaf, 2001), 170–171.

21. U.S. Green Building Council, *LEED (Leadership in Energy and Environmental Design) Green Building Rating System for New Construction and Major Renovations (LEED-NC)*, Version 2.1, November 2002.

22. International Standards Organization, "ISO and the Environment," in *Environmental Management: The ISO 14000 Family of International Standards* (Geneva: International Standards Organization, 2000).

23. James Robertson discusses the ecorent concept in *The New Economics of Sustainable Development*, 137–139.

24. Lewis and Gertsakis profile a range of legislation and policies for "extended product responsibility" and "product stewardship," in *Design + Environment,* 22–27.

25. For a brief overview of tax and subsidies, see Paul Hawken, Amory Lovins, and L. Hunter Lovins, *Natural Capitalism* (London: Earthscan,1999), 159–169.

26. William McDonough also talks about regulation as being simply a government-issued license to kill because it allows the use of many dangerous chemicals. Interview with William McDonough, "How to Dematerialize" in *On the Ground: The Multimedia Journal on Community, Design and Environment*, 2, no. 1 (1997).

27. Turner, Pearce, and Bateman provide a general discussion of discounting in *Environmental Economics*, 97–107.

28. Burningham and Davies review the problem of discounting nature and culture, in *Green Economics*, 73–74.

29. Greco *Money*, 165–171.

30. Burningham and Davies review rationale for low or even negative discount rates in *Green Economics*, 1999, 73–74.

31. Kelly, *The Divine Right of Capital,* 29–32.

32. Simon Dresner, *The Principles of Sustainability* (London: Earthscan, 2002), 10–11.

33. Many authors have provided useful histories of the development of Western economics and the roles of Smith and Marx, among others. See, for example, Jackson, *Material Concerns*; Lutz and Lux, *Humanistic Economics*; and Korten, *The Post-Corporate World.*

34. Gates, *Democracy at Risk*, 83–84, 123–126.

35. United Nations Development Programme, *Human Development Report 2002*, 19.

36. Gates, *Democracy at Risk*, 34.

37. Korten, *The Post-Corporate World*, 143, 158; and Kelly, *The Divine Right of Capital*, 85.

38. Gates, *Democracy at Risk*, 43–46.

39. Ibid., 2000, xxxvii, xxxviii.

40. Ibid., 97–100.

41. Gates notes that "[o]n the Forbes 400 list for 1999 are 149 people who inherited some or all of their wealth (average net worth: $2.5 billion)." Gates, *Democracy at Risk*, 112. See also Kelly, *The Divine Right of Capital*, 170–171.

42. Gates also provides an accessible explanation of depreciation from which this example is fashioned in *Democracy at Risk*, 100–102.

43. Gates, *Democracy at Risk*, 101.

44. Robertson, *The New Economics of Sustainable Development*, 92–93.

45. Robertson discusses how interest payments work to transfer wealth from the poor to the rich in *The New Economics of Sustainable Development*, 93. Greco provides numbers from a German study on how the costs and benefits of interest are distributed in *Money*, 12.

46. Greco provides this quotation but many authors develop the theme of the economy and markets as human creations that can, and probably should, be substantially reorganized. In *Money*, 3.

47. Robertson points out that no one has ever been in charge of making sure the market works fairly and efficiently for all its users in *The New Economics of Sustainable Development*, 98–99; Gates suggests that none of us would choose a system like the one we have now in Gates, *Democracy at Risk*. xxxviii

48. Maxine J. Horn and Jeremy Myerson, *The British Design Industry Survey* (London: Design Council, 2002).

49. Although I've seen no integrated statistics on how much design work is controlled, globally, by large corporations, one can look to individual countries; for example, in the United Kingdom, see Design Council, *Facts and Figures on Design in Britain 2002–2003* (London: Design Council, 2002). The chapter on business shows that roughly 90% of larger businesses (250 employees or more) are making use of design, while roughly 37% of smaller businesses (0–19 employees) are making use of design. In addition, 55% of large businesses have their own design department and 22% employ internal designers or bring in consultants on an ad hoc basis.

50. Korten estimates that fifty-one of the world's largest economies are corporations rather than countries and that three hundred companies control 25% of the world's productive assets. *The Post-Corporate World*, 61, 167. Jerry Mander provides a related estimate in "Net Loss," in *Take It Personally: How Globalization Affects You and Powerful Ways to Challenge It*, ed. Anita Roddick (London: Thorsons, 2001), 40–41. Mander states that "200 corporations now control 28% of global economic activity."

51. Both Korten and Kelly provide good insights into and critiques of corporate structure: Korten, *The Post-Corporate World*, 183–184; and Kelly, *The Divine Right of Capital*, part 1. Lutz and Lux discuss the concept of corporations having the rights of an individual in *Humanistic Economics*, 214–215.

52. Kelly comments on the primacy of stockholders, distribution of wealth from shares, and the liquidity function of the market in *The Divine Right of Capital*, 4–5.

53. Gates provides an overview of the wage gap, its health effects, and the extreme example of Disney in *Democracy at Risk*, 18–21. Kelly also examines the pay pressure on CEOs in *The Divine Right of Capital*, 54–58.

54. Julia Finch and Jill Treanor, "Shares Down 24%, Average Earnings up 3%, Boardroom Pay up 23%," *The Guardian* (London), January 31, 2003, 1.

55. Kelly examines the concept of privilege tied exclusively to ownership (as opposed to productive work or other democratic principles of equality) in *The Divine Right of Capital*, 41–50.

56. Ibid., 48.

57. For a description of the phenomenon of electronic "day traders" in stocks, see James Gleick, *Faster: The Acceleration of Just about Everything* (London: Little, Brown, 1999), 72–74. Kelly also examines the compensation, productivity, and balance sheet treatment of employees in *The Divine Right of Capital*, 21–24.

58. See http://www.patagonia.com/enviro/one_percent.shtml (accessed November 1, 2003); and http://www.onepercentfortheplanet.org/members.html (accessed November 1, 2003).

59. Lewis and Gertsakis profile a range of demonstration projects, as well as university partnerships with companies and designers in *Design + Environment*, 20–22.

60. For a range of tools for managing the business supply chain for sustainability objectives, along with case studies, see, for example, Martin Charter, Aleksandra Kielkiewicz-Young, Alex Young, and Andrew Hughes, *Supply Chain Strategy and Evaluation First Report*, The Sigma Project R&D Report (London: British Standards Institute 2001).

61. For an exploration of the role of public policy with respect to corporations, see Lutz and Lux, *Humanistic Economics*, 202–221; and Robertson, *The New Economics of Sustainable Development*, 62–63.

62. United Nations Development Programme, *Human Development Report 2002*, 68.

63. Gates discusses maximum wages in *Democracy at Risk*, 115.

64. For a wide-ranging discussion of ownerization techniques, see Gates, *Democracy at Work*, 120–143. For a more theoretical discussion about why ownerization is democratically and ethically preferred, see Lutz and Lux, *Humanistic Economics*, 153–177.

65. Robertson documents the fragmentation of public policy, noting that "most government policy makers have traditionally been expected to keep within their own departmental boundaries—to specialize in their own subject and respect one another's 'turf.' Inter-departmental co-ordination has generally had the limited aim of achieving acceptable trade-offs between conflicting departmental policies developed separately." In *The New Economics of Sustainable Development*, 4.

66. Carol Valenta, "Cycles of Water: Stormwater Treatment and Wetland Enhancement," and Joe Castiglione, "Fusion: Merging Art and Engineering in Arizona and North Dakota" in *On the Ground: The Multimedia Journal on Community, Design and Environment*, 1, no. 4 (1995).

67. The United Nations Development Programme notes that "[t]hough membership has fallen in political parties, trade unions and other traditional vehicles for collective action, there has been an explosion in support for non-governmental organizations (NGOs) and other new civil groups." From 1941 to 2000, the number of international NGOs went from 1,083 to more than 37,000. Nearly 20% of these new NGOs were formed in the 1990s. In *Deepening Democracy in a Fragmented World*, 5.

68. www.5ways.info

69. Mander, "Net Loss," in *Take It Personally*, 2001, 70.

70. Dresner, *The Principles of Sustainability*, 169.

71. Morris in "This Isn't Your Father's Free Trade" from *Take It Personally*, 70, 224–227.

72. Third World Network, *The Multilateral Trading System: A Development Perspective*, ed. Martin Khor (New York: United Nations Development Programme, 2001), 5, 20, 23–24.

73. Third World Network, *The Multilateral Trading System*, 23.

74. For comments on the downward pressure on wages see, for example, Robertson, *New Economics of Sustainable Development*, 1999, 100; and Gates, *Democracy at Risk*, 123–124.

75. This fascinating analysis, along with the ethnic imbalance in the concentration of wealth, is well developed in Amy Chua's *World on Fire: How Exporting Free-Market Democracy Breeds Ethnic Hatred and Global Instability* (London: William Heinemann, 2003).

76. For some analysis of the movement concerned about globalization and the 1999 Seattle WTO meeting, see Paul Hawken, "Seattle" (22–29) and Naomi Klein "Welcome to the Net Generation" (32–38) in *Take It Personally*.

77. Examples of microlending are found in Korten, *The Post-Corporate World*, 178–180. A good microloan definition is found in Robertson, *The New Economics of Sustainable Development*, 108.

78. This discussion is based on a very useful and thorough review of money and alternatives to legal tender in Greco, *Money*, 2001.

79. This chapter is adapted largely from John Perry Barlow's article "Selling Wine Without Bottles: The Economy of Mind on the Global Net," New York, New York, December 13–14, 1993.

PART 4 ENDNOTES

1. Frances Westley et al. develop the discussion of human and natural systems in "Why Systems of People and Nature Are Not Just Social and Ecological Systems," in *Panarchy: Understanding Transformations in Human and Natural Systems*, ed. Lance H. Gunderson and C. S. Holling (Washington, DC: Island Press, 2002), 103–119.

2. Tim Jackson, Wander Jager, and Sigrid Stagl provide a good overview of needs theory within the context of consumerism in *Beyond Insatiability: Needs Theory, Consumption and Sustainability*, Working Paper No. 2004/2 (Swindon,

UK: Economic and Social Research Council, Sustainable Technologies Programme, January 2004), 6–16.

3. Jackson, Jager, and Stagl cite Max Neef for the human needs typology that is extended to include the dimensions of being, doing, having, and interacting in *Beyond insstability*, 9.

4. Ibid., *Beyond Insatiability*, 125.

5. Tim Kasser develops the idea that "people who strongly value the pursuit of material wealth and possessions report lower psychological well-being than those who are less concerned with such aims" in *The High Price of Materialism* (Boston: MIT Press, 2002), 5–22.

6. Ibid., 7.

7. John McNeill charts our unusual century well in chapter 1 "Prologue: Peculiarities of a Prodigal Century" from *Something New Under the Sun: An Environmental History of the Twentieth Century* (London: Penguin Books, 2000) 3–17.

8. Mike Ashby and Kara Johnson chart how metals dominated as the engineering materials of choice after they were discovered around 1000 BCE until about the 1960s, when polymers and composites have taken the lead. In *Materials and Design: The Art and Science of Material Selection in Product Design* (Oxford: Butterworth-Heinemann, 2002), 176–177.

9. Stewart Brand, *The Clock of the Long Now: Time and Responsibility* (London: Weidenfeld and Nicolson, 1999).

10. Steve Gorelick, *Tipping the Scale: Systemic Support for the Large and Global* (Devon, UK: International Society for Ecology and Culture, n.d.), 1 (originally published in *The Ecologist*, May/June 1999).

11. Jared Diamond charts the history of writing, and why it "appeared so late in human evolution" (236) in *Guns, Germs and Steel: the Fates of Human Societies* (London: W. W. Norton & Company, 1999) 233–236; and Witold Rybczynski charts the development of writing and literacy in terms of their influence on furniture and architecture in *Home: A Short History of an Idea* (New York: Viking, 1986) 15–19, 39, 123–124. Particulars of the history of written forms (scrolls, codices), writing surfaces (papyrus, vellum, parchment, paper), writing instruments (reed pens, quill pens, ballpoint pens) are drawn from Wikipedia, the free encyclopedia. www.wikipedia.org (accessed July 10, 2006).

12. This description of home furnishings from the Middle Ages is adapted from Rybczynski, *Home*, 24–28, and John Gloag, *A Social History of Furniture Design: From B.C. 1300 to A.D. 1960* (London: Cassell, 1966), 75–85.

13. Rybczynski comments on the gradual separation of houses into rooms with specific functions, heating, and the role of women in *Home*, 88, 91–95. Gloag comments on when and how fashion came to furniture in *A Social History of Furniture Design*, 97.

14. Robert A. Papper, Michael E. Holmes, Ph.D., and Mark N. Popovich, Ph.D. "Middletown Media Studies: Media Multitasking…and How Much People Really Use the Media" in *The International Digital Media and Arts Association Journal,* 1, no. 1 (2004) 5–61. "Eleven hours" refers to selected media including: reading (books, magazines, newspapers), computer (online, e-mail), radio listening, and televisions viewing. It excludes some items such as telephone, video games, and postal mail.

15. Stuart Ewen outlines photography's "affinity to reality and fantasy" and the resulting alienation in *All Consuming Images: The Politics of Style in Contemporary Culture* (New York: Basic Books, HarperCollins, 1988), 90–91.

16. Richard Layard makes the point that "[t]elevision creates discontent by bombarding us with images of body shapes, riches and goods we do not have. It does this both in TV drama and advertisements." *Happiness: Has Social Science a Clue?* Lionel Robbins Memorial Lectures 2002–3 (London: London School of Economics, Centre for Economic Performance, April 2001). See also statistics on types and ages of actors in Screen Actors Guild, *Casting Data* (Hollywood: Screen Actors Guild, 2002).

17. Kasser, *The High Price of Materialism*, 53–57.

18. Ibid., 104.

19. Joseph Campbell, *The Hero with a Thousand Faces* (London: Fontana Press, 1949), 10–11.

20. Mary Douglas and Baron Isherwood, cited in Tim Jackson, Wander Jager, and Sigrid Sagel, *Beyond Instability*, 22. Douglas explores the loss of a publicly recognized structure of symbols, particularly in terms of religion, and how this diminishes "self-knowledge" for the individual in society, in *Natural Symbols* (London: Routledge, 1996), 124–125.

21. Ibid. See also Anthony Giddens, *Modernity and Self-Identity: Self and Society in the Late Modern Age* (Cambridge, UK: Polity Press, 1991), 18–32.

22. Tim Kasser summarizes these arguments before going on to develop a chapter for each of the four main ways that materialistic values harm well-being. Kasser, *The High Price of Materialism*, 28.

23. Robin Cohen and Paul Kennedy, *Global Sociology* (London: Macmillan Press, 2000), 233–234.

24. Ibid., 239.

25. Nigel Whitely provides a good overview of this position in *Design for Society* (London: Reaktion Books, 1993), 30–32.

26. Media Education Foundation, *Advertising: Exposure and Industry Statistics* (Northampton, MA: Media Education, Foundation, n.d.).

27. *Business Week* cited in Michael Jacobson and Laurie Ann Mazur, *Marketing Madness* (Boulder, CO: Westview Press, 1995), 13, 15. Jacobson and Mazur also cite the statistic for growth in advertising spending from 1935 to 1994 and describe throughout their book the pervasive and intrusive advertising techniques.

28. U.S. Census Bureau, Table 937, "Advertising—Estimated Expenditures, Through Medium: 1990 to 1999," from *Statistical Abstract of the United States: 2000.* (Washington, D.C.: U.S. Census Bureau) 2000.

29. The United Nations Development Programme notes that "[f]our private media groups own 85% of UK daily newspapers, accounting for two-thirds of circulation. And in the United States, six companies control most of the media." In *Human Development Report 2002: Deepening Democracy in a Fragmented World* (Oxford: Oxford University Press, 2002), 6.

30. Whitely notes that "[w]hat we might object to is not that consumer-led design is immoral because it caters for desires rather than just needs, but the extent to which a value system attuned to desires has become a predominant cultural and social norm with values that are very largely implicit rather than explicit." Whitely, *Design for Society*, 31.

31. Borgmann notes that fewer skills are needed and thus people are less engaged by the material environment, because of engineering design that "disburdens" the user by hiding technologies that "do the work" and then putting the focus on the style of the outside package (aesthetic design). The overall movement he claims is a move from user engagement to user disburdenment. In "The Depth of Design" in *Discovering Design: Explorations in*

Design Studies, ed. Richard Buchanan and Victor Margolin (Chicago: University of Chicago Press, 1995), 15. Giddens also notes the fact that many aspects of daily life are "de-skilled" in *Modernity and Self-Identity*, 22.

32. John De Graaf, David Wann, and Thomas H. Naylor compare the notions of consumer and citizen, the knowledge of plant types versus corporate logos, and private versus public investment in *Affluenza: The All-Consuming Epidemic* (San Francisco: Berrett-Koehler, 2001), 61–63, 66, 150.

33. Jacobson and Mazur, *Marketing Madness,* 201–206.

34. Examples of participatory design techniques can be found throughout Evans, Burns, and Barrett, *The Empathic Design Tutor* (Milton Keynes, UK: Cranfield University, 2002); and Hugh Aldersey-Williams, John Bound, and Roger Coleman,eds., *The Methods Lab: User Research for Design* (London: Design for Ageing Network, 1999).

35. Albert Borgmann, "The Depth of Design," 18.

36. Campbell, *The Hero with a Thousand Faces*, 10–11.

37. Anne Bikle, Cedar River Basin steward for King County, Washington, conversation with author, February 28, 2005.

38. Renny Ramakers, *Less + More: Droog Design in Context* (Rotterdam: 010 Publishers, 2002), 188.

39. Peter Paul Verbeek and Petran Kockelkoren, "Matter Matters" in *Eternally Yours: Visions on Product Endurance*, ed. Liesbeth Bonekamp, Henk Muis, Ed van Hinte, and Arnoud Odding (Rotterdam: 010 Publishers, 1997), 104.

40. Leonard Koren is cited for this observation in Paul Thursfield, Monica Bueno and John Cass in "Flow: The Emergence of Richness from Simplicity" from *The New Everyday: Views on Ambient Intelligence*, eds. Emile Aarts and Stefano Marzano (Rotterdam: 010 Publishers, undated), 133.

41. Gianfranco Zaccai, "Art and Technology: Aesthetics Redefined," in *Discovering Design: Explorations in Design Studies*, ed. Richard Buchanan and Victor Margolin (Chicago: University of Chicago Press,1995), 10–12.

42. Martin Bontoft and Graham Pullin, "What Is an Inclusive Design Process?" in *Inclusive Design: Design for the Whole Population*, ed. John Clarkson, Roger Coleman, Simeon Keates, and Cherie Lebbon (London: Springer-Verlag, 2003), 520–531.

43. Ed Van Hinte's screenless computer game is noted in Ramakers, *Less + More*, 188.

44. Stewart Brand comments on the idea of using cooked and raw spaces to help meet the shortage of affordable starter homes in *How Buildings Learn* (New York: Penguin Books, 1994), 201.

45. Jonathan Bell, "Ruins, Recycling, Smart Buildings, and the Endlessly Transformable Environment," in *Strangely Familiar: Design and Everyday Life*, ed. Andrew Blauvelt (Madison, WI: Walker Art Center, 2003), 75–76.

46. The concepts of customization are becoming more popular; examples for architecture are covered in Ramakers, *Less + More*, 114. For products, see John Thackara, *Winners! How Today's Successful Companies Innovate by Design* (Aldershot, UK: Gower, 1997), 79–127.

47. Thursfield, Bueno, and Cass, "Flow: The Emergence of Richness from Simplicity,"in *The New Everyday*, 132–137.

48. The idea of people participating to the level of their "optimal challenge zones" is from Eric Raymond, *The Cathedral and the Bazaar: Musings on Linux and Open Source by an Accidental Revolutionary* (Sebastapol, CA: O'Reilly, 2001), 61.

49. Thursfield, Bueno, and Cass, "Flow."

50. Ramakers, *Less + More*, 75.

51. Raymond, *The Cathedral and the Bazaar*, 29–31.

52. David Reinfurt, "I Was Thinking the Other Day about One Possible Scenario for a Collective Future: The Open Source Software Movement," in *Citizen Designer: Perspectives on Design Responsibility*, ed. Steven Heller and Veronique Vienne (New York: Allworth Press, 2003), 165–174.

53. Whitely, *Design for Society*, 42–43. Raymond in *The Cathedral and the Bazaar* highlights recognizing brilliant ideas of others, 47.

54. Dormer, *Meaning of Modern Design* (London: Thames and Hudson, 1990), 14–15, 30–31.

55. A discussion of design versus craft is found in Dormer, *Design Since 1945*, 7–10.

56. John Heskett, *Toothpicks and Logos: Design in Everyday Life* (Oxford: Oxford University Press, 2002), 60–70.

57. For an outline of the effect of Moore's law, the frequency with which the number of components on a computer chip doubles, see Stewart Brand, *The Clock of the Long Now: Time and Responsibility* (London: Weidenfeld and Nicolson, 1999), 12–17, 30.

58. James Gleick develops the idea of our perpetual crisis in *Faster: The Acceleration of Just about Everything* (London: Little, Brown, 1999), 170. Jay Griffiths develops the notion that global media are best served by short fragments of information in *Pip Pip: A Sideways Look at Time* (London: HarperCollins, 1999), 16.

59. Gleick develops the idea of diplomatic pause for thought, instant public opinion, "sound bite" culture, and short-term nature of investing in *Faster*, 97; 98, 74.

60. Jack Hitt, "Say No More," *New York Times*, Feburary 29, 2004.

61. Griffiths proposes, based on the loss of languages and culture, that the sum of human knowledge may be decreasing in *Pip Pip*, 200, 222. Brand proposes a "size" for civilization thus far as ten thousand years in *The Clock of the Long Now*, 30.

62. Griffiths, *Pip Pip*, 200, 222.

63. Brand, discusses the "convergence" in *The Clock of the Long Now*, 20–22."

64. Griffiths develops the idea of fast and slow knowledge in *Pip Pip*, 36-37.

65. Stewart Brand presents the diagram for the order of civilization in *The Clock of the Long Now*, 34–39.

66. Ibid.

67. Anna Muoio, "We All Go to the Same Place: Let Us Go There Slowly," *Fast Company*, issue 34 (May 2000): 194.

68. Gleick notes that, "Some of biology is essentially a pause: sleep, for example. Pauses serve a purpose, breaking the flow." in *Faster*, 105.

69. For discussions on the concept of finesse as a weapon against speed, see Brand, *The Clock of the Long Now*, 22; and Gleick, *Faster*, 82.

70. Brand quotes architect Chris Alexander as saying, "A building's foundation and frame should be capable of living 300 years" in *How Buildings Learn* (New York: Penguin Books, 1994), 194.

71. Physicist Freeman Dyson is quoted in Brand as saying that human beings are the product of adaptation to all six of these time scales. Brand, *The Clock of the Long Now*, 35.

72. Winona LaDuke notes that the Native American Iroquois Confederacy had the maxim "In our every deliberation, we must consider the impact of our decisions on the next seven generations." LaDuke, "Next Independence Day, Look Ahead," *Earth Island Journal* 13, no. 2 (Spring 1998).

73. Brand attributes the "infinite" quotation to Zen Buddhists in *The Clock of the Long Now*, 9. He further explains that although the "infinite" quote is not widely standard to Zen Buddhists, it does have a good provenance among some Zen Buddhists. Brand, personal communication with author, December 6, 2004.

74. Brand, *The Clock of the Long Now*, 8–9.

75. Jeff Gates, *Democracy at Risk: Rescuing Main Street from Wall Street* (Cambridge, MA: Perseus, 2000), 27.

76. Bell says, "Such architecture neatly addresses the dominant paradox of our era—that consumers expect things to be simultaneously new and capable of remembering. In product design, this has given rise to retro styling, fast becoming the prevalent mode of expression as designers and producers seek to revive elements of iconic products for a new market segment." In "Ruins, Recycling, Smart Buildings, and the Endlessly Transformable Environment," in *Strangely Familiar*, 84–85.

77. Brand, *How Buildings Learn*, 215.

78. Liesbeth Bonekamp, Henk Muis, Ed van Hinte, and Arnoud Odding, eds., *Eternally Yours*, 129–131, 157–159.

79. Brand documents the usefulness of being able to see underneath a building's skin in *How Buildings Learn*, 196–200.

80. Richard Wray, "From Kids' Stuff to Boys' Toys," interview with Torben Sorensen, president and chief executive of Bang and Olufsen, *The Guardian* (London) September 25, 2004. In the interview Sorensen notes that one B&O television has been on the market for eighteen years. In addition, one of the company's stereo systems launched in the 1980s is still compatible with the company's newest speakers. The same philosophy pervades Lego, where Sorenson also worked: Lego bricks from forty years ago still fit onto the newest Lego products.

81. Brand, *How Buildings Learn*, 178–189. My description of scenario planning is adapted from Brand's excellent section on its application to architecture.

82. Richard Parkinson, *Egyptian Hieroglyphs* (London: British Museum, 2003), 9.

83. Rosetta Disk information adapted from http://www.long now.org.

84. "Design for our Future Selves" is a project of the Helen Hamlyn Research Centre at the Royal College of Art in London. It is a design competition that addresses the needs and aspirations of older people.

85. Theodore Rozak, "Where Psyche Meets Gaia," in *Ecopsychology: Restoring the Earth, Healing the Mind* (San Francisco: Sierra Club Books, 1995), 14–17.

86. Joanna Macy and Molly Young Brown, *Coming Back to Life* (Gabriola Island, BC: New Society, 1998), 25–38.

87. Chellis Glendinning develops the idea of unhealthy techonological addiction in "Technology, Trauma and the Wild," (42–54) and Ralph Metzner explains the notion of the removal of rights of passage in "The Psychopathology of the Human-Nature Relationship" (55–67) in *Ecopsychology: Restoring the Earth, Healing the Mind,* eds. Theodore Roszak, Mary E. Gomes, and Allen D. Kanner (San Francisco: Sierra Club Books, 1995). Metzner writes, "The notion of a species-wide fixation at the stage of early adolescence fits with the kind of boisterous, arrogant pursuit of individual self-assertion that characterizes the consumerist, exploitative model of economic growth, where the short-term profit of entrepreneurs and corporate shareholders seems to be not only the dominant value, but the only value under consideration." Tim Jackson also highlights our modern disconnection from nature and our inability to survive in the natural world in *Material Concerns: Pollution, Profit and Quality of Life* (London: Routledge, 1996), 35.

88. Anita Barrows, "The Ecopsychology of Child Development," in *Ecopsychology*, 102.

89. Macy and Young Brown, *Coming Back to Life*, 25–38. The authors present a detailed discussion of epressed feeling about the destruction of nature. For an in-depth discussion of the personal, spiritual side of their approach, see chapters 3 and 4.

90. This quiz is an adaption of "Where You At — A Bioregional Quiz" by Leonard Charles, Jim Dodge, Lynn Milliman, and Victoria Stockley, first published in the Winter 1981 issue of *Coevolution Quarterly* and subsequently reprinted in *Home! A Bioregional Reader* (Gabriola Island, British Columbia: New Society Publishers, 1990), 29.

PART 5 ENDNOTES

1. Deborah Gordon first proposed technology, policy, and behavior as three areas for change in "Diversifying Transportation," *On the Ground* 1, no. 3 (1995). J. C. Brezet, A. S. Bijma, J. Ehrenfeld, and S. Silvester propose a somewhat similar framework in *The Design of Eco-Efficient Services: Method, Tools and Review of the Case Study Based*

'Designing Eco-efficient Services' Project (Delft, the Netherlands: Delft University of Technology, Design for Sustainability Program, June, 2001), 27–28. They describe a triangle in which the three points relate to "user practice" (which corresponds to "behavior"), "device" (which corresponds to "technology"), and infrastructure, both physical and institutional (which corresponds somewhat to "policy").

2. For the discussion of codes of ethics and codes of practice, I requested and reviewed a number of codes of ethics from a range of designers' professional organizations. I requested but never received codes from the United Kingdom's Chartered Society of Designers and Fashion Designers of America. Reviewed codes included those from Industrial Designers' Society of America (IDSA), American Institute of Architects (AIA), Royal Institute of British Architects (RIBA), American Institute of Graphic Arts (AIGA), American Interior Designers Association (AIDA), and International Council of Societies of Industrial Design. The British Interior Designers' Association (BIDA) appeared not to have a code of ethics/practice at the time of this research.

3. Peter Dormer, The Meanings of Modern Design (London: Thames and Hudson, 1990), 22.

4. American Institute of Architects, "Canon I: General Obligations," in 1997 Code of Ethics and Professional Conduct (Washington, DC: AIA Office of the General Counsel, 1997).

5. American Institute of Architects, "Canon II: Obligations to the Public, Ethical Standard 2.2 and 2.3," in 1997 Code of Ethics and Professional Conduct.

6. "First Things First Manifesto," Émigré Magazine, issue 51 (Summer 1999).

7. I first heard a useful discussion of the problem of being cast as either a saint or a doomsday prophet from Karl-Henrik Robèrt, founder of The Natural Step (TNS), at a TNS conference in Portland, Oregon, in 1999.

8. Carolyn Merchant, The Death of Nature: Women, Ecology, and the Scientific Revolution (San Francisco: Harper, 1990).

9. Frances Westley et al. explore the notion of human systems as social productions in "Why Systems of People and Nature Are Not Just Social and Ecological Systems" in Panarchy: Understanding Transformations in Human and Natural Systems (Washington, DC: Island Press, 2002), 110–113.

ILLUSTRATIONS: CREDITS AND SOURCES

Photographers with multiple contributions: Finn Brandt, Andy Crawford, and Ann Thorpe

About Island Press Mies van der Rohe Barcelona Chair, iStockphoto.

Contents Toaster, Crawford. • Flags, Jean Schweitzer/iStockphoto. • Paper cup, Crawford.

Acknowledgements Button, Thorpe.

PART 1: INTRODUCTION

Pages 4/5 Crawford.

Pages 8/9 Development gap charts: Harvesting natural resources, United Nations Development Programme et. al., *A Guide to World Resources 2000-2001: People and Ecosystems, The Fraying Web of Life* (Washington DC: World Resources Institute, 2000), 4; Poverty, The United Nations Development Programme, *Human Development Report 2002: Deepening Democracy in a Fragmented World* (Oxford: Oxford University Press, 2002), 17–18; HIV/AIDS, Ibid., 27; Internet, The United Nations Development Programme. *Human Development Report 2004: Cultural Liberty in Today's Diverse World* (New York: UNDP, 2004), from table 12, "Technology: diffusion and creation," 180; Water, UN State of the Environment and Policy Retrospective: 1972–2002, 150–152; Adult literacy, The United Nations Development Programme *Human Development Report 2002*, 22; Income gap, Jeff Gates, citing the UN's 1999 Human Development Report in *Democracy at Risk* (Cambridge, MA: Perseus Publishing, 2000), 32.

Pages 10/11 St. Pancreas Building clock tower London, Thorpe. • Mies van der Rohe Barcelona Chair, iStockphoto. • Anna Corkscrew courtesy of Alessi.

Pages 12/13 Shiny, Crawford. • Rough, Thorpe.

Pages 14/15 Crawford.

Pages 16/17 Blender and bottles, Crawford. • Button and house, Thorpe.

Pages 18/19 Crawford.

Pages 20/21 iStockphoto.

PART 2: ECOLOGY

Pages 22/23 Living systems graphs, from figures 3–5 in *Living Planet Report 2004*, Jonathan Loh and Mathis Wackernagel, eds. (Gland, Switzerland: World Wildlife Fund for Nature, 2004), 2. • Graph background images left to right: Brandt, Dan Schmitt/iStockphoto, Thorpe. • Toaster, Crawford.

Pages 24/25 Carbon cycle: Clouds, smokestack, rock, Thorpe; Oceans, Brandt; Clearcut, Ron Smith/iStockphoto; Leaves, seedlings, soil, log section, PhotoDisc.

Pages 26/27 Ecosphere: Air, biosphere, rock, Thorpe; Ocean, Brandt. • Put in/take out: Earphones, rice paper, chemicals, Crawford; Flame, washing, smokestack, Thorpe; Landfill, Joy Fera/iStockphoto; Radioactive, Thomas Reekie/iStockphoto.

Pages 28/29 Materials chart, from Tim Jackson, *Material Concerns: Pollution, Profit and Quality of Life.* (London: Routledge, 1996), 29. • Refinery, iStockphoto. • Wheat, Bryn Donaldson/iStockphoto. • Planet earth, NASA Visible Earth, http://visibleearth.nasa.gov. • Ecological footprint chart, from Table 2 Ecological Footprint and Biocapacity *Living Planet Report 2004*, 24-31.

Pages 30/31 Catalogs, Crawford. • *All other images as previously cited.*

Pages 32/33 Crawford.

Pages 34/35 Thorpe.

Pages 36/37 Crawford.

Pages 38/39 Sketch, Thye Aun Ngo/iStockphoto. • Mining, Michael Fuller/iStockphoto. • All others, Crawford.

Pages 40/41 World map, iStockphoto. • Sewing, Martha Bayona/iStockphoto. • All others, Crawford.

Pages 42/43 Crawford

Pages 44/45 Organic material cycle: Shearing, Brandt; Yarn, Crawford; Carpet, Thorpe; Soil, PhotoDisc. • Nutrients table: Wood/leather, Crawford; All others, Thorpe.

Pages 46/47 Shark, Ian Scott/iStockphoto. • Shark skin, courtesy of Electron Microscope Unit, University of Cape Town. • Burr plant, Eyecrave/iStockphoto. • Burr on fabric and Velcro, Crawford. • Biome map, Thomas Portlock, based on plate 4 of "World Vegetation" from *Times Atlas of the World*, Seventh Edition (New York: John Bartholomew & Sons and Times Books, 1985).

Pages 48/49 Tree frog, Michael Sacco, iStockphoto. • Diagram phases of the ecosystem cycle, from figure 2-1 in *Panarchy*, Lance H. Gunderson and C.S. Holling, eds. (Washington, D.C.: Island Press, 2002). Reproduced with permission.

Pages 50/51 Ecosystem size/time diagram, from figure 3-9 in *Panarchy* Reproduced with permission. • Pinecones, PhotoDisc objects of nature. • Forest, Brandt.

Pages 52/53 Ecosystem diagram from figure 3-10 in *Panarchy* Reproduced with permission.

Pages 56/57 Iron, Crawford. • *All other images as previously cited*.

PART 3: ECONOMY

Pages 58/59 "Success," Mark Aplet/iStockphoto. • 100s, Allen Johnson/iStockphoto.

Pages 62/63 Tailfin, Patricia Marroquin/iStockphoto. • Skyline, Brandt.

Pages 64/65 American flag, Christine Balderas/iStockphoto. • Genuine Progress Indicator, courtesy of Redefining Progress © 2006. Reprinted by permission.

Pages 66/67 Fabric, Crawford. • Boy, Thorpe. • Mountain, Brandt.

Pages 68/69 Green Dot and PE-LD, Crawford. • FSC logo, courtesy of the Forest Stewardship Council. • Seattle public library: completed in 2004 and designed by Rem Koolhaas' Office for Metropolitan Architecture in joint venture with Seattle-based LMN Architects, image courtesy of the Seattle Public Library.

Pages 72/73 Eames lounge chair and ottoman, Crawford.

Pages 74/75 Brandt.

Pages 76/77 Thorpe.

Pages 78/79 Concentration of wealth and gender of wealth diagrams, adapted from Jeff Gates, *Democracy at Risk*. (Cambridge, Mass: Perseus Publishing, 2000), xxxvii, 34.

Pages 80/81 Missoni and Sophie Conran teacups with saucers, Thorpe. • Designers, Crawford.

Pages 82/83 Brandt.

Pages 86/87 Countries and companies chart adapted from Naomi Klein in *Globalization: Take It Personally*, Anita Roddick, ed. (London: HarperCollins, 2001), 36.

Pages 88/89 Employee and shareholder productivity, adapted from information in Marjorie Kelly, *The Divine Right of Capital: Dethroning the Corporate Aristocracy* (San Francisco: Berrett-Koehler Publishers, Inc), 2001. • Background employee, Crawford. • Background shareholder, Phil Date/iStockphoto. • Executive pay bar chart compiled from data in Julia Finch and Jill Treanor, "Shares Down 24%. Average Earnings up 3%. Boardroom Pay up 23%," *The Guardian* (London), January 31 2003, 1. • Manager, Crawford. • Welder, Luca di Filippo/iStockphoto.

Pages 90/91 Crawford.

Pages 92/93 Financial reports and stacks of paper, Crawford.

Pages 94/95 Building, Ron Smith/iStockphoto. • Woman, Crawford.

Pages 96/97 Senior couple, Simone van den Berg/iStockphoto. • Flags, Jean Schweitzer/iStockphoto. • Billboards, Thorpe.

Page 98/99 Bridge Pavilion by Lorna Jordan, Artist, with Bob Boggess, Architect, and URS Greiner Woodward Clyde, Engineers, 2002. The bridge, with decking of recycled cedar timbers in a herringbone pattern, is part of the Longfellow Creek Habitat Improvement Project in Seattle, supported by the Seattle Arts Commission, Seattle Public Utilities, Seattle Parks and Recreation Department, and the Mayor's Office, in cooperation with URS Greiner Woodward Clyde and Hough Beck Baird. • Fish, Dan Schmitt/iStockphoto. • Wheat, Bryn Donaldson/iStockphoto. • Air, Thorpe.

Pages 100/101 No Wash shirt, courtesy of Kate Fletcher and Rebecca Earley, 5 Ways Project.

Pages 102/103 Lathe and camel, Thorpe. • Western man, Crawford.

Pages 104/105   Crawford.

Pages 106/107   Crawford.

Pages 110/111   Staircase inside the Seattle Public Library, image courtesy of the Seattle Public Library. • *All other images as previously cited.*

PART 4: CULTURE

Pages 112/113   Thorpe.

Pages 114/115   Woman, Crawford. • Human needs table: Subsistence, protection, and leisure, Thorpe; Affection, understanding, and creation, Crawford; Participation, Galina Barskaya/iStockphoto; Identity, Luba Nel/iStockphoto.

Pages 116/117   Nature, iStockphoto. • Time, Phil Sigin-Lavdanski/iStockphoto. • Artifacts, Thorpe. • Communication, Crawford. • Materialism, Thorpe.

Pages 118/119   Crawford.

Pages 120/121   Diagram, Thorpe. • Illuminated manuscript, Crawford.

Pages 122/123   Science and technology, Crawford. • All others, Thorpe.

Pages 124/125   Remote and slide frame, Crawford. • Time spent with the media chart, based on data from Table 5, "Time Spent Per Person Per Media (in minutes) by Telephone Survey, Diary and Observation Methods for Selected Media" in Robert A. Papper, Michael E. Holmes, Ph.D., Mark N. Popovich, Ph.D., "Middletown Media Studies: Media Multitasking . . . and How Much People Really Use the Media" in The International Digital Media and Arts Association Journal 1 no. 1 (2004), 19.

Pages 126/127   Crawford.

Pages 128/129   Man, Crawford. • Chart, developed from information in Tim Kasser, *The High Price of Materialism* (Boston: MIT Press, 2002), 104.

Pages 130/131   Woman, Josef Kubicek/iStockphoto. • Advertising expenditures chart, adapted from Theodore Caplow, Louis Hicks, and Ben J. Wattenberg, *The First Measured Century: An Illustrated Guide to Trends in America 1900–2000* (American Enterprise Institute Press, 2000).

Pages 132/133   Camera, penguin, and apple, Crawford. • Leaves, PhotoDisc. • Black bag, Thorpe

Pages 134/135   Diagram, Thorpe. • Meal, Crawford.

Pages 136/137   Three women, mask, Crawford. • Meditation, Pavel Losevsky/iStockphoto. • Guitar, Nicholas Monu/iStockphoto. • Ceremony, Thorpe.

Pages 138/139   Jelani Memory/iStockphoto.

Pages 140/141   Crawford.

Pages 142/143   Crawford.

Pages 144/145   Sandy Manter/iStockphoto.

Pages 146/147   Gearshift, Thomas Pullicino/iStockphoto. • Handknit, Crawford. • Wood work, Thorpe.

Pages 148/149   Crawford.

Pages 150/151   Celia Martinez/iStockphoto.

Pages 152/153   Maartje van Caspel/iStockphoto.

Pages 154/155   Greater London Authority building, designed by Foster and Partners and completed in 2002, iStockphoto.

Pages 156/157   Image from the NASA Hubble Space Telescope, courtesy of NASA. • Seeds, Thorpe. • Earth from space, courtesy of NASA's Visible Earth at http://visibleearth.nasa.gov.

Pages 158/159   Doing, iStockphoto. • Making by hand, Thorpe. • Diagram of fast and slow layers of civilization, adapted with permission from Stewart Brand's work in *The Clock of the Long Now: Time and Responsibility.* (London: Weidenfeld and Nicolson, 1999), 37. • All other images, Crawford.

Pages 160/161   Crawford.

Pages 162/163   Image of the Hubble Space Telescope, NASA. • Ladakhi Buddha, Thorpe. • Diagram adapted from information in Brand, *The Clock of the Long Now.*

Pages 164/165   Bag from a used sail by Klein and More (Germany), jeans and leather, Crawford. • Construction, Anton Foltin/iStockphoto.

Pages 166/167   Lisa McDonald/iStockphoto.

Pages 168/169   Rosetta Disk images, courtesy of The Long Now Foundation.

Pages 170/171   The Downland Gridshell building (at the UK's Weald & Downland Open Air Museum) by Edward Cullinan Architects with Buro Happold engineers, Alex Sayer quantity surveyors, and The Green Oak Carpentry Company Ltd., completed in 2002. The clear-span timber gridshell structure sits atop a protected archive space, Thorpe.

Pages 172/173   Australian animal carvings, Crawford. • Sunset, Paulus Rusyanto/iStockphoto.

Pages 176/177   Measuring tape, Crawford. • *All other images as previously cited.*

PART 5: FRONTIERS

INDEX

About the Author

Ms. Thorpe's background in sustainable design includes university teaching, research, and support to architects and designers for green building and product stewardship. Along the way she has served as co-chair of a regional chapter of the U.S. Green Building Council and participated in collaborative projects doing eco-redesign of consumer products. Her publications on sustainable design cover a range of topics such as the greening of the Sydney Summer 2000 Olympics, time in design, and industrial ecology. She served as publisher and editor of *On the Ground*, a journal on community, design, and environment. She holds a BS in Design and Environment from Stanford University and an MA in Energy and Resources from the University of California at Berkeley.

Note to Readers

Teachers, business people, policy analysts, and advocates can find out more about using the atlas from its companion Web site: www.designers-atlas.net. For example, the site includes a teaching guide (studio and theory design courses), ideas for business workshops, and notes on bringing design into advocacy and policy organizations. The author welcomes discussions, questions, and comments via the book's Web site or E-mail: ann@designers-atlas.net.